CONFLICT: PRACTICES IN MANAGEMENT, SETTLEMENT AND RESOLUTION

Conflict: Practices in Management, Settlement and Resolution

John Burton and Frank Dukes
Center for Conflict Analysis and Resolution
George Mason University, Fairfax, Virginia

St. Martin's Press   New York

Scholarly and Reference Division,
St. Martin's Press, Inc., 175 Fifth Avenue,
New York, N.Y. 10010

First published in the United States of America in 1990

Printed in the United States of America

ISBN 0–312–04197–7 hc.
ISBN 0–312–04217–5 pb.

Library of Congress Cataloging-in-Publication Data
Burton, John W. (John Wear), 1915–
Conflict: practices in management, settlement, and resolution/
John Burton and Frank Dukes.
    p.   cm.—(The Conflict series; v. 4)
Includes bibliographical references.
ISBN 0–312–04197–7.—ISBN 0–312–04217–5 (pbk.)
1. Conflict management.   I. Dukes, Frank, 1951–   .   II. Title.
III. Series.
HD42.B86   1990
658.4—dc20   89–29436
                                                        CIP

The Conflict Series

1. CONFLICT: RESOLUTION AND PROVENTION,* *by John Burton*
2. CONFLICT: HUMAN NEEDS THEORY, *edited by John Burton*

3. CONFLICT: READINGS IN MANAGEMENT AND RESOLUTION, *edited by John Burton and Frank Dukes*

4. CONFLICT: PRACTICES IN MANAGEMENT, SETTLEMENT AND RESOLUTION, *by John Burton and Frank Dukes*

*Provention
The term *pre*vention has the connotation of containment. The term *pro*vention has been introduced to signify taking steps to remove sources of conflict, and more positively to promote conditions in which collaborative and valued relationships control behaviors.

Foreword to the Series

Samuel W. Lewis
President, United States Institute of Peace

We seem to know much more about how wars and other violent international conflicts get started than we do about how to end them. Nor do we understand very well how to transform settlements that terminate immediate hostilities into enduring peaceful relationships through which nations can continue to work out their differences without violence. The lack of attention to these questions, at least with regard to relations among sovereign governments, is due in some degree to the way international relations as an academic subject has traditionally been studied. By and large, more academic theory and analysis has been devoted to patterns and causes in international behavior with an eye to perfecting explanatory theory than to effective, usable remedies to international conflicts. We have assumed the remedies would become plain once the correct theory was found.

That imbalance is now being corrected. Interest is now growing in the theory and practice of "conflict resolution," a new field concerned specifically with the nature of conflict as a generic human problem and with techniques or initiatives that might be applied productively in addressing conflicts. This new emphasis is reflected in the emergence of alternative dispute resolution methods in the law profession, of peace studies or conflict resolution programs in many of the nation's colleges and universities, of research journals devoted specifically to conflict and its resolution, and of community mediation or problem-solving strategies at the local level and "second-track diplomacy" at the international level.

Providing much of the conceptual foundation for an explicit focus on conflict itself has been a small but growing group of interdisciplinary scholars engaged in a search for formulas and processes that seem to work in ending conflicts among nations and groups. They are seeking to identify those institutional and societal structures that have the best chance of ensuring a lasting and just peace among conflicting interests. Unfortunately, the work of these scholars has not reached the widest circles of policy makers, professionals, students, and researchers who could benefit from the stimulating explorations of the conflict resolution school of thought.

The United States Institute of Peace wishes to commend the four-book Conflict Series: an effort by one of the acknowledged founding fathers of the conflict resolution field to summarize the main insights of the field to date for a wider readership. In these books, John Burton, with the assistance of other major contributors, delineates the distinctive scope of the conflict resolution field, defines its key concepts, explains how the field emerged out of existing approaches to conflict and peace and how it differs from them, summarizes the field's leading substantive insights about conflict and its resolution, collects some of the best readings produced by the field, and probes where the field needs to go in the future to strengthen its theory and applicability to real problems. The series also surveys extant practical techniques for conflict management such as mediation, adjudication, ombudsmen, interactive management, and problem-solving workshops and explores their utility for different types of conflict situations. Of course, the views expressed in these volumes are those of the authors alone and do not necessarily reflect views of the Institute of Peace.

Impressively, John Burton and Frank Dukes completed this broad examination of the conflict resolution field during Burton's year as a Distinguished Fellow of the United States Institute of Peace in 1988–89 while he was also a Distinguished Visiting Professor at the Center for Conflict Resolution at George Mason University in Virginia. No one in the world is better qualified to present the conflict resolution field's distinctive perspectives and unique contributions than is Burton, whom many in the field regard as its first leading explorer and one of its most ardent spokesmen before students, scholars, and governments since its beginnings in the late 1950s. In preparing this series, Burton has drawn on the wealth of his extensive academic training in economics and international relations and his 25 years of research and teaching at universities in three countries, as reflected in his previous ten books and numerous articles. He also has applied the lessons of his practical experience as a diplomat for the Australian government and as a third-party facilitator in efforts to end such conflicts as those in Lebanon, Cyprus, Northern Ireland, and Sri Lanka.

The United States Institute of Peace is a non-partisan, independent institution created and funded by the United States Congress to strengthen the nation's capacity to understand and deal more effectively with international conflict through peaceful means. It serves this purpose by supporting research and education projects that will expand and disseminate available knowledge about the nature of international conflict and the full range of ways it can be resolved within a framework that maximizes freedom and justice. Within this challenging mandate, one of our tasks is to identify serious, innovative, but less well known approaches that may bear further examination and to bring the insights from these approaches to wider circles so that fruitful dialogue among different perspectives is fostered.

John Burton's work complements another Institute project that is mapping all the major "roads to peace" – e.g., international law, diplomacy and negotiations, transnationalism, deterrence theory, non-violence traditions, and international organizations – that have been emphasized in the scholarly literature and world of practice as important methods and tools for achieving international peace. The conflict resolution method and outlook is one of the approaches the Institute wishes to see more widely understood so their respective strengths and limitations can be sorted out and constructive syntheses can be developed. In short, we seek to stimulate much faster dissemination of ideas and cross-fertilization than normally would occur across the barriers of different academic disciplines, professions, governmental spheres, and private organizations that are concerned in various ways with international conflict and its resolution, although they may not necessarily describe their concerns in exactly these terms.

By supporting John Burton's work, the United States Institute of Peace hopes that the perspectives, insights, and new directions for analysis of this relatively new field of conflict resolution will be brought before, and enrich the work of, a wider readership of international relations and conflict resolution students; practitioners in fields such as law, government, labor and industrial management, and social work; policy makers at all levels; as well as scholars concerned with conflict issues.

Washington, D.C.

Preface to the Series

It is not easy for those who are seeking new approaches to move from deterrence theories and practices of conflict *settlement* and *management* to conflict *resolution* theory and practice. The jump to prevention and the predictive capabilities that prevention requires, is even more challenging. These are different fields with different assumptions. While they exist concurrently they are in different conceptual worlds. Some practitioners and theorists seek more effective institutional and management constraints, power negotiating techniques and peace through technologies of mutual threat. There are consensus seekers who employ more sophisticated socialization processes largely within existing systems. Problem-solving advocates pursue more analysis of human behaviors and seek to deduce processes of conflict resolution and provention. There cannot be communication between different approaches, or with policy makers and the public generally, until there is a precisely defined language, appropriate concepts that enable a clear differentiation of the various approaches, and an adequate and agreed theory of human behaviors at all social levels. This is the purpose of these four books concerned with the study of Conflict.

There are four books in this Conflict Series. They are:

1. *Conflict: Resolution and Provention.* This book seeks to provide an historical and theoretical perspective, and a framework for consideration of theory and practice in conflict resolution and provention. It is in five parts: Part I defines the approach; Part II deals with the political context of conflict provention; Part III is concerned with theory of decision making, and with conflict resolution processes; Part IV is concerned with the longer-term policy implications of provention; and Part V draws together some conclusions.

2. *Conflict: Human Needs Theory.* An adequate theory of behavior is required to provide a basis for the analysis and resolution of conflict, and particularly for prediction of conflict and a guide to conflict provention. "Needs theory" is put forward as this foundation. The chapters contributed in this book were written as a result of an international conference convened in July 1988 for that purpose.

3. *Conflict: Readings in Management and Resolution.* A new subject has origins in many fields, and this is an attempt to bring

together some earlier contributions from a broad spectrum of disciplines. A newly developing subject also has gaps requiring attention, and this book includes contributions requested to fill some of these gaps. It also contains an extensive annotated bibliography.

4. *Conflict: Practices in Management, Settlement and Resolution.* It is useful to survey practices generally, even those that proceed from contradictory theories. This book is a general survey of management, settlement and conflict resolution practices.

Conflict, its resolution and provention, comprises an *a-disciplinary* study, that is, a synthesis that goes beyond separate disciplines, beyond interaction between separate disciplines, and beyond any synthesis of approaches from several disciplines. An a-disciplinary approach accepts no boundaries of knowledge. Consequently, it has as yet no shelf in any discipline-based library. These four books seek to make a start.

JOHN BURTON

CONFLICT: PRACTICES IN MANAGEMENT, SETTLEMENT AND RESOLUTION

Acknowledgements

The authors and publishers wish to thank the following for permission to reproduce copyright material: Kettering Foundation, for extracts from "Negotiated Investment Strategy" (1982); and University Press of America, Lanham, Maryland, for extracts from John W. Burton, *Resolving Deep-Rooted Conflict: A Handbook* (copyright 1987).

Contents

Introduction

The intention of this book is to differentiate types of disputes and conflicts, to examine the variety of processes by which they might be tackled, and to match dispute and conflict situations with appropriate settlement and resolution processes.

THE PROBLEMS OF LANGUAGE AND ASSESSMENTS

Even discussing these matters is difficult because we have not yet arrived at a common language by which to communicate either the differences in dispute and conflict situations or the remedial processes we wish to describe and to match. Only when we have tackled this problem of language and labels can we make assessments as to the usefulness and relevance of different remedial processes.

There has been a tendency in the recent literature in the dispute and conflict fields to use the terms "disputes" and "conflicts" interchangeably. Furthermore, "settlement" and "resolution" are also used interchangeably. This leads to the assumption that the notions of dispute settlement and conflict resolution are interchangeable. The American Bar Association has a standing committee on "dispute resolution." The same kinds of dispute are "settled" when courts are involved or when attorneys negotiate on behalf of their clients. The Society for Professionals in Dispute Resolution (SPIDR) has conference topics such as "Conflict Resolution in Today's Economic Climate," when what is meant is dispute settlement. Care with language would make it clear that there is a distinction between disputes which can be settled by, for example, a court, and conflicts, involving non-negotiable human needs, that must be resolved by, for example, some analytical and problem-solving process – a distinction made in *Conflict: Resolution and Provention*, and which we further justify below.

Even arguments or management problems are referred to as disputes or conflicts when what is involved is no more than a choice to be made by persons with shared goals and values. Two engineers argue about different ways of bridging a river. These are everyday experiences in the management of business and social life, and do not warrant the terms dispute or conflict. We must have precision in

1

our nomenclature if there is to be meaningful assessment of situations, and further development of processes.

The reason for our current confusion seems to be that academic and applied interests have been confined to situations that occur within an existing political–social–economic system. *Management* has been the responsibility of whichever authorities are relevant, for instance the owner of a factory or the head of a government agency. *Disputes* over property and damages have been for courts to settle. Ethnic, class and other identity conflicts, have been regarded, not as conflicts, but as challenges to law and order, and therefore the responsibility of national authorities which have available the means of repression. *Conflicts* require in-depth analysis of sources and problem-solving in ways that do not compromise values and human needs. Generally this has not been recognized, and they have been repressed or treated in the same way as interest *disputes*. This being the case, the language distinction has not been important. Conflicts, in so far as this term has had some special meaning, have been equated with wars, and wars have been (wrongly) treated as a phenomenon different from other forms of conflict, requiring deterrent capabilities.

Underlying the thinking that has led to such confusion in terms has been a high level of complacency, on the one hand, and resignation, on the other. While some disputes may be managed, violent conflict has been regarded as a natural phenomenon: it has to be accepted as inevitable, while making what defensive provisions are possible. But now, in complex societies and in a nuclear age, we see the emergence of the study of conflict as a universal phenomenon, different from management problems and dispute situations. We now require precise definitions of situations and processes, and distinctive terms by which they can be categorized.

THE SEARCH FOR CATEGORIES

In searching for a means of categorization we have several choices. We could turn to societal level categories – that is, the family, the community, the nation or the international system. It is categories such as these which practitioners tend to employ, and by which they identify themselves. But this is the traditional categorization that we wish to avoid, for it implies that human behavior is different at these different levels, and should be treated differently. The behavior of the individual within a society in seeking recognition and identity is not different from the behavior of identity groups such as ethnic minorities or nations: there is a common human dimension in all. At any level, including the international, relations that are not cooperative can be in the management, the dispute or the conflict category. Societal levels are not a basis for differentiating disputes and conflicts.

We could turn to the categories of process that have emerged over time. Historically, there has been a trend away from formal judicial processes, toward less formal and more participatory forms such as mediation, conciliation and good offices. Lawyers have called these "weaker" forms, weaker in the sense that there is less authoritative decision making and enforcement. Experience demonstrates, especially at the international level, that parties to a conflict which involves important issues are not willing to allow courts, arbitrators or mediators to make decisions for them. In addition, the increase in numbers of disputes requiring some form of treatment has led to the invention of many alternative forms of adjudication and mediation. If we were to list alternatives to judicial processes in the order in which they were introduced, we would find that there was a continuing progression toward "weaker" forms.

CATEGORIZATION BASED ON ASSUMPTIONS ABOUT THE NATURE OF DISPUTES AND CONFLICT

Categorization of processes according to this historical trend, however, does not touch on the nature and source of conflicts. We seek a categorization that will help to tell us when different processes are appropriate. It is the nature and source of disputes and conflicts that should provide the basis of a categorization.

It follows that a categorization of situations and the processes relevant to them must be derived from an explanatory or theoretical framework of behaviors. Within the theoretical framework of human needs as used in this Conflict Series we have categorized *disputes* and *conflicts* by applying the tests of *interests* and *human needs*. ("Values," such as cultural values, fall between for they do change over time, and there are personal adjustments made. The most strongly held values, however, necessarily imply identity and other human needs, and for practical purposes we treat them as though they are "needs.") On the basis of this categorization of *situations* we define the two main types of *processes*: *dispute settlement* (involving negotiable interests) and *conflict resolution* (involving non-negotiable human needs).

Settlement processes are appropriate for those cases in which authoritative determinations are required in order to preserve social norms. They are cases in which there are no human needs of development that might be suppressed by such enforced settlement. Excluded would be a situation involving any human dimension. For example, in the case of gang violence or a drug offense, imposing a sentence does not deter either the person concerned or others. It results in gaols being filled, but not in the reduction of crime or conflict. Such behaviors involve underlying problems which are outside the jurisdiction of courts, at least any courts that apply norms based on legal precedents which do not take fully into account a human dimension. This would effectively limit courts to interpretations of documents, and consideration of contracts and agreements, and the imposition of fines and sanctions for social offenses, such as traffic and other infringements of the functional norms of society. This is a narrow definition of the relevance of legal processes, but it follows logically from a theory of behavior which hypothesizes that there are certain needs that *will* be pursued and, therefore, certain behaviors that cannot be suppressed. We return to the role of courts and legal processes when dealing with settlement, and also in our conclusions where there are offered some constructive suggestions.

Resolution processes are appropriate when any in-depth analysis of behaviors and relationships is required. This probably requires the assistance of a third party. An extension of resolution processes is involved when decision making is designed to prevent (or *pro*vent) conflict by removing its sources.

CONTROL OF "IRRATIONAL" BEHAVIOR

This simple categorization leaves out two classes of behaviors for which some treatment is required. The first is those anti-social and frequently violent behaviors that are attributed to the insane and the "evildoer." Insanity can in most cases be determined, and some form of treatment and perhaps containment will be necessary. The evildoer is far harder to determine, as evil in an individual may be the direct product of the ontological pursuit of human needs in frustrating social conditions. Even so, treatment and containment in the interests of others may be necessary. This issue was addressed, in so far as it can be at the present state of knowledge, in *Conflict: Resolution and Provention.*

MANAGEMENT PROBLEMS

The second class of behaviors excluded by the dispute (interest)–conflict (needs) categorization arises out of situations sometimes termed disputes and conflicts, but which we label *arguments* or *problems of organization and management* among persons having the same goals and interests. *Management processes* include improved communication, problem-solving, and improved personal interactions within relationships that have generally shared goals. For example, members of a large firm or corporation might come together within a problem-solving framework to sort out differences over organization and objectives. They might resolve their disagreements by debate followed by voting after there is shared information and a higher degree of consensus. Management procedures are appropriate in the great bulk of cases of disagreements that are part of personal cooperation and interactions. Under this heading there are a great variety of processes. Removing such behaviors from the categories of disputes and conflicts does not make them any less significant. On the contrary, they form the numerical bulk of social problems, and lead to disputes and conflicts if not dealt with promptly and effectively.

There are many sub-groups within each of these main categories. For example, at the fringe of judicial settlements are arbitration processes. Associated with management are therapy and counseling in cases where confrontational behaviors relate to personal relationship problems within an organization rather than to any wider environmental frustrations of human needs. We will introduce bases for distinguishing these as we proceed.

DIFFERENT PHENOMENA AND DIFFERENT PROCESSES

Management problems or arguments, disputes and conflicts, each have distinct sources and are different phenomena, even though frequently they may have similar overt or superficial characteristics. Management problems involve differences in choice of alternatives. Disputes involve some interest issue of gain or loss. Conflicts involve the development and autonomy of the individual or identity group of the individual. We are dealing with differences in kind, rather than a continuum from less violent to more violent, less socially important to more socially important.

As these are different phenomena, different processes and procedures are required in dealing with them. A management problem within the factory or a family can be dealt with by communication, perhaps assisted by someone suitably positioned. Disputes within an institutional framework can be settled by bargaining, in the local council by voting, in society by courts. But conflicts affecting the security of identity groups, the identity of the person, the autonomy of an ethnic group, the security of a nation, cannot be resolved by any of these techniques.

The different nature of management problems, disputes and conflicts becomes clear when attempts are made to deal with cases. There are, obviously, provocations in each case. Management problems and the arguments they generate arise largely out of inadequate knowledge, misperceptions and differences in preferences. Interest disputes are readily provoked by broken agreements, unobserved norms, and competition in the use of resources. Remedies include sanctions, punishment and arbitration. At the work place some misunderstanding could give rise to disturbing arguments, and these can be dealt with by some form of organized discussion and leadership direction. The source of the problem and the remedy are within the system. The provocations that give rise to such problems are part of the system, and the arguments are a part of ordinary social and organizational relationships.

In the case of conflicts, however, where there are non-negotiable needs at stake, finding some means of satisfying these is the only means of control. This could require changes in policies, institutions and even in the systems concerned. No amount of coercion or control is likely to suppress conflict and its violence in the family, the street, the community or the total national or international society while there remain underlying causes that prejudice human development. The remedy for conflicts is the removal of the provocations, not just the manipulation of behaviors.

IDEAL TYPES

There are here three different fields requiring different techniques and professional training. But in practice they are mixed. These three categories are ideal types: there are many cases or situations that cannot be placed in any one of these categories. Just as the symptoms of flu could easily turn out to be symptoms of some serious disease, so a seemingly simple problem in relationships is likely to include both interest disputes and conflicts involving human needs, and will not respond to well-meaning attempts merely to improve personal relationships. Family situations of the type a social worker might be treating, perhaps contributed to by poor housing, unemployment and other adverse conditions, can lead to widespread anti-social behaviors. So it is with industrial, communal and national disputes – one spreads to another, and each one has elements of the others within it.

We are faced, therefore, with a most difficult problem in deciding in which field a situation lies, and how it should be treated. The bulk of problems societies face are at the management level. These are the everyday experiences of everyone. They include traffic problems, personality clashes, community problems, and a host of other situations. There is an obvious need for knowledge about how to handle such problems within all social settings. Professionalism in terms of training might not have to be extensive, but it does call for persons who are perceptive and who can remove themselves from the situation sufficiently to assist in management. Training is likely to be in special areas, such as child welfare, single parent families, industrial relations, public policy and others.

The next largest category are disputes of all kinds which might require judicial or arbitration processes, or some alternative third-party intervention. Conflicts, while the most damaging to the social fabric and to persons, are rare by comparison, but probably require the most professional training.

This linking of fields does not diminish the importance of defining separate situation categories, and determining the processes relevant to each. It implies that those working in each should be aware of the specialities of others, and be prepared to consult when required, as happens in other professions in which there are specialities. This, once again, points to the need for well-defined categorizations, for appropriate training that relates to each, and for an awareness of limitations of specializations.

THE PROBLEM AREA

The three other books in this Conflict Series focus on deep rooted conflict resolution defined as analytical and problem solving. This focus reflects the special interest of the Series in the handling of *conflict* as we have defined the term – that is, situations involving inherent human needs, such as individual and group identity and recognition, and developmental needs generally. These are not negotiable. They do not respond to coercive measures or power bargaining and negotiation. They do require analytical problem-solving and the discovery of means or satisfiers that meet the needs of all concerned.

In this book we broaden the focus beyond conflict and conflict resolution, and examine also the range of processes and techniques that are employed by authorities and non-official bodies in the handling of *disputes*. The processes include judicial procedures, arbitration, mediation in all its forms, and the range of dispute settlement processes which have evolved in recent years as alternatives to judicial processes. Let it be noted that these processes traditionally have been employed for conflicts also, because no separation has been made between disputes and conflicts.

Indeed, we broaden the focus even further to include processes that are appropriate in situations that cannot be termed either disputes or conflicts, but which, nevertheless, present personal and group tensions leading to problems to be solved – as, for example, when there are choices to be made. We include these, and the ways in which they can be handled, because arguments can become disputes if not managed promptly and with insight. A protracted argument leads to the taking of positions, and personal identity gets involved. Arguments, like disputes and conflicts, may perhaps require the help of a third party for their settlement or resolution.

We have widened our focus in this book for three reasons. As noted already, there is difficulty in determining whether a situation is an argument, a dispute or a conflict. A problem in relationships, for example some neighbourhood argument, could appear to be a result of misperceptions or disagreements over options available. The treatment in such a case would be some help in arriving at objective considerations and a better understanding. The problem could, however, be the result of deeply ingrained prejudices, and would then require a far more searching approach. Clashes between minority groups trading in competition with each other may appear to be disputes involving interests only, and would appear, therefore, to be subject to arbitration, bargaining and negotiation. But such situations are likely to have deep-rooted sources not immediately apparent, probably involving ethnicity and identity issues. Negotiation on the assumption that the problem is an issue of different interests only could result in outcomes that would make the situation even more intractable. To take another example, an industrial strike may appear to be over a wage claim, while underlying the claim might be major frustrations in the working conditions of employees, unlikely to be resolved by increased wages. Our analysis of conflict resolution is not complete without consideration of the means by which problems in relationships that are seemingly superficial, but which may involve deep rooted conflicts, can be detected and treated.

A second reason for our wider focus in this book is that there is the always present danger that practitioners who employ some particular technique suited to some special case may fail to distinguish clear categorizations, and may move into areas for which their techniques may not be appropriate. This would lead to protracted conflicts. In *Conflict: Resolution and Prevention* it was argued that over the years an environment of conflict has evolved in most societies, leading to exponential rates of increase in the incidence of violence, largely due to past attempts to contain or to suppress deep-rooted conflicts rather than to resolve them. The employment of inappropriate techniques in a conflict situation, especially techniques that are coercive and that merely treat symptoms (for example, drug violence) as opposed to sources (for example, the economic and social environment), is a serious concern. By broadening the focus we can arrive at categorizations that should help practitioners to define more precisely their professional fields.

A third reason for extending the focus beyond conflict and its resolution is to place it in the wider context of judicial and related processes such as Alternative Dispute Resolution (ADR), second track diplomacy, mediation in various forms, community activities to deal with social tensions, and the many other endeavors that seek cooperative relationships at one societal level or another. Interest in many of these processes is new. Few people who are involved in some particular endeavor have knowledge about the activities of others. There is as yet little learning from one approach spilling over to others. In this book we hope to set out the main processes and the circumstances for which they are relevant, and also to point to problems encountered by these practices. Courts and arbitration are well known. Deterrence strategies such as police controls and international mutual threats are well known. The friendly advice individuals give to each other is also familiar. The many different techniques and processes that have recently evolved to supplement these more traditional means of dealing with management problems, disputes and conflicts, are less well known. Societies, and practitioners in particular, need to be aware of what processes are appropriate in different circumstances, what training there should be, what institutionalization is desirable, and what professional ethics should be introduced.

In short, we are extending the scope of the study in this book on processes because we are arguing that processes must be appropriate to the problem. Many of these approaches are pragmatic, innovative and recent, some untested, and most are devoid of any theoretical base on which they can be assessed. We must, therefore, find some means to define situations, to define processes, to determine relevance and to evaluate performance.

The professional treatment of management problems, disputes and conflicts outside judicial and bargaining power processes is a recent development. It has emerged along with the weakening of central authorities as social systems have become more complex. It is part of a long-term trend in decision making toward problem-solving, that is an approach that takes into account all aspects of relationships, including behavioral responses to decisions (see Part III of *Conflict: Resolution and Provention*). It is also part of a long-term trend toward "deregulation" and decentralization, and toward local and informal decision making.

While official practices have been modified, and non-official processes have emerged, intellectually we have not caught up with these developments. There is no clear categorization of situations that could and should be dealt with by courts on the basis of consensus norms, of situations for which informal dispute resolution processes would be more appropriate, and of situations which are best handled informally by persons skilled in overcoming communication and perception problems. Societies are still in an experimental stage in handling social problems. It is still a field in which theorists and practitioners assert their preferences and make their claims in the absence of any widespread understanding or consensus.

THE DANGER OF PALLIATIVES

There is one additional reason for examining situations and processes relevant to them: that we can be alerted to possible dangers of making disputes and conflicts protracted by processes that employ palliatives.

Many management and dispute settlement processes, and even some conflict resolution processes, are applied to local situations with the best of intentions by professionals in these practices. For example, attempts are made to bring young people of different ethnic origin together in a social setting, to improve housing in a particular area, or to promote some community organizations designed to improve living conditions. These are activities that a repressive authority should welcome, for they could make the status quo more acceptable; but they may also keep the conflict simmering without any real progress toward a solution. They divert attention from the underlying structural sources of conflict. There are, moreover, some wider implications of dispute settlement and conflict resolution that should be kept in mind by all practitioners if their endeavors are not to be frustrated by the wider social, economic and political environment. In Part IV, *Provention and Education,* we introduce the notion of Provention, the need to deal with the source of problems, in order to underscore the point that no matter how many disputes and conflicts are settled and resolved in certain circumstances, their settlement and resolution will not prevent others, and may in practice lead to others.

FAILED MECHANISMS

We are making assessments on processes at a critical and transitional stage in the history of social control. Legal processes are relevant to within-system disputes – that is those disputes which are bound to occur within any system, for example, constitutional interpretations, property rights and transactions, straightforward cases of criminal offense, and others which have to be regarded as normal and expected, and which do not involve complex human dimensions. Even these are taxing the capabilities of courts and police as their work loads increase with population growth and with the growing complexities of social organization (due, perhaps, to the increasing number of social problems that are merely contained and not resolved). More recently courts have come under criticism, whether justifiable or not, for their rigidity, for delays, for limited access, and for costliness.

However, it is not just volume which is the problem with courts and judicial processes. Legal processes are not effective means of getting at the root of problems of alienation, violence and their associated deviance symptoms. The explanation of behavior is outside their area of interest. Courts are guided by social and legal norms. Moreover, they are part of the apparatus of coercion; their primary purpose is to control and manage deviance, not to resolve conflict.

It is the perceived limitation of legal processes and the accompanying escalation of violence associated with both disputes (for example, drug-related violence) and conflict (for example, ethnic violence) that has triggered a recent interest in disputes and conflicts. What seems generally agreed is that given increased environmental provocations for violent behaviors, and the failure of constraints, there has emerged in most societies a condition in which the traditional legal system, courts and enforcement agencies, have become over-burdened and increasingly irrelevant.

THE RESPONSE TO FAILURE

The response of authorities to their own failures – that is to escalating violence that arises out of disputes and conflicts – has been of two kinds. First, there has been the traditional one of dealing with symptoms rather than with causes – for example, dealing with drug problems by building more gaols. This has been the traditional response for two reasons. First, it has been assumed that all behaviors can be controlled by deterrence and punishments and, second, authorities seek the preservation of those structures, institutions and policies which exist, despite the fact that these are often a source of conflict. Rates of unemployment exceeding 40 per cent among minority youths within certain locations in the US must give rise to many forms of deviance and conflict, but it has been more expedient to suppress or ignore the unrest than to get to the roots of the trouble by fundamental changes in policies. International problems, such as those in the Middle East and other areas where there are ethnic uprisings, can be described in the same terms.

In the past it was usually possible to deal with the symptoms of problems by suppressing violence, and traditionally, if this did not work, then more of the same medicine was applied. Now, with general awareness of individual developmental possibilities, with more complex situations of ethnicity and class, with increased means of violence available to all, and with increased communications that make possible external support, no amount of the medicine of suppression seems to provide a stable remedy. Dealing with symptoms, in the past, rarely led to success, but continued failure is now destructive of societies, and at a global level is threatening civilizations. Short-term political expediency has costly long-term consequences, whether we are considering ecology or social relationships.

A second and more recent response by authorities to their failures and the increase in disorder and violence, is to withdraw from the scene, and to leave social problems to the "market place", the community and voluntary organizations. The longer-term consequence is as yet unclear. It may be decentralization and more local community activity, but there are already examples of other authorities taking over the decision making arena as a result of military coups when law and order seems to be threatened.

At this stage of failed policies we have no option but to go back to basics and to determine the nature of conflict, which is the purpose of both *Conflict: Resolution and Provention*, and *Conflict: Human Needs Theory* and, having done that, to try, as we do in this book, to arrive at some categorization of disputes and conflicts, and a categorization of processes. This should help to provide a basis on which decisions can be made as to what processes are appropriate to particular situations.

FIVE PARTS OF THE STUDY

This book is accordingly separated into five Parts. Part I deals with *Problems of Management*, Part II with *Settlement*, dealing largely with authoritative and normative decision making, Part III with *Resolution*, meaning problem-solving conflict resolution. It has to be stressed again that these are pure or ideal types. Within each are elements of all the others. In Part IV we deal with *Provention and Education* and in Part V, *Conclusions*, we assess developments in this field.

It is quite impossible to describe adequately the many existing processes, especially those within the management category. The procedure we have adopted is to describe each category in an introduction, and then set out typical examples of processes relevant to that category.

I
Problems of Management

1 Introduction: Problems of Management

We commence our descriptions of processes with those we have labeled *management*: how to handle disagreements and arguments over choices and preferences that result from interactions between parties who have common interests and goals, and who differ only on the means of achieving them. Members of a corporate body debating some policy issue, or members of a United Nations committee on disaster relief, have agreed common goals and must debate options available. Parents arguing over custody usually have a common interest in the development of the child.

In management situations there are personal interactions in which arguments and differences must occur. The assumption is that any problem can be resolved by the interaction of the parties: no deep analysis of behaviors is required. The subject matter is typically sufficiently removed from personal value preferences and the inherent needs of those concerned that majority voting may be an acceptable process. The shared norms involved are the norms of the parties operating within their wider social environment.

Interests and identity needs sometimes underlie arguments, and sometimes prolonged argument provokes them. If any emerge, organizational or management processes are no longer appropriate. It is important, therefore, for arguments to be dealt with quickly, and sometimes a third party is required.

VARIETY OF INFORMAL PROCESSES

In this category we are dealing with usual relationships at all societal levels. The role of the third party, if one is required, is that of the friend of the family who helps overcome some problem. At a social level it may be the role of the social worker helping clients to cope with their environments. These usual and well established roles, however, cannot cope with complexities in relationships as they emerge in modern industrial societies. There is clearly a need for some institutionalized forms of intervention to deal effectively with situations before they escalate and become disputes and conflicts.

Tensions in arguments can easily escalate: an argument that persists causes people to take inflexible positions, and their roles and identities become involved.

The variety of management problems is enormous, and means of dealing with them accordingly vary. There are family and community mediations, and "mediation to shape public policy", (this being the title of a special number of *Mediation Quarterly*, 20, 1988), with their appropriate processes. Examples of the latter are environmental problems, water resources sharing problems, waste disposal and others that require decision making by public authorities who have to reflect local concerns, and the processes are a means of determining these. In many ways these processes are an adjunct to institutional decision making.

To determine appropriate procedures in each different management case it is necessary to have a clear statement of the problem, an identification of those concerned, advice from specialists such as social workers and engineers, and all the normal procedures of decision making. To mitigate a social or political situation it is sometimes expedient to bring in a third party who can help assess the issues and the options available. In many instances authorities have their own third parties, that is an agency that can assist in decision making processes.

There are likely to be disagreements, however, even in the most straightforward of management problems that reflect not just choices but hidden interests, as for example, in an environmental project when there are persons involved who have interests in development, others who attach a value to environmental preservation, and local publics whose interests would also be affected. If this is the case, a more structured process will be required.

Keltner has published a useful paper on "Mediation – Toward a Civilized System of Dispute Resolution" (1987). His description of cases and processes points to the restricted and limited nature of this approach. His list of areas for training are: credibility, empathy, listening, feedback, interrogation, timing, speaking skills, message carrying, non-verbal communication and persuasion. It is to be noted that these are all process skills. Management problem-solving procedures did not evolve from any new understanding of the nature of the problem of conflict, but largely because of greater social complexities and the failure of local authorities to cope with their management problems. Forms of management problem-solving are essentially techniques for facilitating communication and compromise. As such, the training required is limited. Thus, the American Bar Association Standing Committee on Dispute Resolution reported that: "Approximately 600 students from 38 states were trained in conflict management, communication, and mediation in a day-long dispute resolution day" (1988).

This limited qualification has two dangers. First, in some apparent management situations, behavioral aspects of conflict and of structural sources of conflict may be present but not appear. A management third party should be qualified to be on the lookout for such situations. Second, a minimum qualification too frequently becomes a justification for tackling more complex problems.

This would suggest that these processes may have a limited function, confined to problems that involve negotiable interests, and not ones that stem from complex human relationships, and the interaction between human needs and structural conditions.

PRAGMATISM

With such a range of management problems, and with limited skill training, it is inevitable that practice will stem largely from personal intuition and pragmatism, making description of process difficult.

It is this pragmatism that separates management processes from judicial settlement and conflict resolution. In these latter cases, as we shall see, rules of procedure are more and more being recognized as essential, rules that must be followed. There is little room for pragmatism in a delicate conflict situation.

While a high degree of pragmatism is to be expected in dealing with ordinary management problems it is, however, this pragmatic aspect that creates problems within this field of studies. Some practitioners employ one technique and others quite different ones in similar cases. Professional standards are difficult to establish. We wish now, for two reasons, to divert and to discuss pragmatism. First, it is important to avoid pragmatism in problem-solving conflict resolution, and second, pragmatism has implications, even for management processes, that need to be noted.

In some cultures pragmatism is more acceptable than is a deeply analytical approach to a problem, for it allows "all flowers to bloom", and enables contending approaches to survive, even though theoretically, logically and even empirically falsified. It enables unlicensed "skills" to be practised with impunity, as was automobile driving in its early days, at least until unacceptable damage is apparent, and ethical considerations are brought to attention.

Many public policies are pragmatic and not necessarily thought through. There is now considerable evidence that criminals placed under strict detention become less, and not more, desirable citizens. Yet the detentions continue at a cost which could be used both to help to eliminate the conditions which led to the deviance in the first place, and to alter the behaviors of the particular persons concerned. Detentions are a pragmatic response to a situation without thoughtful anticipation of consequences. So it is with many pragmatic practices as with management problems. They may or may not be beneficial to those concerned and to society. Success and failure are not easy to assess, but they can be judged within a framework that deals with the sources of disputes and conflicts, and for this reason pragmatism needs to be examined.

Note that these observations apply equally to pragmatic practices employed by professional diplomats at the international level, where they are described in the international relations literature as the "art of the possible".

A justification of these processes is that they are practical, and that a third party, if one is required, is in a position to be flexible and to meet the desires of clients. Pragmatism has in recent years taken on a positive meaning, as though it were a desirable trait or practice.

The reasons why this shift has occurred, and the thinking behind it, are important for our analysis. Pragmatism implies an absence of knowledge, of theory and of predictive capacity. In pragmatism truth lies in testing and post hoc assessments. A second characteristic is that it is an approach made necessary once there is a break with existing norms and practices which have proved unworkable, such as repressive and coercive means of control.

In other words, pragmatism is the process of exploring alternatives almost at random, though intuition and experience may guide. If these alternatives prove useful or beneficial they should be followed, even in the absence of any reasoned or theoretical justifications which would throw light on longer-term consequences. If they fail others must be sought, again by pragmatic means. Faced with a problem or a specific conflict, the pragmatist employs intuition, unconsciously held theories, trial and error, innovation and expediency.

This is a process that may be acceptable in solving some problems. If one is lost in a forest, trial and error could be a useful procedure.

But trial and error applied to dispute or conflict situations, in which the quality of life and life itself may be at stake, is unacceptable. Post hoc assessments are a bit late. Predictable results are required. While accepting pragmatism as part of existing realities we cannot accept the realities with complacency. Perhaps in management situations pragmatism has an important role, and we merely note at this stage that in resolving a conflict processes should reduce the pragmatic element, and provide instead some insights that can lead to more structured analysis, procedures and policies, and, therefore, to greater predictability. The third party in such situations is accountable.

PRAGMATISM AND THE POWERFUL

The training offered in management skills is to conduct meetings, to promote accurate perceptions and to increase group concentration and memory. It does not include skills in understanding the nature of human conflict from which conflict resolution processes must be deduced. Management skills are at the service of those who seek to maintain the systems and institutions which are the source of the conflicts being treated, as much as they are at the service of those who seek to alter the conditions which led to conflict. Indeed, these skills have already largely been captured by those in powerful positions in industry and the community who can afford their employment, just as in the past legal processes have tended to serve the interests of the more affluent. The main clients of management procedures are corporations; local governments, which have to justify their activities to those whom they represent; and developers, who must contend with those who have concerns about the environment; and others who might find legal processes less favorable and more costly. Because these skills are applied sometimes without an awareness of structural and institutional sources of the problems being tackled, they are likely to lead in the longer term to even more costly disputes and planning mistakes, and when underlying ethnicity issues are involved, perhaps to some social disruption.

These observations are not meant to decry management processes in removing tensions, but to make clear the dangers that have to be guarded against. When we come to dispute settlement and conflict resolution processes we will see that there are built-in safeguards, the observance of consensus norms in the first case, and costing processes in the second, which tend to minimize power as an influence in negotiation and problem solving.

PRAGMATISM AS A PHASE IN KNOWLEDGE DEVELOPMENT

Pragmatism is a natural and inevitable phase in the development of practice. It reflects a rejection of existing norms and rules which are found to be unworkable. Unless, however, it seeks to discover explanations of failure, it cannot lead reliably to improved practices. It is in this sense a transition phenomenon. It is the phase in a paradigm shift at which there is dissent, but not yet a clear switch to a new paradigm. Pragmatism fills a gap. It is a temporary expedient.

This legitimacy of pragmatism, however, is self-perpetuating. Once established, pragmatism moves from being defined as uninformed "meddling" (to use a dictionary definition) to being defined as a positive "science." This is dangerous, as it suggests that there are means of solving problems even when there is no theoretical base on which to rest.

There are signs that the essentially pragmatic approaches are giving way to far more fundamental analyses. In the field of public policy, Carpenter and Kennedy (1988) have adopted problem-solving approaches (p. 27), though public policy does not normally raise major issues of conflict as we define it here. The authors deal with "strongly held values" – notions of right and wrong – in public disputes (p. 10). Susskind and Cruikshank (1987) argue that such processes should be "restricted to distributional issues, not fundamental values, or issues of basic human rights" (p. 77).

Little by little pragmatic processes will give way to more structured ones as the nature of relationships and their complexities becomes better understood. Already the US National Institute for Dispute Resolution (NIDR) and Society of Professionals in Dispute Resolution (SPIDR) are trying to develop standards and qualifications for what are called "neutrals" – that is, third parties.

PUBLIC DISPUTE CENTERS AND DEMOCRACY

Even assuming that management processes and training in their use are adequate, there are some wider implications regarding their use.

One of the goals of management processes is "to enhance community involvement in the dispute resolution process" (Goldberg, Green and Sander, 1985, p. 5). Indeed, those involved in these processes attach importance to their democratic nature. Community participation is regarded as essential to decision making on environmental and other topics of community interest: "In our view, it is more important that an agreement be perceived as fair by the parties involved than by an independent analyst who applies an abstract decision rule" (Susskind and Cruikshank, 1987, p. 25).

This is clearly taking away from representative government its prime role of reflecting the public interest. There is not necessarily anything wrong with this, especially when representative government is greatly influenced by interest groups, and when governments are more concerned with their immediate political rating than with the longer-term community interest. Frequently informal processes are adopted when there is a policy making stalemate. What in fact happens, however, is that these informal and pragmatic processes play into the hands of interest groups, and give a legitimacy to agreements by reason of community consultation. A local government, not wishing to take responsibility for the establishment of a waste disposal site, invites in a public policy facilitator, and with his/her help identifies the parties and representatives of the community. This can be most manipulative. The process becomes a means by which an authority can have its way without appearing to have taken sides in some community dispute. It is also a process that plays into the hands of the more powerful and influential. Local authorities may be unduly subject to interest pressures, but far better hold them politically responsible than introduce some unofficial decision making process that is under the control only of an unaccountable "neutral" brought in to oversee the process. The longer-term implications of decision making of this order are most disturbing: community processes that are inevitably power political processes become a substitute for political accountability.

SOME SPECIAL APPLICATIONS

In the remainder of Part I dealing with problems of management we describe mediation (Chapter 2), divorce mediation (Chapter 3), victim-offender reconciliation (Chapter 4), community mediation (Chapter 5), environmental and public policy mediation (Chapter

6) and interactive management (Chapter 7). The strengths and weaknesses of management processes, and the kinds of skills that are considered adequate, will become clearer.

2 Mediation

INTRODUCTION

The term "mediation" has been popularly used to describe almost any third-party activity short of armed intervention. We hesitate to deal with it as a process. The generic use of the term indicates the state of confusion, and the absence of precise categories in the field. It is sometimes just as broadly defined by practitioners and researchers as by the general public. For instance: "Mediation is the assistance of a neutral 'third party' to a negotiation" (Bingham, 1986, p. 5), or "third party assistance to two or more disputing parties who are trying to reach agreement" (Pruitt and Kressel, 1985, p. 1).

Some practitioners are more specific, if only because their definitions encompass their own particular domains of interest. We thus have statements such as these:

Mediation involves the intervention of a third party who first investigates and defines the problem and then usually approaches each group separately with recommendations designed to provide a mutually acceptable solution (Blake and Mouton, 1985, p. 15);

a process by which an impartial third person (sometimes more than one person) helps parties to resolve disputes through mutual concessions and face-to-face bargaining (Coulson, 1983); and

Mediation is the intervention into a dispute or negotiation by an acceptable, impartial, and neutral third-party who has no authoritative decision-making power to assist disputing parties in voluntarily reaching their own mutually acceptable settlement of issues in dispute (Moore, 1987, p. 14).

This range of definitions (and these are only a sample of the field) exemplifies the difficulties inherent in discussing a subject when there exists such basic disagreement about its scope. We can point to problems with each of these definitions. Consider them in turn: mediators often are not neutral, even in the broadest sense of the term; one or more of the parties might well be trying not to reach agreement; many mediators refrain from making substantive (as opposed to procedural) suggestions; in certain kinds and instances of mediation, concessions are avoided in favor of integrative solutions;

and occasionally, as in the mediation-arbitration (med-arb) process, mediators do have authoritative decision making power.

Much of the debate about the merits of mediation is confused because it is not clear what is the essence of mediation. Terms such as "neutrality", "voluntarily", "concessions", and "separately", rather than serving to define mediation, argue for a particular quality of intervention. Such arguments may or may not be worthwhile; however, we suggest that they be removed from the realm of mediation's definition and made an explicit part of the debate about the merits and problems of mediation in relation to particular processes.

Like arbitration, mediation must date to the furthest reaches of prehistory. What can be a more natural response by concerned friends witnessing destructive conflict than to try to help the disputants settle their differences? From Popes to Prime Ministers, from chiefs to children, such intervention has been a common feature of social life.

Mediation is not the exclusive province of Western cultures. Among many examples that might be given are Chinese community mediation (where the third party takes an active, often coercive role in the substantive issues), the Kpelle moot courts (Danzig, 1973), the Nuer leopard-skin chief (Kolb, 1983a) and many other kinds of procedures (see, for example, Nader, 1969; Gulliver, 1979; Abel, 1982b). However, with the exception of the Kpelle courts, whose philosophy of conciliation within the community has served, albeit loosely, as a model for neighborhood justice centers (Goldberg, Green and Sander, 1985), these approaches to disputes and conflicts have had little influence on the development of current practices in the United States. Despite the interest by anthropologists in the mechanisms by which other cultures maintain order and treat disputes and conflicts, they exist or existed independent of the current evolutionary mainstream.

The sources of this mainstream are many, and it is unclear exactly how it developed. Did the concept of neutrality, to take one important aspect of mediation, derive empirically from repeated attempts to attract disputants to the table? Or was it derived from conciliators and mediators, such as the Mennonites and Quakers, whose religious background challenged them to view the behavior ("sin"), rather than the person, as the problem? Or was it inherited from therapeutic procedures which stress acceptance of the individual and absence of blame by the therapist? And what influence has systems theory (which views individual and group behavior as a product of reciprocal interaction among all participants in a situation) had in averting blame and establishing impartiality?

There are no easy answers to these questions, and other aspects of mediation share this uncertainty. In some cases development of processes in separate fields, such as family or public policy mediation, has been along parallel but separate paths; in others, practices in one field have reinforced those in another; while in some cases, concepts or practices in one area have been borrowed wholesale by another.

The attempt to define clearly the roots and lineage of the various mediation practices is needed to demonstrate commonalities within various fields and among different levels of practice. But an overall view of the entire arena of mediation incorporating each of these smaller fields does not yet exist. What can be traced are the histories of the usage of these processes within various fields of practice. The divorce, community, victim–offender, public policy, and school fields in particular have become defined as separate entities, with their own individual literatures, associations of practitioners, educational and training institutions, and conventions. We devote separate sections to each of these fields.

THE STATE OF THE ART

Mediation is used informally in virtually every area of human interaction. And the number of settings in which formal, institutionalized mediation is used has been increasing rapidly since the 1970s. Mediation may be associated in the public's eye with individuals such as U Thant, Henry Kissinger, and Terry Waite – well-known personalities working in hotspots of international conflict. In fact, however, the spread of mediation to other fields owes much more to the quieter example of labor–management mediation than it does to the publicity-conscious wheeling and dealing of these other third parties.

Mediation is used in dealing with a number of intra-community problems, such as divorce and child custody issues, consumer–merchant problems, and landlord–tenant disputes. In the public sector, mediation is used in areas such as labor–management relations and city–county annexation disputes. In the environmental field, mediation has been used to manage differences over siting, waste management, and Superfund clean up of toxic waste dumps, as well as to aid the development of Environmental Protection Agency regulations. Many businesses now use mediation internally, as one part of their employee and/or consumer grievance proceedings, as well as for dealing with inter-corporate disputes. Institutions such as prisons and schools have used mediation to deal with problems as diverse as prison uprisings and school bussing. A growing number of elementary and secondary schools have created programs that teach children to act as "conflict managers" by formally mediating problems among their fellow students.

At the community level, which relies primarily on volunteers, mediation is being practiced by professionals in related fields – attorneys, counsellors, social workers – as well as individuals from virtually all walks of life. Many community programs have a religious base and draw their mediators from church membership. The "peace" churches, the Quakers, Mennonites, and Brethren, supply a dispro-portionate number of mediators in a variety of fields, including the international (Brubaker and Kraybill, 1987).

Even fields as specialized and professionalized as labor and divorce mediation draw their mediators from diverse sources. Attorneys, professors, clergy, and former union activists all practise labor mediation, although the "ideal" experience is as a labor or manage-ment negotiator (Kolb, 1983a). Divorce mediation is practised by volunteers and professionals alike, with custody and visitation issues drawing more attention from therapists, and other aspects from attorneys (Emery and Wyer, 1987). Environmental mediation draws practitioners from a variety of experiences, including environmental activists and former labor–management mediators. In the inter-national area, professional diplomats in the official realm are comple-mented by a range of unofficial mediators and conciliators, many of whom work from a religious base.

Many public officials who have always performed a quasi-mediator role in dealing with the public now explicity recognize this role and receive training in mediation skills and techniques. An increasing number of judges perform "judicial mediation" (Wall and Rude, 1985) for out-of-court settlement of cases.

Depending upon the field and locality of practice, certification of mediators may or may not be required by a state or by an appropriate professional organization. Some national organizations, including the Academy of Family Mediators and the Family Mediation Association, have established certification requirements for their members. The Society of Professionals in Dispute Resolution (SPIDR), while resisting a single set of standards, does suggest principles of qualification (NIDR, 1989). But in some areas any who want to may call themselves mediators and advertise their services in any area.

Community dispute resolution centers, often also called community mediation or neighborhood justice centers, commonly depend upon volunteers to handle intake and to conduct their mediation sessions. Required training for such volunteers may vary from minimal – one ten-hour course – to more extensive – forty or more hours to begin with, additional inservice training, and co-mediation with an experienced mediator.

A number of public agencies in the United States have been instrumental in the development of various forms of mediation. The Federal Mediation and Conciliation Service (FMCS) was founded in 1917 under the name of the "U.S. Conciliation Service" and under the aegis of the Department of Labor. The title change in 1947 accompanied its establishment as an independent federal agency. Its jurisdiction includes other federal agencies, private industries engaged in interstate commerce, and private non-profit health facilities, a work load handled by its relatively small staff of nearly 300 full-time mediators.

At one time, FMCS mediators intervened only in labor–management disputes. The announcement of federal mediators being brought in during a potential or actual strike still indicates FMCS involvement. But the agency has been broadening its role. Its proactive stance now includes negotiation training, and in many cases agency personnel work with labor and management before contract negotiations in what they term "preventive mediation". Preventive mediation is designed to help parties avoid the conditions that create disputes by improving working relationships.

Other activities sponsored by the FMCS include a grants program to support joint labor–management committees and FMCS or private mediators trained to mediate age discrimination complaints for federally funded programs. The agency also maintains a roster of recommended arbitrators, through their Office of Arbitration Services, for parties choosing arbitration. Despite the increased activities and responsibilities assumed by the FMCS, however, funding in the 1980s actually declined. The future of the agency is thus unsettled.

The Community Relations Service (CRS) of the Department of Justice was created in 1964 with a mandate to intervene in disputes and difficulties related to discrimination based on race, color, or national origin. They can enter a case either upon request or upon their own initiative. They are involved in many kinds of cases, from school desegregation problems in numerous communities and the major riots of the 1960s, to single incidents such as the Miami riot of 1980, the Nazi march in Skokie, Illinois, and the Wounded Knee violence. Because they are mandated to work in confidence and without publicity, they have had a lower profile than the impact of their activities might deserve.

In a significant recognition of the actual sources of many of the problems they were seeing, the CRS restructured their activities in 1968. They moved away from the "fire-fighting" role of crisis intervention to work at the level of the underlying causes (Pompa, 1987). They identified five areas of the greatest frustration for minorities: the administration of justice; education; fair housing; economic development; and communications, or access to the media. For a variety of reasons, however, by 1972 the agency was forced to return to crisis response, with limited preventive work.

At least 35 states and the District of Columbia have asserted statutory authority for mediation by the end of 1988 (NIDR, 1989). At least 21 states provide for mediation of industrial disputes, many of them through state boards of mediation; 10 or more have statutes concerning family mediation.

The largest general organization of mediators is the Society of Professionals in Dispute Resolution (SPIDR), whose membership includes a mix of arbitrators, mediators, facilitators, and academics. The annual conventions, and the published reports of these conventions, demonstrate the wide range of beliefs and practices of its members.

The Academy of Family Mediators, a relatively new organization, at one time was entirely dedicated to divorce mediation and divorce mediators. However, it has broadened its scope to include areas such as school based mediation and business mediation.

THE MEDIATION PROCESSES

Mediation, then, is not a single process, but several kinds of third-party intervention. A number of researchers have attempted to make sense of the wide range of mediation processes by categorizing mediator roles. Kolb (1983a) claims that mediators espouse one of two distinct understandings of their practice. Some view it as a science. Most view mediation as an art; dealing with different circumstances for each case, the mediator must feel his or her way through the obstacles posed by personality, issues, and political and economic limitations.

Zartman and Touval (1985) suggest that mediators take one of three roles: communicator, formulator or manipulator. Pruitt (1981) distinguishes between mediators who emphasize the importance of the process and those who focus on content. Bolduc (1989) suggests four mediator styles: "fair treatment", "mutual self-interest", "just-outcome", and "just relationship".

Some researchers attempt to understand mediation by the kinds of strategies and tactics used. Wall (1981), in his analysis of mediation, has provided an exhaustive survey of various mediator strategies, techniques and functions. These procedures include not only such commonly accepted tactics as identifying the real issues and summarizing the agreement, but much more controversial ones as well: exploiting the weaker side, obfuscating the negotiator's position, publicly indicting negotiators for being too tough, and misrepresenting and distorting information.

A number of people have divided the mediation process into stages. Moore (1987) proposes the following twelve stages:

1. Initial contacts with the disputing parties
2. Selecting a strategy to guide mediation
3. Collecting and analyzing background information
4. Designing a detailed plan for mediation
5. Building trust and cooperation
6. Beginning the mediation session
7. Defining issues and setting an agenda
8. Uncovering hidden interests of the disputing parties
9. Generating options for settlement
10. Assessing options for settlement
11. Final bargaining
12. Achieving formal settlement.

Kraybill (1984), in training materials developed for mediators on behalf of the Mennonite Conciliation Service, suggests five stages: introduction; story-telling; caucus (not mandatory); problem-solving; and agreement.

Keltner (1987) suggests seven phases of mediation: setting the stage; opening and development; exploration of the issues; identification of alternatives; evaluation, negotiation, and bargaining; decision making and testing; and terminating the process.

The Community Board Center for Policy and Training advocates four phases in addition to an opening and closing. Phase 1 is for preparing the disputants to work together by developing rapport; Phase 2 is facilitating communication; Phase 3 is reflection on work and learning and preparation to resolve the conflict; and Phase 4 is developing a mutual resolution.

Another way to understand mediation is to represent its practice along a continuum of polar ideal types: "agreement-centered" and "relationship-centered", which are similar to what Silbey and Merry (1986) term "bargaining" and "therapeutic". The primary goal of the former is to avoid the potential harmful consequences of continuing a dispute or conflict by reaching agreements tolerable to each party. Agreement-centered mediation is associated with labor–management collective bargaining, and is often called the "labor" model (Lentz, 1986). Relationship-focussed processes do not ignore the goal of reaching agreement, but the primary emphasis is on creating the kind of relationship needed to develop, implement, and sustain an integrative solution to continuing problems between or among parties. Of course, mediators can and do combine elements of both practices. But the distinction is useful as a means of highlighting two different philosophies of mediation.

We provide descriptions of some of the different mediation practices (divorce mediation, community mediation, and public policy mediation) later, in Chapters 3, 5 and 6. However, we think it useful to present here representatives of these two ideal types. The first, the "agreement-centered" or "labor" model, is that used by the FMCS to deal with labor–management disputes. The actual procedures described by the FMCS themselves suggest the agency's stress on its newer, more relationship-centered role, as they do not entirely conform to other descriptions of the labor model (Lentz, 1986; Kolb, 1983a and 1983b). The FMCS (1981) provides this brief summary of its procedure:

> While methods and circumstances vary, the mediator will generally confer first with one of the parties and then with the other to get their versions of the pending difficulties. With these problems firmly in mind, he will usually call joint conferences with both agency and union representatives present.
>
> The mediator functions informally, meeting separately and jointly to help the parties find some mutually acceptable solution. He or she explores all possible areas of agreement.
>
> It is part of the mediator's job to listen, review, analyze, suggest,

advise and reason.

In addition to working hard to help the agency and the union agree to contract terms, the mediator strives to create permanent improvement in the bargaining relationship and in the day-to-day working relationship between the parties.

The mediator can often get stalled negotiations going again . . . improve the atmosphere . . . encourage discussion . . . explore alternative solutions . . . suggest ideas that have worked elsewhere . . . provide needed data and other expertise and information.

Through the use of FMCS services, agencies and their unions, working with the mediator, can undertake programs to resolve mutual problems in their relationship. The mediator can give advisory assistance on specific problems and encourage the use of joint labor–management committees. Mediators can provide training and information to improve the knowledge and skill of both parties, can identify trends and developments, can encourage early bargaining to avoid deadline tensions.

The process used by the CRS serves as an example of the second of the two ideal types, "relationship-centered". The CRS uses six factors to determine whether a situation is suitable for mediation (Pompa, 1987). First, the issues must be negotiable and able to form the basis of a written agreement. Second, the rhetorical climate must be at a level conducive for the parties to negotiate. Third, the situation must have been defined as a crisis. Fourth, the protesters must be ready to end the confrontation before negotiating. Fifth, the protest leaders must be sufficiently representative of the minority community to sign an agreement that will last. And sixth, the establishment negotiators must have decision making authority. The CRS describes their process as follows:

Role of the CRS Mediator

The CRS mediator is responsible for establishing and interpreting ground rules and procedures for the negotiation sessions. The mediator schedules, arranges, and chairs the joint mediation sessions. When necessary, the mediator may arrange various kinds of resource assistance to the parties. The CRS mediator serves as moderator or referee to ensure that procedural rules are observed and to guide discussion toward constructive consideration of remedies and solutions. In no sense is the mediator an arbitrator, judge, or decision-maker. CRS recognizes that only the parties themselves can reach a mutually satisfactory settlement, accomplished by full examination of the issues, open-minded exchange of views, and acceptance of reasonable remedies or solutions to recognized grievances and needs.

The Mediation Process

Mediation is a voluntary process in which the parties to a dispute attempt to resolve their differences through discussion, clarification, and orderly negotiation. Unlike an adjudicated settlement of disputes, successful mediation does not consist of "winners" and "losers" but of parties who have carefully examined and resolved a defined set of issues and practices. While mediation may address alleged past offenses, its main focus is prospective, forging a consensus on reasonable and necessary actions for the future.

Usually as a first step, the mediator will meet with each team and perhaps also with its parent body or general membership. The mediator will listen carefully to everyone, seeking understanding in depth of their real concerns and needs and of the positions of the group on the issues. The mediator's main objective throughout is to enhance the possibility that the parties will come to understand better each other's situation and proceed to hammer out a mutually acceptable settlement. From these preparatory talks with each party, the mediator will work up an approved agenda covering all matters which are to be addressed during joint negotiations. All outstanding issues are open for negotiation.

Joint mediation sessions, usually held at a neutral setting, seldom last longer than three hours, depending on the effectiveness of the session and the wishes of the participants. How many such sessions and what time span will be required to complete the agenda are difficult to predict. Much will depend upon the complexity of the issues, the severity of conflicting positions, and the determination of each team to find or create workable solutions.

Where possible, it is sometimes desirable to hold the joint sessions in a concentrated time frame or on consecutive days. It often may be necessary to recess sessions for a time to consult with the parties or advisors, consider proposals, draft prospective agreements, or for other compelling reasons.

During the mediation sessions any team or the mediator may request a caucus in order for the team members to consult with one another in private. The mediator is available to the teams during caucuses for consultation, if desired. If a team wishes to discuss any matter with the mediator in confidence, such information will not be disclosed except as clearly authorized. Such communication is encouraged. The more fully the mediator is permitted to understand the real concerns and positions of each party, the more useful the mediator can become in raising questions or offering ideas which will help forge an agreement. In some situations, the mediator may find that better progress can be made in separate meetings with the respective teams than in joint sessions.

Mediation sessions are closed to the news media and other outside parties, except for resource specialists or observers agreed to in advance. While mediation is underway, no participant or other person may report or discuss the content of the proceedings or positions of the parties with newspeople, the public or others not directly involved. This does not limit team members from conferring as need be from time to time with their parent body or key decision-makers whom they represent. Usually the participants choose to have only the mediator respond to press inquiries.

Formalization of an Agreement

Matters finally agreed upon in mediation are set forth in a written document signed by the parties and witnessed by the mediator. Generally, the agreement is prepared for the court's approval and entered as a Consent Decree. A legally sufficient court decree can be enforced in a court of law. Generally, the agreement includes provisions for ongoing local monitoring of the agreement's implementation and procedures to be employed, including the use of CRS, in the event disagreements arise over execution of the accord (CRS, undated).

CONCLUSIONS

Mediation's growing acceptance in fields as diverse as civil rights, divorce, prisoner grievances, and land-annexation disputes, indicates that an increasing number of people, mediators and disputants alike, are finding it a useful means of dealing with disputes or conflicts. Indeed, mediation has been promoted as though it is a miracle cure of society's ills. A partial listing of its claimed merits includes the following (Center for Dispute Resolution, 1986): economical decisions, rapid settlements, mutually satisfactory outcomes, high rate of compliance, comprehensive and "customized" agreements, practice in and learning of creative problem-solving procedures, greater degree of control and predictability of outcome, personal empowerment, preservation of an on-going working relationship or termination of relationship in a more amicable way, workable and implementable decisions, agreements that are better than a simple compromise or win/lose outcome, and decisions that hold over time.

Despite these accolades, a number of questions and problems remain. For instance, is a mediator responsible to a larger public than those immediate parties to a dispute? Argument over this question polarizes those who claim no duty beyond these immediate parties and those who claim responsibility for unrepresented interests (see SPIDR, 1984 and 1985, for discussion). Those experienced with the labor model of mediation, with its clearly-defined issues and parties, are more likely to focus solely on the participating disputants than are mediators in fields in which the parties and issues are not well-defined.

There is some concern that a rigidly defined mediation process applied indiscriminately to a variety of settings denies valid cultural differences, and in so doing is inappropriate for many groups. Indeed, much of mediation as it is institutionalized and practiced today assumes standards and behavior alien to various cultures. Folberg and Taylor (1984) suggest differences in the ways that different cultures react to a number of elements, including the idea of outside help, a mediator's role, interpersonal conflict, mediator credentials, the techniques of mediation, and such seemingly innocuous matters as schedules and payment of fees.

At one time, mediation differed from other processes in that participation was at least nominally voluntary. This distinction may not have been apparent to those individuals, groups, and nations who were subtly, or not so subtly, coerced into participation. But to many mediators, voluntary participation is an ideal whose observance is both ethically and practically necessary for success. Hence, the increasing practice – in child custody disputes, for example – by which courts insist upon mediation prior to an adjudicated hearing, strikes some mediation advocates as being both unfair and impractical.

Another concern common to the public policy, divorce, and community fields, is that mediation transforms collective grievances into individual problems (Abel, 1982a). By dealing with these grievances on a case-by-case basis, the larger problems are ignored and allowed to fester unresolved. Also, some fear that by using evaluative criteria such as "disputant satisfaction" to measure its successes or failures, mediation risks ignoring the meaning of real interests and rights (Tyler, 1988).

Other questions or potential problems of mediation include the exploitative potential of the process by more powerful sections of society, the expansion of state control into private lives, and the denial of due process (see Roehl and Cook, 1985, for discussion). It is hard to disagree with Kressel and Pruitt (1985, p. 196), who find that "the enthusiasm and inventiveness of mediators has thus far outdistanced the ability of researchers to comprehend the mediation process and to accurately assess its value." Clearly, wholesale and uncritical acceptance of mediation risks turning it into a process sold as a remedy for anything that is ailing, rather than a tool at the service of deliberately-chosen and explicit goals.

We turn now to examine, in the light of these introductory observations, several specific types of mediation that fall within the management area.

3 Divorce Mediation

INTRODUCTION

The range of ways that decisions about divorce issues are made is representative of the entire spectrum of management, settlement, and resolution practices. The decision making mechanisms include out-of-court negotiations and litigation, where judgement is rendered as part of the adversarial process; procedures where a counselor or mediator works with a couple before making recommendations to a judge; and processes where the couple, and even their children, are maximally involved in a well-facilitated forum for exploration of their divisive issues.

Koopman and Hunt (1988) contrast traditional and emerging principles regarding divorcing families. They note several important changes, including the movement from evaluation based on fault to one based on need/equity; a past perspective giving way to one based on the present and future; a process focus moving from punitive/reactive to problem-solving/proactive; and a movement away from a prescriptive authority role to one facilitative of client self-determination.

Three major factors are responsible for these changes and the increasing interest and use of divorce mediation:

1. Several aspects of divorce law have recently been changing. No-fault laws have eroded the influence of "fault" in determining custody, and the "best-interests" standard by which most courts handed custody to mothers has been under attack (Emery and Wyer, 1987).
2. Psychological research has demonstrated the adverse effects of divorce on children. Their exposure to continuing fighting between their parents is associated with adjustment difficulties (Emery and Wyer, 1987). A process less adversarial than the courts may result in less contention, and hence less trauma to the children. Indeed, some have found that the actual provisions of the custody or visitation agreement have less effect on the children than parental agreement and cooperation (Mumma, 1984).
3. There is a general trend in other fields, exemplified by practices in community and public policy mediation, towards disputants

having a greater say in the determination of their management problems, disputes and conflicts. Although impossible to measure, there clearly is a spillover effect from these other fields (Koopman and Hunt, 1988).

Divorce mediation is performed by three separate groups: mental health professionals, attorneys, and volunteers and professionals from other fields who have received specialized mediation training. A number of states and localities provide mandatory or optional court-sponsored mediation, particularly in cases involving minor children. Many community mediation centers do custody and divorce mediation, and private mediators deal with the standard divorce issues of separation, custody, alimony, and property division.

The Academy of Family Mediators, founded in 1981, is the preeminent education and accreditation organization in the field. The Academy sponsors annual conferences and the publications *Mediation Quarterly* and *Mediation News*. Standards for divorce mediation have been prepared by the Association of Family and Conciliation Courts (1984) and by the American Bar Association, Family Law Section (1984).

THE PROCESS

Because divorce mediation is practiced by individuals with a variety of backgrounds, there is wide variation in the types of processes used. An attorney's approach might involve no more structure than meeting with the couple and suggesting the best way to divide property and settle other issues. At the other extreme are those who practice "mediation counseling" (Mumma, 1984), approaching the realm of family therapy in their efforts to change patterns of confrontational interaction. In between is a wide range of practices.

Although the study of divorce mediation is interesting researchers more and more, there is as yet relatively little literature that incorporates process description, theoretical foundations, and analysis of results. The work of Emery and his associates (Emery, Shaw and Jackson, 1987; Emery and Wyer, 1987) is one exception, and this section will draw heavily upon the characteristics of their process.

The legal requirements and options of custody and divorce are complex. Although ideally the parties have their own attorneys to represent their legal rights and interests, many participants are either too poor or simply unwilling to do so. Therefore, the divorce mediator must bring considerable knowledge of the law to the mediation, without actually offering legal advice.

When practical, male and female co-mediators are favored in order to avoid giving the parents the impression of gender bias, as well as to offer the other advantages of co-mediation. These other advantages include allowing one mediator to focus on content and the other on process, aiding in training new mediators, improving the skills of experienced mediators, and removing what may be a heavy burden of responsibility from a single mediator. Cost limitations, however, mean that most often there is just one mediator.

Not all potential participants are suitable for mediation. Factors which might hinder or make impossible a fair mediation include severe discrepancy in relative bargaining power, such as when one of the couple maintains control of all of the finances; alleged child abuse; severe individual psychopathology; and low intelligence (Emery and Wyer, 1987).

The married couple by themselves are normally the participants in mediation. Occasionally, members of the extended family participate. Some mediators also directly involve the parents' attorneys. Rarely are the children included, although in some cases they are consulted. Indeed, in some cases mediators emphatically emphasize that the parents should not include the children in the decision making process, suggesting that to do so is to abdicate responsibility and unnecessarily involve children in highly tense situations.

Some programs do, however, involve the children. Mumma (1984) suggests how a family systems approach to custody mediation, which recognizes the role and influence of each participant in developing, maintaining, or changing the system, must bring together all family members. If some participants are not involved in the process, he argues, dysfunctional patterns of communication and behavior cannot be observed and changed. Such involvement also allows the parents to focus their attention away from their positions and on to the needs of the children.

The length of sessions varies, depending on the phase of the mediation (introductory sessions might take less time), mediator preference, and parent availability. Although seven or eight sessions of two hours or more might be required to work properly through difficult cases, mediators have found that in allowing more than five or six sessions one or both participants might become dependent upon the process and reluctant to conclude their business.

For Emery and his associates (Emery, Shaw and Jackson, 1987) the initial introductory session often is highly structured. It consists first of an introduction to the process, where the parents are presented the contrast between an imposed decision by the judge and an agreement which reflects their own and the children's needs. A mediation contract which professes their understanding of the process and agreement to not subpoena the mediators to any future hearing is then signed by the parents. "The first session gives parents a chance to voice their concerns, become more cognizant of the 'real' issues, gain confidence in the mediation process, and begin emotional preparation for later problem-solving" (Emery, Shaw and Jackson, 1987, p. 19).

The parents are then presented the ground rules, which are established both to make the sessions a safe place for the parents to discuss emotionally-charged issues and to establish control for the mediators. These rules provide a framework for the process, but may not be enforced fully if flexibility is required.

The next step is to focus on the children, during which time the parents discuss their children informally. This can result in the parents discovering or renewing their common concerns about the children.

During the next stage, the parents each get five or ten minutes of uninterrupted time to present the issues as they see them. The mediators then begin to redefine the issues at hand. They replace loaded terms such as "custody" with terms such as "parenting", and reframe the problem as "an inability on the part of the parents to negotiate an agreement, not as an issue regarding what to do about the children" (Emery, Shaw and Jackson, 1987, p. 13).

Confrontation at this stage is encouraged, as it may be necessary before problem-solving can occur. Confrontation also signals important issues, and can demonstrate for the mediators the parents' style of relating to each other. However, balance must be created to allow the necessary expression of feelings without destroying the entire process.

At the end of the problem definition stage the mediators summarize and redefine the areas of agreement and disagreement. Caucusing with each parent then allows more opportunity for emotional ventilation, establishes personal rapport between mediators and parent, and uncovers underlying issues which might not have been revealed in the joint session.

The mediators then emphasize areas of difference and agreement. Feedback about the mediators' understanding is sought. A brief negotiation about interim child arrangements concludes the first session.

The middle sessions are less structured. Emery and his associates join other divorce mediators (Koopman and Hunt, 1988) in using Fisher and Ury's (1981) model of principled negotiation. The key aspects of their model are separating the people from the problem (help parents distinguish their spousal role from their parental role); focusing on interests, not positions (in particular, focus on the children's welfare); inventing options for mutual gain; and whenever possible using objective criteria for testing alternatives.

Agreement is written out in lay terminology. Parents are given time to consult attorneys and change their minds before it becomes part of the court decree. It is standard practice to include a clause in the agreement that specifies a return to mediation before litigation should any further dispute occur, and it is common for couples to return to work out new agreements under changed circumstances.

CONCLUSIONS

As in other areas, the question of mediator qualifications is an issue of some controversy (Lemmon, 1988). A number of unregulated organizations and individuals sponsor both divorce mediation and training for such mediation. It is not uncommon for mediators to be trained by others with little training and less experience, and in most jurisdictions anyone may practice and advertise private divorce mediation without any qualifications whatsoever. There is considerable argument as well about the appropriate roles for volunteers, attorneys and mental health professionals in divorce mediation. Emery and Wyer (1987) suggest a likely future in which attorneys dominate private divorce practice, as their profession increasingly accepts the concept. Mental health professionals, who currently dominate court-based programs, will mediate custody and visitation disputes.

As is typical of other fields, evaluation of the mediation process presents problems as well. Hunt, Koopman, Coltri and Favretto (1988) suggest the use of criteria such as comprehensiveness of agreement *vis-à-vis* the issues and parental roles and responsibilities; agreement durability, flexibility, and modifiability; need satisfaction; workability of agreement; level of family conflict; and level of child adjustment. As with other fields, speculation still exceeds research, but in divorce mediation perhaps more than any other field this is changing (Kelly 1989).

There is disagreement among mediators about the mediator's duty to the children (Paquin, 1988), with some claiming that the parents themselves are responsible for the determination of custody and others arguing for the mediator's role as child advocate. Among those in favor of the advocacy role there are disagreements about whether and when direct involvement with the child is appropriate. Children are susceptible to pressures from one or both parents and other family members, they may blame one of the parents with whom they actually have a good relationship, they may feel dependent on the parent whose care they are in at the time they are asked, and they may feel obliged to help the parent who shows the greatest signs of distress.

A corollary to the involvement of children is the appropriate use of joint custody. Emery and Wyer (1987) suggest an unwarranted bias by mediators in favor of joint custody, and warn of dangers such as inconsistent parenting and children's anxiety about switching households.

Another debate within the field concerns the suitability of mediation for situations involving power disparities. In particular, it is argued that traditional male–female marital roles often leave the wife unprepared to bargain on an equal basis with the husband (Schulman and Woods, 1983; Leitch, 1986). The National Center on Women and Family Law (1983) declared that mediation is inappropriate in any divorce and family law dispute. Others who have recognized this problem have devised explicit guidelines, strategies, and tactics to empower the less powerful participant (Davis and Salem, 1984). As divorce mediator Stephen Erickson argued during a divorce mediation training in 1987, given a mediator sensitive to a disputant's lack of experience with financial affairs or inexperience in bargaining, mediation can provide a forum for breaking the pattern of dependence, whereas litigation may merely replace one dependency with another (from the husband to the attorney).

In many cases divorce is as conflictual and traumatic a situation as an individual is ever likely to be involved in. Divorce would hardly seem the most promising arena for the development of a collaborative decision making forum, in which partners who cannot stand any longer to live with one another must confront one another in person and reach agreement on numerous divisive issues. Yet divorce mediation is clearly an established and rapidly-growing field. Furthermore, the field has attracted some of the most imaginative practition-ers and theoreticians of any of the fields in which mediation is used. Innovations within the field abound, such as the use of groups to decide custody issues (Campbell and Johnston, 1986). The growing acceptance of divorce mediation is perhaps the clearest statement of how poorly the litigation process has dealt with determining such divisive issues as property settlement and custody of the children.

4 Victim–Offender Reconciliation

INTRODUCTION

The Victim–Offender Reconciliation Program (VORP) brings together in a face-to-face meeting a person who has been convicted of a crime and the person or persons who were victims of that crime. An attempt is made to mediate some form of restitution for the victims, and to achieve a reconciliation satisfactory to the victims, the offender and the representatives of the legal system.

The concept of victim–offender reconciliation is a product of three contemporary movements within the criminal justice domain: an increased concern for victims and their role in the criminal justice system; growing dissatisfaction with established ways of punishing and/or treating the offender; and awareness of new alternatives to standard methods of dispute settlement and management.

The last few decades have seen the growth of a field of study, termed "victimology", as a kind of counterweight to the extensive research that had previously been done on offenders, deviance, and punishment. Researchers in this field have compiled an extensive bibliography and even have their own journal: *Victimology: an International Journal*.

Early studies (see review in Mendelsohn, 1963) focussed on victim susceptibility to and precipitation of the crime. In recent years these kinds of studies have aroused controversy, raising the ire of those who see the least suggestion of culpability by the victim in spouse abuse, rape, and other crimes as further exploitation of the already traumatized victim.

More recent interest in the victim has taken the form of advocacy for their rights. This interest has resulted in the creation of institutions such as the National Organization of Victims Assistance (NOVA) and the National Center on Child Abuse and Neglect. Programs existing nationwide to aid the victim include victim/witness assistance, rape crisis support centers, victim ombudsmen, victim advocates, and shelters for battered wives.

Despite this increasing concern for victims, numerous problems still exist. Studies of victim dissatisfaction with the criminal justice system have confirmed what many knew or suspected for some time: that victims are often ignored and/or mistreated by the system intended to protect them (Knudten and Knudten, 1981).

Criminal victimization can be, and often is, a traumatic experience. Even crimes normally treated as rather minor, such as vandalism or car theft, can leave the victim feeling shock, anger, fear and helplessness. Yet criminal justice procedures often exacerbate these same feelings by removing the victim from any significant participation in the treatment of the crime. The victim has little or no part in arresting the offender, and must put up with long delays before a trial is held. Testimony is given at the convenience of the court; repeated visits by the victim are often necessary. Guilt, sentencing, and restitution (if it is even considered), are all determined by others. It is not surprising, then, that the levels of victim dissatisfaction with the criminal justice system are so high, and that changes are being demanded.

The standard paradigm for treating the offender is that of punishment by incarceration. Society justifies this punishment by claiming that imprisonment serves three purposes (Barnett, 1981): as a deterrent to further crime; as a means of removing the offender from the opportunity to continue criminal activity; and as a means of rehabilitation.

While the validity of various theories can be argued, the reality does not support any of these justifications of punishment. The prison population of the United States has risen nearly 50 per cent in a decade, and significant crime continues to increase, as does the rate of recidivism.

When an offender is locked away the possibility of restitution for the victim also disappears, along with any chance of teaching the offender accountability for the consequences of his or her actions. Furthermore, prisons rarely foster rehabilitation. The chief probation officer of a Central Virginia Corrections unit, explaining his interest in alternatives to incarceration, claimed "I have never yet seen anyone come out of prison a better person than when he went in" (Tom Wilson, Chief Probation Officer, personal communication). Zehr and Umbreit (1982, pp. 63–4) echo this sentiment:

Indeed, prisons often provide an unreal climate of brutality, intrigue, dependence and control which make participants not more but less able to live as law-abiding citizens in a free society, and this may contribute to rather than reduce crime. Moreover, prisons are rapidly pricing themselves out of the market.

Elsewhere in this Series, and in later chapters in this book, the wider question is raised as to the sources of crimes and conflicts, and whether too much emphasis is being placed by society on punishment, and not enough on conditions likely to promote crime and conflict. Incarceration and coercion seem to be accepted by society, not as a last resort but as the only resort.

VORP HISTORY AND GOALS

In 1974, a Kitchener, Ontario, probation officer decided that a case of vandalism (known as the "Elmira" case) involving two juveniles could best be handled by having the offenders meet with the victims and work out restitution among themselves. With a mediator's help, the two young men met with each victim, and within six months completed restitution. Results were so gratifying that this kind of face-to-face meeting was tried again. After a few more test cases, a VORP committee was formed that received a government grant to support a pilot project.

As is so often the case, one person's idea and initiative touched a general concern. Interested residents of other localities began starting similar programs. As the number of programs grew the need was seen for a central information and assistance service to aid those in other communities. The PACT (Prisoner and Community Together) Institute of Justice, of Elkhart, Indiana now operates the Victim–Offender Reconciliation Resource Center to provide materials and assistance to those interested in VORP.

In addition to PACT, the MCC (Mennonite Central Committee) Office of Criminal Justice of Elkhart is involved in promoting and supporting VORP, and Judeo-Christian principles are specifically invoked in much of the VORP promotional literature as the foundation of those programs currently in existence. There are now several dozen Victim–Offender Reconciliation Programs in the United States, thirty or more in Canada, and at least fifteen in Great Britain.

The initial Victim–Offender Reconciliation Project in Kitchener, Ontario began as a joint venture of the Mennonite Central Committee of Ontario and the Province of Ontario Ministry of Correctional

Services. Their stated purposes were (McKnight, 1981): to provide a useful method for dealing with crime in the community; to bring the victim and offender together in an attempt to reach reconciliation and agreement about restitution; to use a third party to foster reconciliation; and to deal with crime as a conflict to be resolved.

With the example of the first program as a guide, other communities have refined these goals and used the VORP process to satisfy other purposes. Literature from PACT Institute of Justice, as well as from proponents writing in independent journals, emphasizes these other purposes.

The primary stated goal is reconciliation between victim and offender (PACT, 1984): "The actual restitution agreement that is worked out by both is a tangible by-product of the reconciliation process." Another goal, increasing victim participation in the criminal justice system, will benefit, it is claimed, both the victim and the system. The victims of crimes often have questions left unanswered in standard criminal proceedings, questions about why their house was chosen for burglary, or why it was their car which was vandalized, or how the offender got into the home. Feelings of victimization, shock, anger, sadness, and fear that often have no outlet can be released in expressing them to the offender.

Restitution, the third goal, should reflect, if worked out between victim and offender, what a victim really wants and expects (and may actually collect) more accurately than restitution ordered (or not ordered) by a less knowledgeable third party, such as the probation officer.

If rehabilitation, yet another goal, is to occur, then the offender first must face up to having committed a wrong and take responsibility for righting that wrong; the goal here is to promote accountability by the offender.

The final goal, empowerment of the offender, dovetails with increased victim participation. Under the current criminal justice system the offender who has feelings of guilt, shame, and sorrow, has no means constructively to alleviate them. VORP is intended to allow the individual a means of expressing and acting upon them.

THE VORP PROCESS

Although it is easier to begin the analysis with the precipitating crime, the very idea of potential reconciliation implies differences more deeply rooted than a single criminal incident itself. These might be long-simmering differences between acquaintances which some triggering event finally explodes; or they might be class differences between people who have never met, and whose opinions of each other are based on stereotype and prejudice; or they might involve differences in deeply held values.

VORP is not a program whose procedures are etched in stone. Restrictions on the age of offenders accepted into the program, and on the severity of crimes handled, vary from one locality to another. Community support, the capabilities of the program administrators and the mediators, and the attitudes of judges, probation officers, prosecutors, victim/witness coordinators, and other court personnel determine acceptance criteria and procedures for each locality.

Arrest of the offender and the admittance of guilt are two obvious prerequisites before victim–offender reconciliation may be considered. If offenders deny guilt, even upon conviction, rehabilitation through accountability – taking responsibility for the consequences of what they have done – will not be possible.

If upon arrest the offender admits guilt, pre-trial diversion into the program might be made. This is particularly true for juveniles, whose processing through the criminal justice system allows more discretion and flexibility. Due process protections for adults make it difficult to institute VORP procedures before guilt is formally established. Adult referrals to the program thus usually come after conviction, but may come either before sentencing or after sentencing. VORP might be required as part or all of the sentence, in which case fulfilling the VORP contract becomes a condition of probation.

Although the literature stresses the voluntary aspects of the meeting for both victim and offender, in practice this is often not the case. According to Coates (1985, p. 7):

> Contrary to the rhetoric of VORP staff which emphasizes the voluntary nature of participation, offenders participate because they believe they must . . . For the most part offenders are ordered formally to participate.

For victims, however, the program is truly voluntary; no one can force them to participate. After the offender has either agreed to or been ordered to participate the next step is for the mediators to meet with the offender. They can ascertain the willingness and desire to make amends, and then relay that information when first contacting the victim. On rare occasions the victim has already requested a meeting with the offender; most often the potential benefits to both victim and offender must be stressed and fears allayed before the victim agrees to participate. Approximately 60 per cent of victims contacted do agree; this figure ranges from 50 per cent to 100 per cent depending on the program (Umbreit, 1986a).

In most programs the majority of the mediations are performed by trained volunteer mediators. After meeting with both victim and offender separately, the mediation is held. Approximately two-thirds of these meetings are held at the victim's home or business. After the mediators introduce the parties and explain the mediation process and goals, both sides get a chance to tell their view of what happened. At this stage expression of feelings is encouraged.

Should restitution be in order, and in nearly all of the cases some restitution is sought, the two parties attempt to work out the amount and schedules of payment, assisted by the mediator. The form of restitution can vary: in some cases payment by money is made, in others the offender performs some service for the victim (such as repairing damage caused by the crime), or some form of community service might be agreed upon. If agreement is reached, a contract is signed by the two parties and the mediators, and case disposition is returned to the court.

Monitoring the payment of restitution is done either by VORP staff or by the probation office, since gaining and fulfilling an agreement might be a condition of probation. Once repayment is completed the case is closed.

The typical case mediated in VORP involves non-violent misdemenors and felonies. Recently, however, some people have been extending the limits of victim–offender meetings to include severe crimes.

Since 1983 the Genesee County Community Service and Victim Assistance program has used what is termed "victim–offender conciliation mediation" for such offenses as criminal negligent homicide and sexual abuse (Larmer, 1986). The rationale for this program includes "their belief that there is often a far greater need to express feelings, understand the event, and work toward closure among victims of such traumatic crimes" (Umbreit, 1986b, p. 204).

Typical of such cases is that of a drunk driver and the widow of the man killed as a result of his negligence. The widow's conclusions support the rationale (Umbreit, 1986b, p. 204):

It was only at that moment when I was able to confront the man who killed my husband, to express my anger and to see the guilt he was experiencing that I was able to move beyond the bitterness that lay deep in my heart and move toward peace in my life again.

CONCLUSIONS

Coates's study (1985; all additional statistics come from that study unless otherwise indicated) claims that only in about one-third of the cases do the participants report any positive change in attitude toward each other. One problem that contributes to this low rate of success is the confusion between the stated goal of reconciliation and the actual goals held by victim, offender, and criminal justice personnel. Case descriptions by participants demonstrate that real world concerns often outrank lofty ideals. For staff and mediators, the highest ranked goal is that of humanizing the criminal justice process through face-to-face meetings; but for victims, it is to recover losses. Offenders wish most to avoid harsher punishment, and criminal justice officials most want to provide restitution to the victims. In general, reconciliation thus occurs mostly as a by-product of other concerns.

While there may not be reconciliation, in 92 per cent of the meetings restitution contracts are signed. Furthermore, 94 per cent of these victims were satisfied with the amount agreed upon. But in nearly one-half of the cases there was difficulty in keeping to the repayment schedule. Because non-VORP court-ordered restitution suffers from the same problem, it is difficult to draw valid conclusions from this data; however, victims report the lack of follow-up and enforcement of restitution as the least satisfactory aspect of VORP.

VORP does indeed involve the victim in decisions which would otherwise be made solely by the court system. However, in most cases referral is made after conviction, so the victim still must go through standard criminal justice procedures before participating in VORP. The second and third most frequent complaints by victims about their experience are the long delays from the crime's occurrence to final resolution, and the length of time given to participation in the VORP process.

According to VORP proponents, the offender must first admit his or her guilt and accept responsibility for righting the wrong that has been done. That process cannot be coerced; participation in the process must be voluntary. In fact, however, most offenders are referred to VORP as part of their sentence, and many of them view it as punishment which they accept only in order to avoid prison. Despite this gap between theory and practice, however, the mediation can be a powerful awakening. Some offenders do realize for the first time that others have truly suffered as a consequence of their actions, and some of the victims recognize the humanity of those who committed the crime.

Offender empowerment is a difficult goal to assess. Offenders themselves are often victims of political decisions that deprive whole classes of people from power, of "structural violence" (Galtung, 1976), and of institutional indifference. There is concern that VORP, like other alternative sanctions, is in fact used to "widen the net" of social control; for instance, it might bring into the system of punishment those whose charges would otherwise have been dropped. And it is the offenders, not the victims, who report the most fear coming into the mediation.

But many offenders as well as victims do see their participation as beneficial. When evaluating their overall experience in VORP, two-thirds of each group stated that the meeting was not conflictual. Some 83 per cent of the offenders and 59 per cent of the victims were satisfied with the process, with another 30 per cent of the victims reporting themselves somewhat satisfied. Interestingly, however, almost everyone, whether victim or offender, claimed that they would choose to participate in VORP again if they had to do it over again.

VORP is flawed in many ways. Coates (1985) found wide differences between program intentions and realities. The ideals trumpeted by its adherents often give way in practice to more prosaic concerns of reality. "Reconciliation" as the goal attracts volunteers, but it is the promotion of "restitution" and "alternatives to incarceration" which gets funding. What actually occurs in day-to-day practice is a product of the give and take between the desired and the possible.

Legitimate concerns about widening the net of social control, about blame placed on those who may themselves be victims, about the lack of objective program evaluation, and about the use of volunteers in sensitive mediation roles, can be given no authoritative rebuttal. The reply, instead, is the question "How well is the current system working?" That answer, as weak as it may be, is difficult to refute.

And every so often comes a case where, whether by good intentions or mediator skill or just plain serendipity, all the elements come together at the right time and the right place. The victim and offender meeting face-to-face and learning about each other's feelings results in true reconciliation. Deindividuation promoted by the impersonal procedures of the criminal justice system stops; the participants learn to see each other as people. The offender faces up to the very real hurt the victim has suffered; the victim discovers the punishment the offender is undergoing and the reasons for the offense. When true reconciliation occurs, the offender admits responsibility and expresses sorrow, and the victim recognizes the humanity of the offender and forgives. And the program seems worthwhile for all the parties involved.

5 Community Mediation

INTRODUCTION

While we would prefer to use the term "mediation", we follow McGillis (1986) and others in using "Community Dispute Resolution" broadly to encompass a variety of programs with similar features. These programs, with names such as "Community Mediation", "Neighborhood Justice", and "Community Boards", all have in common the use of a non-adjudicative forum, such as conciliation or mediation, to deal with a wide range of interpersonal and familial disputes, and the involvement of community volunteers as third parties. However, the use of this term should not disguise the significant differences in purposes, goals, and practices of various programs.

The Community Dispute Resolution movement began as the product of many disparate influences. Among these were the recognition of the increases in problems such as interpersonal violence and community disintegration; dissatisfaction with the available means to deal with these problems; and inspiration from the examples of other practices in our own and other societies. Indeed, there have been so many different goals and purposes stated for Community Dispute Resolution that at times it looks like a solution in search of a problem. Bush (1988), for example, identifies seven categories of stated goals used for evaluating quality of outcomes – individual satisfaction, individual autonomy, social control, social justice, social solidarity, personal transformation, and administrative economy – with many more sub-objectives within these categories (See also Wahrhaftig, 1982; Tomasic and Feeley, 1982; Shonholtz, 1984 and 1987; McGillis, 1986; and Esser, 1988, Table II).

In an attempt to make sense of this array of goals, Harrington and Merry (1988) have identified three categories of what they term "ideological projects" within the field of Community Dispute Resolution: the delivery of dispute services, social transformation, and personal growth.

In the first category, services are contrasted with the courts, and the goals are expressed in terms of efficiency, relief of court congestion, and a more appropriate forum for certain kinds of disputes. Centers which accept the first ideology are justified, and structured, as alternatives or adjuncts to courts.

The goals of the ideology of social transformation are a restructuring of human society through the creation of a new sense of community, community empowerment, decentralized judicial decision making, and the replacement of professional dispute resolvers with indigenous community members. Included here would also be such goals as the reduction of interpersonal violence and interpersonal reconciliation.

The ideology of personal growth and development emphasizes personal empowerment and achievement of skills, and suggests that mediation can be more humane and more responsive to needs than courts.

Obviously, then, Community Dispute Resolution programs vary considerably from one another. Besides these different ideologies there are contextual variations found in any program or service, differences in community characteristics such as size and ethos, and differences in sponsorship. They are sponsored by or affiliated with such diverse groups as churches, courts, private organizations, social service agencies, and the general community.

According to Megan Sylvester of the American Bar Association's Special Committee on Dispute Resolution (personal communication), there are in the United States over 700 community programs of various kinds. As experiments in social innovation, many of the earliest centers were able to attract, and became dependent upon, foundation and federal funding. When the experimental stage ended, so did the funding, and some of the earliest centers folded. The ones that did not, as well as the many newer ones, have developed a number of different ways of paying their expenses, including the affiliation with other public and private institutions (Wahrhaftig, 1987). While funding remains a major concern for most centers, many states and localities in the United States now allocate regular public moneys to ensure their continued existence (NIDR, 1988b).

However, the Community Dispute Resolution movement does not have the same type of institutional bases that other fields and practices have. Community Boards of San Francisco is perhaps the most influential organization in the field, despite the fact that it is not a national institution. Besides advocacy for community empowerment (Shonholtz, 1987), it sponsors trainings and produces a wide range of resources, including manuals and videos. Many Community Dispute Resolution Centers are modelled on them.

The National Association for Community Justice (NACJ), after a start hampered by "lofty goals, an over-ambitious program, and little funding" (NACJ, 1989), is attempting to be the kind of national institution that the Academy of Family Mediators or the National Association for Mediation in Education are in their own fields. The Directors plan for the NACJ to serve as a forum for sharing information about a wide range of subjects, including research and legislation.

Because of the diverse goals and settings, generalizations about the field do not adequately highlight important elements of individual programs. Neither do the practices of a single program represent the entire field. Nonetheless, we present a single example of a community mediation process in order to fulfill the intentions of this book, which include the demonstration whenever possible of actual practices. We will present the process used by a center in Central Virginia.

THE PROCESS

The purpose of this center was stated in its by-laws (Community Mediation Center, 1985):

> an effective, cost-saving alternative to traditional methods of resolving interpersonal disputes, and particularly in offering a simple, accessible, and inexpensive method of dispute settlement to members of this public community not generally available, particularly to lower income individuals, and in diverting from the judicial system certain minor matters, thereby helping to relieve crowded court dockets and allowing more effective use of legal resources, all without pecuniary gain or profit to its members or to any private individual.

Although the language is abstruse, the participants who approved this statement were quite clear about the principles behind the wording. In order to accomplish their purpose, the following objectives were identified (Community Mediation Center, 1985):

1. To provide mediation as an alternative to litigation.
2. To provide training and mediation to people in existing institutions to help them resolve conflicts within their institutions.
3. To help mediate specific issues for different organizations within the community.
4. To address problems of the following types:

   (i) Domestic (between parents and children, within families, and

among generations);
(ii) Neighborhood (such as noise, pets, and nuisances);
(iii) Landlord–tenant (such as security deposits, repairs, and damages);
(iv) Juvenile (such as fights and vandalism);
(v) Consumer–merchant (such as faulty merchandise, service and repair);
(vi) Such other problems as may come to the attention of CMC and as may lend themselves to mediation.

5. To involve citizen volunteers in the mediation process.
6. To train volunteers from the community to help in the mediation process.
7. To educate the public in order to create new attitudes towards alternative methods of dispute resolution.
8. To do any and all lawful acts and things and to engage in any and all lawful activities which may be necessary, useful, or desirable for the furtherance, fostering or attainment of any and all purposes for which the organization is organized as stated generally and specifically above.

The process used by the volunteer mediators is not original; it is based upon community mediation techniques pioneered by such practitioners as Kraybill (1984).

This model of mediation uses co-mediators. Co-mediation has several advantages: it can provide new mediators with experience; prevent perception of unfairness that a single mediator's race, gender, or occupation might provoke; balance one individual's weaknesses with another's strengths; and increase effectiveness through co-evaluation. Most of the volunteers have no previous mediation experience; co-mediation can bolster confidence in a novice by ensuring that no one person feels solely responsible for the mediation's success or failure.

Each session is designed to be highly structured. There are four separate stages. The introduction is intended to build trust in the mediators and in the process of mediation. In this stage the mediators attempt to create a safe climate for each of the participants through establishment and acceptance of ground rules. After the introduction, the story-telling stage allows ventilation of feelings and informs the mediators (and each party) of the issues under dispute.

At this point, and at any time afterwards, the parties may caucus with the mediators, if either side or the mediators feel the need to do so. If the mediators do meet alone with one side, they will then meet alone with the other, so as to not give the impression of favoritism. Problem-solving then follows, as options are created and evaluated. Finally, if agreement is reached, the implementation is detailed and a contract signed.

CONCLUSIONS

The failures of established procedures that deal with problems such as repression, injustice, and violence, has made alternatives to those procedures such as Community Dispute Resolution look very appealing. However, many critics have suggested that Community Dispute Resolution programs actually function to undermine their purported goals. There is some concern, for instance, that people are being denied legitimate rights to access to the courts, or that these programs provide a second-class forum for citizens who cannot afford the justice provided by litigation. Another criticism is that these programs transform disputes involving public interest into private concerns, to the public's detriment. Some question whether these centers really aid the disputants, or whether they deflect criticism of systems and institutions which are themselves the source of the conflicts. Perhaps the most far-reaching criticism is presented by one side of the current debate about whether Community Dispute Resolution represents an unjustified and invidious extension of state control over individuals' lives, or a positive alternative to the excesses of existing state control (for critical examination see, for example, Abel, 1982a; Harrington, 1985; Hofrichter, 1987; Delgado, 1988; Gallagher, 1988; and Sarat, 1988).

Unfortunately, we do not yet have the answers to these questions. The procedures of mediation, and micro-level activities of negotiation, concession, and mediator tactics, have received a good deal of attention (for overviews of such research see, for example, Wall 1981; Kolb, 1983b; and Pruitt and Kressel 1985). But given the nature of some of the claims made for Community Dispute Resolution, it is difficult or impossible to demonstrate empirically whether goals have been met, and even if they have, whether Community Dispute Resolution activities are responsible for achieving those goals. The little research that has been done about some of these more nebulous goals is often of questionable validity. For example, McGillis (1986) notes the difficulty in defining and assessing elements such as "improved quality of justice". He then demonstrates his point by defining four measures of the quality of justice, none of which addresses what is arguably the most important element, the righting of wrongs.

In his review and analysis of the research literature, McGillis (1986) can claim only that results indicate some superiority for dispute resolution programs relative to adjudication in terms of disputant perceptions and case processing time. He suggests the need for far more research. Esser (1988), in his survey and review of the research literature, finds that results are either ambiguous or downright contradictory, and that we are able to draw very few definite conclusions about Community Dispute Resolution's success in meeting goals (for overviews of the empirical research, see "Finding Empirical Answers to Important Questions", in Goldberg, Green and Sander, 1985; McGillis, 1986; Tyler, 1988; and Esser, 1988).

Current analysis of Community Dispute Resolution focusses on dispute processing: assessing the success or failure of certain processes, mostly mediation and arbitration, applied to various kinds of disputes, particularly in terms of quantifiable variables such as cost, time, and disputant satisfaction. Esser (1988) details the assumptions implicit in this conceptual framework: there are certain types of distinct procedures used for resolving disputes, with distinctive characteristics which make them appropriate for certain types of disputes and inappropriate for others. Through research, we can learn which processes fit which disputes, while ineffectiveness can be explained and reforms derived from the resultant dispute processing theory.

Others have recognized the problems with these assumptions. Sarat (1988) criticizes what he terms the "new formalism" of this conceptualization. He attacks it for ignoring the dynamic nature of conflict, for failing to recognize the flexibility and adaptivity of dispute processes, and for implicitly accepting the "conflict is bad" paradigm. In brief, it is a conservative view of disputes, disputing, and dispute handling, that inherently favors the status quo to the detriment of legitimate challengers and challenges.

Esser (1988) demonstrates how the views of the "new formalism" affect research and policy making. He suggests that the conceptual frameworks of Community Dispute Resolution evaluators who produce empirical results, while facilitating understanding of certain aspects of dispute processes, distract attention from other important aspects. Those who use these results, including other researchers, administrators, and policy makers, then share the same limited vision. This framework thus limits the understanding of dispute processing.

However, these criticisms, while valid within their own framework, themselves accept too limited a conception of Community Dispute Resolution. They leave unchallenged, and in fact reinforce, the conception of Community Dispute Resolution programs as dispute processing vehicles alone. This framework is inaccurate and inadequate because it does not encompass the full scope of Community Dispute Resolution centers' activities. These are not merely places where people come to have their disputes processed. Each center has its own history: the goals and ideology which inspired its beginnings; the people who came together to create it; the search for funding and, often, institutional affiliation; and the relationships with residents and other organizations in the community, including local government and, inevitably, local bar associations.

Each center has volunteers who are socialized into the ideology and practices of their particular program, as they are recruited, trained, and given opportunities to work with disputants. Each of these centers affects the community through publicity and public education. They can raise community consciousness about problems that have been ignored, and model means for dealing with these and other problems. They can be a resource for other agencies. They provide opportunities for employment and advancement for those interested in pursuing various kinds of careers in the field.

In addition to these indirect influences shared by all of the centers, many have branched out into other areas. Some of them have become involved in public policy disputes having to do with problems such as school system mergers and commercial development of historical areas. More and more handle a wider range of disputes than was part of their original mandate, dealing with problems such as divorce and spousal abuse. Others specialize in certain kinds of programs, such as Victim–Offender Reconciliation Programs (VORP). Many do trainings in negotiation, conciliation and mediation, for the general public as well as for specified populations, including businesses and government personnel. A growing number sponsor school mediation and conflict management programs.

These new applications mean a changing role for Community Dispute Resolution. Until the conceptual framework by which Community Dispute Resolution is understood acknowledges these new roles, their import will remain undiscovered.

6 Environmental and Public Policy Mediation

INTRODUCTION

Imagine the following scenario:

A major highway running north to south connects a series of cities and towns throughout a 200-hundred-mile area. As these population centers have grown, manufacturing plants, retail stores, and various other businesses have tended to cluster around the highway as it entered and exited town.

The state highway department, prodded by the legislature and the governor, has constructed a series of bypasses around the most troublesome areas, so that traffic can travel the length of the highway nearly uninterrupted by stoplights or heavy congestion. However, one large obstacle remains: a university town whose recent accelerated growth has taken planners by surprise. During rush hours it now takes half an hour to an hour to cover the same distance that a decade ago might have taken ten minutes.

The highway department initially proposed constructing a western bypass that would allow through traffic to avoid the local problem. Twenty years ago, such a proposal would have almost certainly been approved with minimal opposition, and the bypass built, subject to minor changes by a few influential local landowners and politicians.

Today, however, the general population is at once more environmentally sensitive and politically knowledgeable. An area environmental council warns against the disruption of a sensitive watershed such a bypass will bring; landowners voice their fear of destruction of farmland; other residents speak of the need to protect the beauty of the area.

State legislators pressure the highway department to conduct a $3 million study of all highway alternatives, including an eastern bypass and an expressway that would use the existing highway. A citizens' group is formed to fight the bypass; during the campaign for governor of the state all the candidates promise to "reassess the situation" and speak out against "wasteful spending" and "insensitive bureaucracy".

Those in favor of the western bypass have been slow to mobilize their efforts, in part because things had seemed to be going their way. The growth of the anti-bypass movement, however, spurs them into action. A coalition of businesses which would be relocated by an expressway and various interested non-western residents of the area incorporate their own pro-bypass group. Legislators representing the northern and southern sections of the highway demand the bypass. And some question the impact on the environment of such a concentrated area of traffic, and the destruction of the tree-lined median, should the expressway be built.

Advertisements from both sides seek public approval. Citizens write the highway department, the newspapers, and various elected officials. Public hearings become grounds of combat, during which each side competes for the honor of the largest and loudest supporting crowd. The community is divided.

Not only is this scenario real, it is being played out in other forms and in other locations through the US and other countries. How will this end? Twenty years ago, the decision would have been forced by whichever group could muster the most influence, by hook or by crook, with the decision making system of legislative committees and administrative departments that fund and build these highways.

Today, however, such is not necessarily the case. It is more likely that an influential legislator, a local politician, a member of the environmental council, or perhaps a journalist, will have heard of other similar cases involving both local and extralocal concerns, environmental issues, and polarized interest groups, where the disputing sides were able to achieve, with the help of a third party, some sort of mutually agreeable solution. One of many such groups that mediate these types of disputes may be called in to discuss the possibility of mediation. The mediators might examine the kinds of parties and issues involved, weigh the merits of the existing means of handling the case and, possibly, propose a mediated forum for dealing with these parties and issues.

This scenario represents yet another shift in the manner of determining public policy. Long the domain of whichever conglomeration of interests wielded the greatest political power, the field has been disciplined more and more during the last several decades by planning specialists. Friedmann (1988) traces the genesis of this transformation to Jeremy Bentham, who shifted the basis for ethical judgement, and hence evaluation and choice, away from rules and intention to the results of action. This shift, in conjunction with the Enlightenment's acceptance of science, spawned a revolutionary concept: that society's problems could be solved through the application of scientific methods of research, application, and evaluation.

A number of fields developed as this idea flourished, and as social and economic problems became more and more complex. Today, we have general fields of public administration and planning, with specialities such as policy analysis, systems analysis, land use, and urban development. The system into which these specialists are supposed to fit implicitly imagines a society that operates something like this: the public reveals its problems to its elected representatives; these representatives assign the search for solutions to the technical experts; the representatives select the solutions from a range of proposals; and they assign the task of carrying out the solutions to other management experts.

The reality, of course, is far different from the image. As illustrated by the scenario described above, problems involving environmental concerns are rarely if ever decided by even-handed judgements about what is "best" for the environment, even if such a "best" can be determined. Indeed, it would be surprising if they were. These are political issues, whose solutions are determined by familiar processes of influence. The desires of interest groups such as businesses, trade associations, elected authorities, and environmental activists, rarely give way to scientific and technical advice.

Also left out of this scenario is the reaction of the public to solutions imposed upon them, in most cases by bureaucrats or by others with little or no interest in the affected community. Of course, one part of the public – those with economic power and political influence – has always enjoyed consideration in any type of decision making process, and that is no different today than it ever was. But in certain areas, those groups who traditionally have had little voice in how the decisions that affect them are made, are organizing, protesting, delaying, blocking, and sometimes changing both the process and the resultant decisions.

The death of the activism of the 1960s and 1970s has been greatly exaggerated. Current activism has been muted, if at all, only in the recognition it receives; in fact, today there are far more advocacy groups representing local, national, and global interests than ever before.

Of course, some of these groups, such as Political Action Committees (PACs), lie squarely within the political mainstream. But many of the groups who do not are nonetheless successful in influencing policy. They rely not only on traditional activist tactics such as confrontational protest, but on more conventional means of coercion and persuasion such as mobilization at the polls, letter-writing campaigns, and direct lobbying. And even groups without the resources to work at this level can often block implementation of legislative, administrative, or corporate actions through threatened or actual litigation. The head of the Environmental Protection Agency (EPA), William Ruckelshaus, during a 1982 conference sponsored by the Conservation Foundation, estimated that 80 per cent of the hundreds of regulations issued by the EPA are challenged in court.

The choice to involve in the decision making process those who will be affected by policy decisions is therefore, in many cases, a practical necessity. Elected public officials at all levels, administrators of government agencies, and representatives of business interests are each realizing that confrontation is not the most efficacious way to achieve their own desired goals. And whether through institutionalized procedures or on a case-by-case, ad hoc basis, the use of third-party mediation for issues of public policy is becoming ever more common (Laue, 1988).

The range of such issues is quite wide. Laue (1988) notes three current uses of mediation: for shaping policy, for implementing policy, and for dealing with site-specific policy disputes. Bingham (1986) suggests six types of policy issues related to the environment:

1. Land use issues, which include annexation, sewage treatment, highways, solid waste and landfills, historic preservation, and hazardous waste siting.
2. Resource management issues, which include fishing rights, timber management, and watershed management.
3. Water resource issues, such as water quality and supply, flood protection, and thermal effects.
4. Energy issues, including coal conversions and nuclear energy.
5. Air quality issues, such as odor, stationary source emissions control, and acid rain.
6. Toxics, including asbestos, pesticides and herbicides, and hazardous materials cleanup.

She also distinguishes between site-specific problems, which deal with a single case, and larger issues of state or national policy. Typical of the latter would be the National Coal Policy Project, during which over 100 participants working in nine task groups reached agreement on over 200 specific issues.

Bingham's (1986) study of environmental mediations identified 161 mediated cases, of which 115 were site-specific and 46 were policy cases. Surprisingly, only 21 per cent of the site-specific cases she studied involved environmental groups and private industry. Overall, environmental groups participated in 35 per cent of those cases studied, private corporations in 34 per cent, and agencies of federal, state, and local governments in 82 per cent.

As Bingham points out, although the participants reached agreement on almost 90 per cent of these issues, few of those agreements were successfully implemented, and some environmentalists criticized the results.

Mediators are drawn from a variety of sources, including private organizations and several statewide offices of mediation (NIDR, 1987). Even the staid and powerful Army Corps of Engineers now employs its own full-time team of facilitators, both to train Corps officers in consensual problem-solving practices and to mediate specific disputes over Corps activities.

A number of organizations work in this field, but there are no national associations dedicated specifically to public policy mediation. Perhaps the most influential organization is the National Institute for Dispute Resolution (NIDR), which is involved in many other fields as well. In 1984 NIDR granted money to five states to establish statewide offices of mediation. NIDR's *Forum* also covers public policy mediation issues.

In the environmental area the leading organization is the Conservation Foundation's Program on Environmental Dispute Resolution. It absorbed the group RESOLVE (Center for Environmental Conflict Resolution) in 1981, and together with the Environmental Protection Agency (EPA) spawned Clean Sites, Inc. (an organization dedicated to cleanup of the United States' worst hazardous waste sites) in 1984.

Besides mediating specific disputes, the Conservation Foundation has sponsored "policy dialogues" such as the Agricultural Chemicals Dialogue Group, the National Groundwater Policy Forum, and the National Wetlands Policy Forum. It also facilitates negotiated rule making for issues such as underground injection of hazardous wastes, asbestos removal, and consumer protection rules issued by the Federal Trade Commission. Staff also have provided training in negotiation skills to such varied groups as EPA personnel and environmental groups. In addition, the Foundation sponsors the newsletter *Resolve* and a biennial National Conference on Environmental Dispute Resolution.

Clean Sites, Inc. a private, non-profit organization, was founded specifically to give help in the multi-billion Superfund hazardous waste cleanup program. While it also gives technical assistance, the organization facilitates negotiations among the EPA and parties responsible for waste. Their promotional literature terms this aspect of their work "technical mediation".

PUBLIC POLICY MEDIATION PROCESSES

As is the case in other fields, we must caution that public policy mediation is not a field with one single set of procedures. At one extreme, there are the "traditionalists" (Lentz, 1986) who claim that their goal is merely one of getting parties to reach agreements, and that the quality of the agreement is of secondary concern. At the other extreme, there are the "revisionists" (Lentz, 1986), those who frankly admit to a political agenda dictated by their own values, such as a concern for an ailing environment.

Lentz contrasts the clearly-defined situations typical of labor–management mediation with the more nebulous issues and contexts that environmental mediators must deal with, and finds that a single process cannot be discovered for the latter. In the former the primary issues are economic; data is therefore readily available; there are two sides to deal with; each side has at least one common goal, avoidance or end of a strike; the new contract provides a focus for the negotiations; and parties have fairly balanced power.

In environmental as well as other public policy cases, on the other hand, issues are often complex, and can involve mutually exclusive and strongly held values; data is often complex and difficult to obtain; numerous separate parties may be involved; there is no common deadline, such as a strike, to impel negotiations; goals may be quite different; and parties often have greatly different resources and power. In addition, the negotiators on each side of union–management disputes often are experienced with both the negotiation and mediation processes, while environmental issues can involve parties who either have no experience at all or, in the case of environmental advocacy groups, are familiar only with confrontational tactics. As mediation becomes more popular, however, this latter factor is changing.

Susskind and Ozawa (1985) describe a number of procedural concerns common to mediated public disputes. These include problems of representation, difficulties in setting the agenda, obstacles to joint fact-finding, difficulties in binding parties to their commitments, and obstacles to monitoring and enforcing agreements.

Laue *et al.* (1988) point out as well that there are few established forums for mediation, and that a major problem for the mediator and parties is to find or construct an appropriate forum acceptable to all. They suggest a set of conditions necessary for this forum: informality, collaborative rather than adversarial procedures, emphasis on analysis, protection from legal and constituent pressures, and a skilled third party.

Bingham (1986) suggests that, despite significant differences in approaches to environmental dispute resolution, all approaches do share certain elements: voluntary participation, consensus building, joint problem-solving, and negotiation. The use of consensus, rather than voting, is the key element of these processes (Bradley, 1988). The knowledge that all of the parties in the mediation must agree to all decisions both reassures those who fear that they will be outvoted and motivates the group as a whole to work to satisfy each party's interests.

Bradley (1988, pp. 52–3) suggests nine common principles derived from a comparison of processes used in five American cities during the 1980s. These are:

1. Ensuring representation of all affected parties
2. Engaging all the parties to cooperate in setting the agenda of the process
3. Developing a problem-solution orientation
4. Keeping the process educational, open, and highly visible
5. Using fact-finding techniques
6. Ensuring use of a consensus decision making model
7. Guiding the process phase by phase with distinct time limits
8. Focussing the process of implementation
9. Using neutral third parties to guide the process.

We offer as a complete example of a public policy mediation process the step-by-step procedures written by members of the Harvard Program on Negotiation (Madigan *et al.* 1986). These are divided into three phases: pre-negotiations, negotiation or consensus building, and post-negotiation.

The Pre-negotiation Phase:

Step 1: The nature of the conflict and the likely scope of the negotiation must be clarified by the parties themselves, perhaps with the assistance of a mediator.

Step 2: The important stakeholding groups must be identified – either by self-nomination or by a mediator. If they choose to participate, each group chooses representatives to sit at the negotiation table.

Step 3: The negotiating parties recruit and select a non-partisan mediator or facilitator to help organize and ultimately manage the process.

Step 4: Agree to a timeline and a set of groundrules to govern the negotiations.

Step 5: The parties agree to an agenda which identifies the range and order of issues to be addressed in the negotiations.

Step 6: The parties, working with the mediator, identify possible resources to support the negotiation.

Step 7: The parties identify information needs and engage in joint fact-finding.

Step 8: Provide parties with pre-negotiation training.

The Negotiation or Consensus-Building Phase

Step 1: The parties and the mediator work toward a single negotiating text to help focus the discussions.

Step 2: The parties explore each other's underlying interests.

Step 3: The parties consider mutually beneficial trades and attempt to invent potential agreement "packages".

Step 4: Draft the final agreement.

Step 5: Parties review, ratify, and sign the final agreement, securing feedback from constituents, where necessary.

The Post-Negotiation Phase

Step 1: Binding the parties to their agreements.

Step 2: Link the agreement to other individuals and institutions with formal implementation power.

Step 3: Design and set in motion a mechanism for monitoring implementation of the agreement.

Step 4: Design mechanisms for future renegotiation or remediation if necessary.

Step 5: Evaluate the negotiation process.

NEGOTIATED INVESTMENT STRATEGY

The "Negotiated Investment Strategy" is the formal title of a process initiated by the Charles F. Kettering Foundation in 1977. Its stated purpose is to bring together representatives from the public and private sectors for face-to-face negotiations over the complex and unique problems characteristic of intergovernmental disputes.

There are six key elements to the Negotiated Investment Strategy: the mediator; the negotiating teams; an informal exchange of information before any formal proposals; face-to-face negotiations; a written agreement; and public review, adoption, and monitoring of the agreement.

The process, as presented by the Kettering Foundation (1982) typically proceeds as follows:

1. Organizing for Negotiation

(1) A local team, representing the public and private sectors, identifies issues, problems, and opportunities.
(2) Participation of federal and state governments is secured.
(3) An impartial mediator is selected by all of the parties.
(4) Core negotiating teams are organized (often appointed) by those with authority (e.g., in a city the chief authority would be the mayor, in a state it would be the governor).
(5) Each team participates in team building and agenda setting.

2. Informal Exchange of Information

(1) During the first meeting, teams request and exchange information about the issues at stake.
(2) Between the first and second meetings, teams prepare preliminary position statements.
(3) During the second meeting, teams present and discuss preliminary positions.

3. Bargaining Process

(1) From the second meeting on, the teams begin to negotiate their differences.
(2) Between the second and third meetings, teams continue to resolve their differences, mainly by working in sub-committees. As this occurs, the local team prepares a written proposal and submits it to the state and federal teams. They, in turn,

respond in writing with proposals. As consensus is achieved, a memorandum of agreement can be circulated. During this period the mediator is an active "go-between," helping the teams to discover mutually satisfactory outcomes.

(3) At the final meeting, teams resolve the few remaining differences through intensive bargaining and reach a final agreement. Or

(4) It is possible that the teams will not be able to resolve their differences and reach an agreement.

4. Public Review and Monitoring of Agreement

(1) After the third meeting, a final agreement is drafted.

(2) During a public ceremony, the final agreement is signed by the chairperson of each team and adopted by the appropriate authorities.

(3) After the public ceremony, the agreements are monitored by the respective teams. It may be necessary from time to time for the mediator to step in to see that implementation occurs.

The Negotiated Investment Strategy has been used by the state of Connecticut to distribute federal block grant funds to its social service programs; by Gary, Indiana, to develop a strategy to improve the city's quality of life; and in several other localities for similar purposes.

REGULATORY NEGOTIATIONS (REG-NEG)

"Regulatory Negotiations", or "Reg-Neg", or "negotiated rule making" is a process by which representatives of interests who would be affected by government agency rules are brought together in a mediated forum to consensually develop those rules. The beginnings of regulatory negotiation as a formalized process coincided with the recognition of the obvious: that the decisions made by government agencies, establishing rules and regulations, were political in nature (Harter, 1986). In the early 1980s, the Administrative Conference of the United States, under the prodding of individuals and agencies dissatisfied with the adjudicatory nature of rule making, began to develop a model decision making process that would seek collaborative participation and consensus agreements from interested stakeholders.

According to Susskind (1986, p. 7), there are four key ingredients to the process:

> the participation of credible spokespeople representing the relevant stakeholding interests, a non-partisan facilitator or mediator acceptable to all the parties, a sustained process of face-to-face interaction aimed at maximizing the shared interests of all the parties, and an explicit procedure for linking informally negotiated agreements to the formal processes of government decision-making.

Haygood (1988, p. 79) summarizes the process in six stages:

1. Identification of a rule that might be appropriate for negotiation
2. Convening (assessment of whether and how negotiations would be conducted)
3. Notice of proposed rule making
4. Organization of the negotiated rule making committee (decisions on committee membership, training of committee members, agreement on groundrules)
5. Negotiations
6. Publication of proposed rule.

According to Harter (1986) the impetus to use the reg-neg procedure may come from within or outside an agency. If the agency is interested, it can appoint a convenor who studies the feasibility of the process, by analyzing the types of issues and parties likely to be involved. The convenor will use the following criteria as the basis for deciding whether or not to use mediation (Harter, 1986): a maximum of 25 represented interests; interests sufficiently organized such that they can be represented during negotiations; issues that are ripe for decisions; a realistic deadline, which usually means a time after which the agency will decide the regulations on its own if progress has not been made; no party must compromise on issues "fundamental to its existence"; the agency supports the process; and the parties will agree to participate in good faith.

If the convenor decides that reg-neg is feasible, the agency may publish in the *Federal Register* a notice describing the process, the issues, and a list of parties who have already agreed to participate, and invite participation by other unrepresented interests.

The convenor may also be chosen as the facilitator of the group. The group will generally be chartered as an advisory committee under the Federal Advisory Committee Act (FACA). Under FACA rules plenary meetings are open to the public, while separate work groups may meet privately.

The goal is to reach consensus agreement on the preamble and all major issues. "Consensus" is defined as either approval or the absence of active opposition by each interest. What this means is that each interest, no matter how little power it may have outside the process, can veto any proposal.

Agreement does not necessarily mean that the agency will adopt the committee's rules as their own. Even if they plan to do so, the proposed rules must be published so that any party, whether a member of the committee or not, may argue otherwise. In practice, however, it would be difficult to contravene the decision of a group truly representative of the relevant interests.

The reg-neg process has been used to develop regulations concerning the Clean Air Act, pesticides, public lands, asbestos in schools, and other issues. Less formal facilitated regulatory negotiations have been used at the state and local levels as well (Susskind, 1986).

THE NATIONAL ISSUES FORUM

The "National Issues Forum (NIF)" was initiated to increase public awareness of and participation in major public policy issues. Sponsored by the Kettering Foundation and administered by the Domestic Policy Association (DPA), these Forums each year focus on three topics of current public concern. The DPA publishes issue books and discussion guides, which are used in community discussions held across the country twice yearly. Representatives of these local Forums convene in a yearly National Forum where they report to members of Congress and the Administration.

An interesting corollary to the NIF is the National Issues Forum Literary Program, which is designed to involve adult literacy students in the public discussion. The Forum materials are designed so that they can be incorporated into adult basic education curriculum, and each topic is also covered by a videotape. 1989–90 topics are drugs, the environment, and day care.

CONCLUSIONS

Public policy mediation, perhaps more than any other practice, has attracted criticism and warnings. There is a deep concern by environmentalists that mediation of certain issues means inappropriate compromising of fundamental values. Amy (1987) suggests that mediators promote a view of environmental conflict that disadvantages environmental interests. He notes that much of the funding for experiments in environmental mediation has come from large corporations, and that the Conservation Foundation and the National Wildlife Federation, the two environmental groups most in the forefront of environmental mediation, are considered to be on the conservative side of the environmental movement. The concern is that the real and deep differences of competing views of society – development and consumption versus preservation and communal values – will be subsumed by the insistence on finding common ground.

Amy (1987) claims that past innovations in citizen participation, including public hearings and advisory committees, have not resulted in true power-sharing. He warns that some mediators who have a professional self-interest promote mediation as a cure-all, despite its limitations (1987, p. 225):

> The business community can use environmental mediation to distract environmentalists from other political strategies, to distort the nature of the issues at stake, and to give the illusion of legitimacy to development projects. Those in government can use mediation to give the appearance of public participation and to undermine public opposition to controversial policies.

Bingham (1986), while more positive about the use of mediation, is also aware of these problems. She prefaces her discussion of how a process may be evaluated by presenting three common perspectives on conflict and its resolution. In the first perspective, specific disputes actually represent fundamental conflicts over the distribution of power, and dealing with specific disputes while leaving intact the existing structures or policies may represent a failure. In the second perspective, conflict is a natural occurrence in pluralistic societies, and increasing the range of interests and variety of views about any issue can be productive. Success then depends upon the joint gains by all parties. The third view holds that clarifying shared values and building trust among parties can restore a basically consensual society to its normal mode.

Most evaluations of success and failure, for both specific cases and for the field in general, ignore the first possibility. Assessments of environmental mediations, including Bingham's (1986), commonly use such criteria as whether or not an agreement is reached, or how satisfied disputants are with the agreement and/or process. These criteria can imply only one or both of the latter two views. And the larger question about fundamental conflicts of value remains in most cases, unasked, and in all cases, unanswered.

7 Interactive Management

INTRODUCTION

As we prepare to enter the twenty-first century, a number of researchers and practitioners are attempting to integrate advanced information processing technology, including the use of computers, into decision making processes. This integration has occurred in both bilateral negotiations and in those assisted by a third party (see, for example, Straus, 1974; Sebenius, 1981; Raiffa, 1982; and Goeltner, 1987).

A prototypical example of such a case occurred when Hammond and his associates (Hammond and Adelman, 1976) intervened in a dispute in Denver, Colorado, over the type of handgun ammunition to be issued to police. The two sides, each advocating a different bullet, had become increasingly antagonistic as technical uncertainty exacerbated existing community cleavages. Ballistics experts argued social policy and legislators argued ballistics. Hammond devised a process that compared various stated preferences of the disputants with basic ballistic data. In so doing he separated the choice of criteria for social policy, the legislative function, from the scientific-technical function of ballistics experts. The results demonstrated that one bullet (out of 80 tested) was clearly superior to the others, according to both sides' criteria, and the dispute was dissipated.

As an institutionalized example of this kind of practice, we have chosen the process titled "Interactive Management" (Warfield, 1976; Broome and Keever, 1986; Christakis and Keever, 1984). Although unique in its design, it is representative of attempts to deal with problems whose solutions involve large amounts of data, technical or non-technical. It is particularly suited for analysis because its careful design has been well documented by its developers, and because by its extensive usage it has progressed beyond the exploratory stage of many proposed processes.

THE PROCESS

Interactive Management is intended for what is termed "Class II", or complex problems, which require knowledge from multiple disciplines within an organization, which cannot be solved by following existing methods, and which challenge past assumptions. This is comparable to what Argyris (1983) terms "double loop" learning, problem-solving which questions the framework in which the problem presents itself.

The process incorporates elements generally considered necessary for effective problem management: each party defines its own view of the situation; there is communication of that view to the other parties, leading to an understanding of each other's view; and there exists a certain minimum amount of shared perception of relevant problems. The process then provides for the generation of a number of potential options for solutions, making realistic choices among those options, and the opportunity to plan to implement these choices.

Interactive Management uses the term "SIGMA 5" to represent five components of the process: a group of 5 to 15 active participants, with as many as 25 other observers and consultants; the computer and software; an array of consensus methodologies; a facilitator; and a specially designed room, called "Demosophia", featuring space for graphic display.

There are three phases of the process, derived from the three primary tasks of management first identified by Simon (1960): understanding the problem, or "Intelligence"; designing solutions, or "Design"; and "Choice". During each phase participants are assisted in the generation and clarification of ideas, in idea structuring and comparison, and in communication (Broome and Keever, 1986).

This generation and evolution of ideas is managed by combining elements of seven methodologies (Warfield, 1982):

Ideawriting is performed individually and in silence by all participants in response to a carefully designed question. After five or ten minutes, papers are exchanged, and the process is repeated until all participants have examined every paper. The facilitation team then edits and organizes the ideas for later presentation. By eliminating excessive group influence by dominant personalities and encouraging people who are reluctant to speak out in groups, brainwriting can be more effective than similar techniques, such as brainstorming.

During the *Nominal Group Technique* stage the group not only generates ideas, but also clarifies and ranks these ideas. Each individual silently generates ideas in writing in response to the trigger question. The facilitator then records the ideas in round-robin fashion, without allowing any discussion or criticism, one individual and one idea at a time. After all contributions have been recorded, each of the ideas is discussed, clarified, and critiqued, again one at a time. The group then votes to prioritize the ideas.

In *Delphi*, a questionnaire is mailed to individual members of a group. Their responses are analyzed, the questionnaire is revised, and it is mailed once again to group members. The process continues until the group's criteria for completion is satisfied. This method allows participation by individuals who might not be able to attend a meeting at a specific time and location, and can allow anonymity as well.

These three procedures are not peculiar to Interactive Management. Neither are all required at any one application. The four computer assisted processes outlined below, however, are unique, and they form the core of the design. Although distinct from one another, each process builds upon those it follows.

The fourth method is titled *Interpretive Structural Modeling*; the fifth, *Options Field*; the sixth, *Options Profile*; and the seventh, *Tradeoff Analysis*. These begin after ideas have been edited and organized into related groups. These ideas are displayed and compared two at a time. Participants are then asked to suggest the relevant relationship (by priority, similarity, or other means) between the two. This program/participant interaction eventually produces a relationship map, including all the original ideas, which is displayed for everyone to see. The group then discusses and, if necessary, edits the map to their satisfaction with the aid of the facilitator and without the computer.

After each available option is placed into the conceived dimensions of a potential design, the dimensions are arranged by clusters of interdependence, which are themselves placed in the sequence in which the design choices will be made. Each Options Profile represents one possible design. The Tradeoff Analysis Method documents how the chosen alternative was selected, which allows review by retracing the steps.

CONCLUSIONS

The Interactive Management structure necessarily limits the kinds of situations and participation suitable for its application. Warfield (1976) identifies what he describes as two types of conflict that occur when groups form objectives: "semantic conflicts" and "conflicts of value". According to Warfield, these semantic differences can be reduced by rewording to capture the intentions of the participants more clearly. On a large scale, that is exactly what the Interactive Management process can do: it can capture the intentions of the participants in the room by promoting shared understanding of their combined knowledge. However, if one then discovers that these intentions are not compatible, Interactive Management has no procedure for probing the foundations of the disagreement. Problems and disputes whose basis is a misunderstanding of the meaning of complex issues should thus be more suitable for the Interactive Management process than disputes or conflicts rooted in substantive differences.

The Interactive Management process requires 5 to 15 active participants, with perhaps as many as 25 non-participating observers. With the limited number of participants, questions common to all processes – Who are the parties involved?; Should only the active stakeholders participate, or should other parties who have legitimate interests in the outcome be included?; Who are the most suitable representatives of these parties?; Do the officials with the power participate, or is it more efficacious to have unofficial but influential participants? – allow little room for selection error. It also reduces the field of potentially suitable problems.

Interactive Management and other management processes may have a role in providing assistance at certain stages of disputes amongst persons and parties with shared goals. These decision facilitating processes might be incorporated into a conflict resolution process at appropriate times of need. For instance, they might be used to separate policy and value differences from differences over data interpretation (NIDR, 1988a), or after agreement on basic principles they might help with the generation and selection of options.

In addition, it is possible that Interactive Management could be useful in attacking problems that are the source of destructive conflict. If it assists groups in solving problems that would not otherwise be solved, or in ensuring that critical decisions are the product of the proper balance of expertise and diversity, then Interactive Management might assist the prevention of problems before they reach critical stages.

However, the Interactive Management process contains elements potentially destructive of its own efforts. A fixed agenda greeting participants coming to the Interactive Management table implies shared goals, which in reality might not be present within the group of participants. Brokering of the agenda and other aspects of the process with only one or two leaders could be unsuitable in a situation involving serious differences. Trust in the process and in the facilitator will not be given as it might in an organizational setting. Thus, much more thorough preparation with the participants than is normally required for Interactive Management may be essential for its success in conflictual settings.

The physical setting in which attempted problem-solving procedures are held has been shown to be an important factor in their success or failure (Druckman, 1986). Distance from representational demands and from media coverage is sometimes necessary to ensure the privacy that allows participants openly to discuss sensitive subjects. The requirements of the room "Demosophia" restrict setting flexibility. That restriction could be an important liability.

When a process is not completely understood by the participants in that process they can feel disempowered. Reliance on computers can frustrate and anger participants, who may feel that the programs distort their intentions. Confusion may result in increased antagonism among the participants, directed against the facilitators and each other. In a competitive setting, factionalism could easily be increased by continued disagreement over procedure and meaning, without even considering the substance of the issues. Unless the participants are either a disempowered group used to having others decide their lives for them, or very experienced with Interactive Management, the process could itself generate resistance to attempted problem-solving.

This, then, is the greatest potential problem involved in using Interactive Management: that certain requirements of the Interactive Management process – reliance on technology that might be unfamiliar to the participants, limited access to Demosophia, and confusion about the process and the technology – would themselves engender such distrust that the process could aggravate rather than relieve the problems that brought the participants together in the first place.

II
Settlement

8 Introduction: Settlement

THE LEGITIMIZATION OF SOCIAL NORMS

In the Introduction we argued that judicial settlement processes were appropriate for disputes over interests. We also anticipated that we would examine the link between judicial settlements and conflict resolution processes, hinting that we would find, over time, an increasing legitimization of judicial processes even beyond interest disputes as insights into human behaviors became more widespread and were incorporated into judicial decision making and legal practices. Indeed, the overcrowding of gaols is already forcing authorities and courts to consider alternative assessments of, and means of handling, crime, disputes and conflicts. Suggestions are emerging that offenders are also themselves victims of social and economic circumstances over which they have no control. Alternatives such as supervised community service and therapy are being introduced. This may be a small step in the direction of removing causal conditions.

Legitimization of social and legal norms has been the result of an historical trend. Settlement processes have shifted in most countries from somewhat arbitrary authoritative impositions – for example, by a feudal lord, a dictator or a dominant power elite – toward the application of consensus norms founded in history and culture. The trend is a continuing one. It cannot be assumed that in any society social and legal norms founded on precedent and culture reflect a contemporary consensus. That would be the case only if the norms took wholly into account the inherent needs of individuals in society. At best social and legal norms reflect an acceptance of societies and their institutions, with all their failings, and only in this sense carry with them a degree of legitimization.

One problem is that changes in norms based on precedents cannot keep pace with altering conditions. Their enforced application tends to reduce the legitimization of authorities. When norms do alter in response to altering conditions and popular demands – when, that is, they acquire consensus support – their authoritative imposition can be regarded as a legitimized exercise of authority, establishing agreed boundaries of behavior. Included in such authoritative impositions are interpretations of documents, agreements and laws, always

somewhat subjective and interest-oriented, but nevertheless a legitimized exercise of such authority.

THE LEGAL IDEAL

Applying the thesis of this Conflict Series – that institutions must be
adapted to human needs and not the other way around – an ideal
legal system would be one in which all norms or rules were derived,
when feasible and appropriate, from the basic norm that inherent
human needs must be satisfied. As observed in *Conflict: Resolution
and Provention*, it is only by postulating human needs as a basis for
assessment that an objectively-based definition of justice is possible.
Tradition, precedents, past elite interests and other determinants of
norms would then be required in law to give place to the satisfaction
of human needs in an ideal system. An alienated person, led through
alienation to commit some crime, would not normally be placed in
punitive custody, which would further alienate, but would receive
whatever rehabilitation treatment was required. More importantly,
there would be in legal findings an implied obligation on authorities
to tackle the source of the alienation so as to prevent further cases.
Social systems based on such norms would be wholly legitimized, as
a high value would be attached by persons to the resultant social
institutions.

Except in circumstances in which poverty of material resources
impaired the satisfaction of their members' needs, this ideal type was
probably approximated in small tribal societies in which relationships
were those of extended kinship relationships with legitimized tribal
leaders. Elders could be arbiters, with their decisions resting on
religious sanctions in some cases. They were not considered "leaders"
imposing the law on unwilling "subjects", but representatives of the
community and its self-generated norms.

Whether this was so or not, societies will not be returning to such
a paradise. Social relationships are no longer confined to tribal
relationships, and the struggle to maintain quality of life must increase
with resource exploitations. But conceptions of such an ideal do
direct attention to the nature of the problem contemporary societies
face – the problem of legitimization of institutions and the ways
in which judicial systems, rather than being chiefly punitive, can
investigate and direct attention to sources of disputes and conflict
within and between societies.

HUMAN NEEDS AS PROVIDING A NORM

The introduction of a human dimension into the study of conflict and its resolution makes a fundamental difference both to explanation and to process. It is now a pervasive trend in all branches of social studies, altering them in a fundamental way. This human dimension must also invade law and political decision making, domestic and foreign, as it becomes part of conventional wisdom. It certainly must change attitudes toward deviant behaviors and their treatment. The human needs framework shifts definitions of justice from a normative base to one that reflects behavioral considerations. Or, to put it differently, the definition of justice posits as a basic norm or rule the principle that inherent human needs must be satisfied if law and order is to be sustained and societies are to be stable and not violent.

Faced with realities and failures in maintaining law and order, societies are beginning to ask whether it is "just" (not to mention practical) to punish children who live in poverty for peddling drugs, or would it be "just" to hold politically responsible authorities who have failed to provide proper schooling, housing and jobs, the absence of which gives rise to these behaviors? It is a curious conception of justice when authorities impose through their courts punishments for crimes that are brought about by circumstances for which they are responsible.

THE WEAKENING OF LEGAL NORMS

Legal norms that place constraints on behavior range from specifying the side of the road on which to drive to many applications that are far more subject to social change. Over time there is change in legal norms even in the absence of changes in law as is legislated by authorities. The norms governing child custody, for example, originally favored the father as the sole source of support, then the mother during the last century as the parent usually closest to small children. More recently, with mothers working outside the home, the emphasis has shifted to case-by-case determinations based on general assessments of the interests of the child. It was for reasons such as this that the original English courts of equity declared that they would not be bound by precedent. Determining custody on the basis of the unique elements of each case eliminates precedent as the basis of norms, and substitutes a behavioral or human norm (the development of the child).

The erosion of norms based on precedent, however, leads to conditions in which courts, in theory existing to interpret and enforce consensus norms enacted into law, become interpreters of individual needs and the common good rather than of historic norms, and become, therefore, quasi-legislatures. The attempt to adapt norms to altering behaviors which increasingly defy control further weakens legal norms, and compels courts to improvise future-oriented solutions, as do legislatures. Issues such as "right to life" versus "right to choice" and interpretations of constitutions generally, cannot be dealt with in the context of any widespread consensus, for there is none. The interpretation of law becomes an ideological battleground in the absence of a clearly articulated consensus norm.

To the extent that precedent norms disappear, and in the absence of some other overriding human needs norm, cases of deep rooted conflict must be defined as being outside the jurisdiction of courts or alternatives to courts, though sometimes relying on a court for eventual validation and enforcement. As we suggest later, this may be a transition stage prior to courts and attorneys moving, along with a popular consensus, toward consideration of the human dimension.

ALTERNATIVE DISPUTE RESOLUTION PROCEDURES

This transition has led to what are known as "Alternative Dispute Resolution" (ADR) procedures. These are somewhat less pragmatic than the less structured management processes. They include arbitration and adjudication, together with forms of conciliation which can be applied to lesser financial claims, neighborhood disputes, and non-criminal but anti-social behaviors.

They are described as "alternative" because their primary purpose has been to ease the burden on the legal system by adding forums that are more attractive than courts, but which do essentially the same job: that is, they settle some types of disputes on the basis of accepted norms without necessarily dealing with fundamental causes. Courts themselves sometimes insist that, before there is recourse to courts, these other processes be used. In the words of Goldberg, Green, and Sander (1985, p. 5) ADR has four separate goals:

1. to relieve court congestion as well as undue cost and delay
2. to enhance community involvement in the dispute resolution process
3. to facilitate access to justice, and
4. to provide more "effective" dispute resolution.

We have placed ADR in this section dealing with settlement because of its association with courts. There are some ADR centers that pursue public policy issues and at the same time enact an ADR role in association with courts (Susskind and Cruikshank, 1987, p. 227). At first glance it might appear that many "alternative dispute resolution" procedures could be more advantageous to disputants than are formal courts, and more likely to result in acceptable outcomes. There could be less formality, less confrontation, and perhaps some opportunities to address psychological issues. Susskind and Ozawa (1985, p. 196) assert that:

> Mediated negotiation is appealing because it addresses many of the procedural shortcomings of the more traditional approaches to resolving resource allocation conflicts. It allows for more direct involvement of those most affected by decisions than other administrative and legislative processes, it can provide settlements more rapidly and at lower cost than the courts, and it is more flexible and adaptable to the specific needs of the parties in each unique situation.

PROBLEMS OF ASSESSMENT

These considerations raise some fundamental questions of psychology, of process, and perhaps of ethics.

Psychology first. How do we know that an outcome of what appears to be an interest dispute, an outcome brought about by persuasion of those directly concerned, and by mediation and negotiation, is a lasting outcome? For example, may it not be that "caucusing" and third-party discussions with participants separately turns out to be manipulative, and inviting the breakdown of an agreement at a later stage (see Goldberg, Green and Sander, 1985. p. 145)? May it not be that the participants are in two roles, those who are subject to manipulation in a social setting or by direct caucusing, and those same persons when they are out of these settings? If this is the case and participants are representatives of parties, the agreements they arrive at could be rejected. May this not explain why such processes, when applied to an interest dispute such as a wage dispute, become so prolonged, and generate role positions and problems of personal recognition, thus transforming an interest dispute into a conflict over non-negotiable issues?

This raises a question of process. Trial and error, pragmatic, mixed and non-defined processes could be dysfunctional, even when dealing only with interest disputes – that is, disputes over material goods which do not in themselves involve any psychological dimension. Caucusing approximates manipulation, and so can recording of "consensus" agreements if they do not give the same weight and approval to reservations and disagreements. May it not be that the analytical training and processes which are essential in the treatment of a conflict with psychological dimensions are equally important in an interest dispute?

Ethical issues in any intervention relate to qualifications, skills and processes, and their applications, as we shall argue in our Conclusions (Part V). A third party must avoid being "used" by a powerful party, and also must avoid representing a status quo position. A third party must also avoid injecting his or her idiosyncratic value judgements. There is in this field of intervention a great deal of confusion between ethics and values. Perhaps it cannot be avoided, but it does seem strange that it is acceptable for governments to select judges because of their prejudices and "values", meaning their ideologies. If subjectivity becomes a feature of alternative means of dispute resolution also, then clients will avoid them.

There are some deeper issues of political philosophy. Is conflict resolution a tool to be employed by or on behalf of institutions and authorities, or on behalf of persons and their development and quality of life? This question feeds back directly into process. Are individual needs and values dominant, or are those of institutions? Should there not be, in all cases, whether dealing with parties directly or not, an emphasis on analysis and the deduction of options?

A TRANSITION STAGE BETWEEN JUDICIAL AND RESOLUTION PROCESSES

Societies have entered a crucial transition stage in which courts are losing their jurisdiction over disputes and conflicts, partly because of overcrowding, partly because of costs, to a large degree because courts are not problem-solving bodies, and partly because it suits more powerful parties to invent their own procedures. In *Conflict: Human Needs Theory* several scholars argue that alternative dispute and conflict resolution practices are pursued sometimes to deal with disputes and conflicts that are the consequence of system faults. In such cases, they tend to bolster institutions and systems that otherwise would be forced to undergo desirable change. In such conditions it is the powerful, those who can manipulate the system, who survive while the underprivileged become even more deprived.

In many cases in which one party voluntarily seeks a judicial decision, as when a party seeks redress against another party in a civil case, the defendant is likely to avoid if possible an authoritative decision based on interpretations of consensus norms. This is clear at the international level, where nations are reluctant to submit to the interpretation and application of norms when their perceived national interest is affected. The growing unpredictability of legal results in a period of weakening norms (which also makes litigation more time-consuming and costly) also leads many defendants to seek more controllable procedures.

The end result of weakened norms and of prejudice entering into settlement processes can only be further system distortion, more discrimination, and economic and social policies designed to bolster the economy, but not the development of all members of the society. The consequences are far-reaching. In the shorter term there are increasing inequalities of income and opportunity, leading to social consequences such as decreasing educational and health standards, and increasing crime and violence; and in the longer term either an authoritarian military takeover, or a mafia-type society in which power groups protect themselves from each other, while the powerless individual becomes a member of an alienated caste.

THE DANGERS OF ARBITRATION

The same legitimization and behavioral considerations are involved in the question of when to use arbitration. In some areas – for example, industrial disputes – arbitration is an accepted process. Over time it seems to become more and more flexible in applying consensus norms and in actual procedures. Its increasing use reflects the desire to break away from the strict application of precedents and norms, and to rely far more on bargaining and negotiation.

Indeed, in some industries there has been a tendency to replace arbitration with forms of mediation, a procedure that relies even less on legal norms. The resultant settlement, however, risks being more an outcome of the relative power of the protagonists than would be the case if consensus norms were applied.

There is one further serious difficulty. Arbitration and mediation that are outside the context of consensus norms can lead to agreements that cater to the interests of the protagonists at the expense of the total society and the future. This was how Italian fascism emerged in the 1930s, when the interests of employers and employees in particular industries were achieved at the expense of the total economy. The same result obtains now, when disputes that should be settled on the basis of societal interests are settled in the interests of the immediate parties (see Fiss, 1984). The great danger of the "Alternative Dispute Resolution" movement as a substitute for legal processes is that it can unintentionally help to promote even further a Hobbesian state of nature.

TOWARD FREEDOM?

In this perspective the movements toward deregulation in Western economic systems, and the parallel movements toward "democracy" in communist countries that were welcomed by Western governments and peoples in the late 1980s, were more a reflection of the breakdown of consensus government and the erosion of legal norms than a trend toward more representative and responsible government. They were, therefore, a prelude to far greater defensive interventions by authorities in the future. These interventions could take one of two forms, according to prevailing ideologies and power influences. They could move in the direction of "constructive interventions" (see *Conflict: Resolution and Provention*, Chapter 11), with provention being a major endeavor, or toward a survival of the fittest system within a power elite or military dictatorship, in which conflicts would be settled by coercive processes.

The challenge both to judicial systems and alternatives is whether they can move from historical and elite norms towards norms based on the needs of the individual, and thus earn a legitimized status. Otherwise they are likely to be merely a stage in the development of even more power-oriented settlement processes. If alternatives remain in the shadow of courts, and if they are captured by the legal profession in the interests of powerful clients, they will be processes devoid of consensus norms, and governed by elite interests. Indeed, they may come to approximate the fascist model that was a disaster nationally and internationally.

This is the context in which we wish to determine the types of cases which are appropriately dealt with by settlement processes – courts, arbitration or non-neutral interventions. The following three chapters on adjudication, arbitration and ombudsmanry raise these issues while describing the processes.

9 Adjudication

INTRODUCTION

The courtroom, whether used in civil or criminal disputes, provides the prototype of a settlement procedure. Because a voluminous literature adequately describes, analyzes, and critiques the full range of courtroom processes (in relation to court alternatives see, for instance, Nader, 1980; Auerbach, 1983; Goldberg, Green and Sander, 1985; Harrington, 1985), we will do no more than describe them briefly. The court deserves recognition as the predominant forum in most societies in which disputes and conflict are handled with or by a third party. In making our overall assessment we come to the view that ultimately the adjustment by courts to new insights on human relations may be a more practical objective than new forms of institutionalization.

THE ROLE OF THE COURTS

There currently exists a stream of thought – fostered by advocates for groups such as abused spouses, minorities, and consumers who have attacked mediation and other so-called "soft" procedures for perpetuating power imbalances – that only the courts are capable of dealing with their issues. However, as Goldberg, Green and Sander (1985, p. 153) point out:

> to the extent the adjudicatory process is susceptible to such manipulation by powerful, repeat players (such as insurance companies, large corporations, and the government), it raises serious questions of whether adjudication perpetuates or ameliorates inequalities of power.

A study of the Council on the Role of Courts (1984) titled *The Role of Courts in American Society*, suggests that there are two distinct views by which the direct functions of courts may be seen, the "traditionalist" and the "adaptationist".

In the traditionalist perspective, courts are best limited to a narrow range of functions: bipolar disputes involving real injuries, handled by adversarial procedures, and settled by the application of ready standards or principles. The courts should not intrude on the domain of other institutions by involving themselves in legislation and administration.

The adaptationist viewpoint highlights the social setting and the changing function of courts as they interact with institutions such as legislatures and executive agencies. The failures of other institutions leave a vacuum that the courts should fill. The question of what courts should do, then, should not be determined by what they do best, but by what needs to be done to build and maintain a proper public and private order.

Types of cases a court might hear, in this view, are as follows (Council on the Role of Courts, 1984, pp. 85–86):

1. Disputes not susceptible to resolution by private ordering; e.g., disputes among strangers and those involving irreconcilable claims about principles.
2. Disputes that should not be settled privately because society has an important stake in governing them by authoritatively imposing public standards; e.g., disputes arising between parties who are significantly unequal in resources for bargaining, or involving one party significantly dependent on the other, or resulting in a privately agreed-upon solution that imposes unacceptable costs on others or that violates established norms of public policy.
3. Disputes that permit courts to create "bargaining endowments" by setting standards in a few cases, thereby facilitating the private system of bargaining and settlement.
4. Cases that recognize and will encourage the airing of grievances that society ought to be interested in articulating.

The Council on the Role of Courts could not offer definitive conclusions about which cases belong and which do not belong in the courts. Instead, it determined six categories of inclusion and exclusion, ranging from cases suitable for courts in any view to cases unsuitable in any view.

It further suggested two sets of criteria of fitness, "functional" criteria and "prudential" criteria. Functional criteria are those factors which determine whether a court is suited or unsuited to hear and decide the case. Prudential criteria are those factors that determine whether a court is more or less suited to hear and decide a case than other institutions. Functional criteria include objectivity, the necessity for authoritative standards, and the determination of past (as opposed to future) events. Prudential criteria include costs, particularized consideration (as opposed to repetitive or routine issues), preference of the parties, the vitality of other institutions, the immediate resolution of a specialized problem, and direct versus indirect action (by indirect meaning the influence of courts in pressuring settlement, deciding jurisdiction, or designing a process).

The Council suggested that constitutional issues involving life or death, liberty, or property, are suitable by any criteria. In addition, parties claiming legal entitlement who are in deadlock over non-continuing events, such as contract claims, should have their cases decided by adjudication.

Some cases that suit the functional criteria do not belong in the courts, according to the Council. For instance those cases involving monetary claims, in which the claim is less than the costs of proceedings, belong in less time-consuming and costly forums. Cases in which the determination of legal issues is unimportant, such as the administration of estates or routine cases of traffic violations, belong elsewhere. A third class of cases involves "harms that can generally be insured against", such as worker's compensation or traffic accidents, in which the facts rather than legal issues are under dispute.

Courts can be a processing forum for, and serve as a back-up to, cases referred elsewhere. The knowledge that failure will result in an adjudicated decision can facilitate agreement. Types of cases given as examples by the Council included child custody and product warranty disputes. Courts might also be "architects of process" by determining or sanctioning a procedure that will eventually determine the outcome.

Some cases not suitable for the courts, according to the traditionalist viewpoint, on the adaptationist view do belong there. These are the cases of structural reform and extended impact affecting institutions such as schools, hospitals, and prisons. In these cases the courts act as on-going administrative authorities, setting specific requirements for change and monitoring compliance with those requirements.

The Council suggests that "problems that have not been shaped into disputes resting on a claim of legal entitlement ought not be aired in court" (Council on the Role of Courts, 1984, p. 121). In addition, many entities and offices, such as parole boards and public prosecutors, are immune from suits arising from the consequences of their authoritative action.

COURTROOM VARIATIONS AND ALTERNATIVE PROCEDURES

Although most people are familiar with the standard trial format – "the formal examination before a competent tribunal of the matter in issue in a civil or criminal cause in order to determine such issue" (Webster's Dictionary) – it is useful to realize that there are extensive differences in trial procedures among different courts in the United States. There are even greater differences between forms of adjudication in the United States and various other places in the world. Contrary to popular belief, the adversarial proceeding is not universal throughout the Western world. It is worth noting that some of these other procedures have provided a model for courtroom alternatives in the United States (such as the Kpelle moot court, see Danzig, 1973).

The "pre-trial conference" is exactly what it sounds like: a conference involving all the major parties to the dispute who meet with the judge before going to trial to prepare for trial. Increasingly, the pre-trial conference has become a method of averting the costs and consequences of a full trial. Presentations are made informally to the judge, who may recommend a settlement. This procedure is used in cases involving business and insurance claims, and may be used with a private judge as well.

"Neutral experts", also known as "fact-finders", are used in disputes where judgement requires specialized expertise. In the US, federal courts can appoint such an expert in certain prescribed situations, with or without approval of the disputants. The expert gives advice and opinion (as opposed to binding decisions) during a trial, informs the parties of his or her findings, and may testify and be cross-examined before the jury. Again, this procedure may be done privately as well.

A "special master" may be appointed by the court for various purposes; again, one purpose may be to create options for settlement of difficult and complex cases. The special master may or may not be approved by the two parties, and might be given leeway in function; for instance, one might choose to mediate a case instead of recommend a specific settlement.

A "moderated settlement conference" may be initiated by either litigants or the court. A third-party panel, usually attorneys, hears presentations by counsel for each side and gives a non-binding, advisory opinion to be used by the parties in their settlement negotiations. Any statements and evidence used during the proceedings are considered confidential and inadmissible at later court hearings. The court will usually be informed only of the conclusion of the proceedings – that is, whether or not the disputants reached an agreement.

Unlike other alternative procedures, a "summary jury trial" retains both the judge and the jury. Each side makes brief presentations of its civil case to the court, including the jury and those with decision making authority on the other side. While the jury deliberates, the parties may make attempts to settle. If not, the jury, if it can agree, then delivers a verdict. After the verdict, lawyers may question the jury. Presumably, the perspective of the jury allows each side to judge better how the merits of its case would appear to an actual jury. The results of this procedure then prepare each side for negotiations with one another or, if then failing to reach agreement, for a full trial.

The summary jury trial may be appropriate when there are substantial differences of opinion over expectations of the jury's interpretation, or one or all parties have unrealistic expectations but insist on their day in court (Lambros, 1986). These facts can be determined in pre-trial conference, and a judge may even have the authority to mandate the procedure and empanel a jury prior to a "real" trial (Lambros, 1986). Because the procedure is kept brief, rarely lasting as long as an entire day, its success can save time and expense.

Lambros suggests that these proceedings may also be converted into a "summary bench trial" by using the judge without the jury. This modification may increase the popularity of this procedure.

A variation of this procedure is "private judging", also called "rent-a-judge". Disputants wishing to avoid the delays of standard judicial procedures hire their own magistrate, usually a retired judge. In some states, this procedure has been institutionalized such that the decision is legally binding; in this case, however, appeal may be made just as if the decision had been rendered by a sitting trial judge.

Some critics fear that the privatization of justice may create a two-track system of justice: one system for the wealthy, the "second-class justice" system for the poor. The concern is that continued acceptance and development of the movement towards private practices such as rent-a-judge and mini-trials may leave in its wake a deteriorating system of public justice.

Gnaizda (1982) raises two philosophical objections to rent-a-judge which apply to all private adjudicatory procedures: the potential destruction of the single integrated system of justice based on common law, and the possibility that easy access to private forums for justice would undermine reform of the public system. There is even an argument against allowing a more expedited private settlement: it may unfairly allow those who can afford it to set precedents affecting other litigants. The League of United Latin American Citizens, the San Francisco chapter of the National Association for the Advancement of Colored People, the Sacramento Urban League, the American G.I. Forum, and others have condemned rent-a-judge for these reasons (Gnaizda, 1982).

Many court systems have "settlement weeks" to attempt to clear up cases which have been on the docket for a long time. First instituted in Orange County, California, where it is a regular part of the court calendar, this innovation is now used in dozens of courts throughout the US. Judges and volunteer lawyers "attempt to facilitate settlement which is ultimately decided by the two parties; 4218 out of 10 248 cases (41.16 per cent) reached settlement for the period from 1986 through December 1988" (American Bar Association, Standing Committee on Dispute Resolution, 1989).

One category of court alternatives is that of non-binding, private adaptations of standard courtroom procedures. Various trial procedures can be kept, modified, or dropped completely depending upon the needs of the participants and their joint agreement.

Heading this category is the "mini-trial", increasingly used in business disputes involving large corporations. Participants themselves determine procedures. They select a neutral advisor to preside over the trial and exchange key documents before the trial session. When the cases are presented to the advisor, and in some instances to a mock jury, each side appoints key personnel with decision making authority to hear the presentations. Following the session, the two sides can negotiate with one another, or the advisor's opinion might be sought. The proceedings can be used as a pre-indication of what might be expected if the case were to proceed to adjudication. In some cases the process of preparing and presenting the cases allows the parties afterwards to engage in better-informed negotiations.

The mini-trial developed out of frustration with the inadequacies of both failed negotiations and costly, time-consuming courtroom proceedings. Although a number of firms provide a standardized mini-trial service, the participants are usually free to determine the exact form of procedures themselves.

The American Arbitration Association (AAA) provides a list of 16 rules by which they administer the mini-trial. These are intended for use by business organizations or government agencies. The AAA suggests that the parties may alter any of these provisions (AAA, 1986):

1. The mini-trial process may be initiated by the written or oral request of either party, made to any regional office of the AAA, but will not be pursued unless both parties agree to resolve their dispute by means of a mini-trial.
2. The course of the mini-trial process shall be governed by a written agreement between the parties.
3. The mini-trial shall consist of an information exchange and settlement negotiation.
4. Each party is represented throughout the mini-trial process by legal counsel whose role is to prepare and present the party's "best case" at the information exchange.
5. Each party shall have in attendance throughout the information exchange and settlement negotiation a senior executive with settlement authority.
6. A neutral advisor shall be present at the information exchange to decide questions of procedure and to render advice to the party representatives when requested by them.
7. The neutral advisor shall be selected by mutual agreement of the parties, who may consult with the AAA for recommendations. To facilitate the selection process, the AAA will make available to the parties a list of individuals to serve as neutral advisors. If the parties fail to agree upon the selection of a neutral advisor, they shall ask that the AAA appoint an advisor from the panel it has compiled for this purpose.
8. Discovery between the parties may take place prior to the information exchange, in accordance with the agreement between the parties.
9. Prior to the information exchange, the parties shall exchange written statements summarizing the issues in the case, and copies of all documents they intend to present at the information exchange.
10. Federal or state rules of evidence do not apply to presentations made at the information exchange. Any limitation on the scope of the evidence offered at the information exchange shall be determined by mutual agreement of the parties prior to the

exchange and shall be enforced by the neutral advisor.

11. After the information exchange, the senior executives shall meet and attempt, in good faith, to formulate a voluntary settlement of the dispute.

12. If the senior executives are unable to settle the dispute, the neutral advisor shall render an advisory opinion as to the likely outcome of the case if it were litigated in a court of law.

13. After the neutral advisor has rendered an advisory opinion, the senior executives shall meet for a second time in an attempt to resolve the dispute. If they are unable to reach a settlement at this time, they may either abandon the proceeding or submit to the neutral advisor written offers of settlement. If the parties elect to make such written offers, the neutral advisor shall make a recommendation for settlement based on those offers. If the parties reject the recommendation of the neutral advisor, either party may declare the mini-trial terminated and resolve the dispute by other means.

14. Mini-trial proceedings are confidential; no written or oral statement made by any participant in the proceeding may be used as evidence or in admission in any other proceeding.

15. The fees and expenses of the neutral advisor shall be borne equally by the parties, and each party is responsible for its own costs, including legal fees, incurred in connection with the mini-trial. The parties may, however, in their written agreement alter the allocation of fees and expenses.

16. Neither the AAA nor any neutral advisor serving in a mini-trial proceeding governed by these procedures shall be liable to any party for any act or omission in connection with the mini-trial. The parties shall indemnify the AAA and the neutral advisor for any liability to third parties arising out of the mini-trial process.

CONCLUSIONS

The influence of the legal system is not limited to the courtroom setting. The threat of a trial and judgement, with its attendant risks and costs, impels many negotiations to a conclusion; only 5 to 10 per cent of disputes that are filed in court are concluded by trial (Goldberg, Green and Sander, 1985, p. 152). Although these cases never reach the judge or jury, they are evidence of the court's influence. The legal system, to a great degree, shapes how disputes are conceptualized, how they emerge into consciousness, and how they are transformed (Felstiner, Abel and Sarat, 1981).

A broadcast of the public television series "Ethics in America" in 1989 exemplified this influence. A panel of experts, including journalists, justices, judges, practising attorneys, clergy, and philosophers, was examining the hypothetical case of a man who had murdered a woman. The panelists were asked to imagine that this person had just committed the murder and was coming to them for help.

After a few brief comments about such non-legal matters as the murderer's condition and moral obligations, the analysis shifted and remained focussed entirely on his legal rights and how he might be best defended against prosecution. The omission of any other considerations, such as what might be best for him as an individual, or about the victim and her family and friends, spoke more eloquently than words of the power the legal system has to affect the way we think about problems.

The courtroom's influence can also be seen in the impetus that recognition of its weaknesses has provided towards the creation of a number of alternative procedures, commonly called "Alternative Dispute Resolution", or "ADR".

Many critics of the legal system favor a kind of Gestalt switch of figure and ground, in which the legal system and courtroom procedures are seen as the alternative, and negotiation and consensual, problem-solving approaches to disputes and conflict are recognized as the norm. US Supreme Court Justice O'Connor (American Bar Association, 1987), although retaining the old language, echoes this sentiment:

> The courts of this country should not be the places where the resolution of disputes begin. They should be the places where disputes end – after alternative methods of resolving disputes have been considered and tried.

There is an alternative, which we broach in our final assessment, that legal norms give place to behavioral norms – that is, that the institutions of the courts be retained, but that their orientation be changed. This could only be accomplished by a wider education of lawyers.

As a first step in any reconceptualization, we suggest that the concept "Alternative Dispute Resolution" should be limited to that large class of processes that includes variations of standard courtroom procedures. The bulk of these processes are designed primarily to decrease court case loads, offer speedier decisions, and reduce expenses of the participants. They do not offer any great change either within or without the legal system: rather, they provide better means of putting together the pieces of an already existing system.

10 Arbitration

INTRODUCTION

Arbitration is the most practised of all the institutionalized processes examined in this volume, in both the United States and the rest of the world. The American Arbitration Association (AAA) handles thousands of cases each year, and lists over 60 000 arbitrators on its National Panel of Arbitrators. The Better Business Bureau (BBB) has trained and uses over 15 000 volunteers. The Federal Mediation and Conciliation Service (FMCS), better known for its mediation of labor–management disputes, also maintains a roster of some 1 500 private citizens whom they recommend to arbitrate labor–contract disputes. More than 95 per cent of labor–management contracts in the US provide for arbitration of contract interpretation disputes (Goldberg, Green and Sander, 1985). Arbitration clauses are included in most commercial contracts (Coulson, 1982).

There is a long history of third-party arbitration. The Greek city-states used arbitration, and the Pope often served as arbitrator between European states in medieval and renaissance times. George Washington included an arbitration clause in his will in case of disputes among his heirs (Cooley, 1986). Since the Hague Convention for the Pacific Settlement of International Disputes (in 1899) arbitration has been formally established within the international arena.

Industrial arbitration was established on a statutory basis in the United States with New York and Massachusetts laws of 1886 (Mercer, 1987). But its use was not widespread until the Second World War, when labor and management took the no-lockout pledge and agreed to have the government decide the merits of labor disputes that affected the war effort (Haughton, 1984). The War Labor Board imposed grievance arbitration where no arbitration agreements existed, and both sides kept these agreements in post-war contracts.

The Uniform Arbitration Act, adopted by the National Conference of the Commissioners for Uniform State Laws in 1955 (amended 1956), provides that arbitration may be compelled if there has been prior agreement to use it but one of the parties refuses to participate. The Magnuson–Moss Warranty Act of 1975 established the legitimacy of private arbitration for consumer/business disputes, in effect letting an industry mandate arbitration before redress is sought in the courts. The Administrative Conference of the United States (1986), recognizing that federal agencies decide "hundreds of thousands of cases annually", far more than the courts, suggested that Congress permit executive branch officials to arbitrate disputes on the government's behalf (Congress S.2274 §585, 1988).

Labor grievances, baseball player salary fights, automobile warranty complaints, insurance problems, construction industry contract disagreements, and international business disagreements are only a few of the better known areas of disputes in which arbitration is practised.

Most arbitration is performed by volunteers. Lawyers dominate the commercial fields, but specialists in other fields are often required for special cases. Kahn (1984) notes that most professional arbitrators come from one of three categories: old hands from the labor relations field, such as mediators or union representatives, who seek a second career in this related field; professors; and those who enter the field directly through internships or under the auspices of a mentor. Many community mediation centers or neighborhood justice centres also train volunteer mediators in arbitration procedures.

The National Academy of Arbitrators (NAA), along with the AAA and the FMCS, published its "Code of Ethics for Arbitrators" in 1951; it was revised in 1972–74 and is now titled "The Code of Professional Responsibility for Arbitrators of Labor–Management Disputes". This code applies to all NAA, AAA, and FMCS arbitrators (Greenbaum, 1984).

THE PROCESS

Arbitration developed free from any explicit theoretical framework. It developed instead as a pragmatic response to certain kinds of costly disputes and conflicts, and the recognition of two factors by disputing parties and the larger community affected by their dispute: the costs of their continuing dispute were higher than either wanted to bear; and no other established mechanisms were likely to end the dispute.

There are two categories of problems settled by arbitration: "interests" and "rights". "Interests" issues are those involving allocation of resources, such as disputes over the negotiation of salary terms or other employment conditions. "Rights" issues involve disputes over the interpretation of existing contracts.

Arbitration can be conducted with a single arbitrator or a panel of arbitrators. How the arbitrators are selected varies depending upon the type of case, the setting, and previous agreement between the contending parties. For instance, the disputants might each select one member of a panel, with the panel themselves selecting the third; or, they might select one mutually acceptable arbitrator from a list of available people; or, the arbitrator might be assigned to the case by some other authority. The arbitrator may be exempt from civil liability arising from the case (Cooley, 1986).

Most of the disputes settled by arbitration involve just two parties disputing with one another. Arbitration is used to settle disputes at all levels – individual against individual, individual against organization, and organization against organization.

At one time arbitration was an entirely voluntary procedure. An arbitration hearing used to result either from prior contractual arrangements between the two parties, or from an agreement made in response to a particular case. Now, however, court-annexed arbitration programs mandate an arbitration hearing for certain kinds of civil disputes prior to formal adjudication. There are also non-judicial programs such as the "Auto Line" program run by the BBB. One party (the consumer, in this case) may be forced to use the arbitration process before seeking redress in court. And some state legislatures have mandated arbitration in case of a public employee contract impasse. If voluntary, the results may be binding or non-binding – that is, the decision may have legal standing or it may be simply advisory.

Each arbitration may be divided into four phases: the agreement to arbitrate; selection of the arbitrator; the hearing; the decision.

Each side's presentation is normally made in person, but some proceedings allow written argument or even a telephone presentation. Rules vary: representation, witnesses, and documentation are often allowed. Depending upon the law, witnesses may be subpoenaed, and they may be required to testify under oath. Pre-hearing discovery may be allowed, but extensive discovery negates the procedure's advantages of speed and simplicity (Cooley, 1986).

The arbitrator's decision is presumably made upon the basis of evidence and arguments; however, some arbitrators prefer to be guided as well by indicators by the parties as to what may or may not be acceptable (Getman, 1985). In some cases informal mediation may be performed by certain arbitrators.

The decision may be rendered immediately, or the case may require a good deal of reflection and research upon the part of the third party, and may take weeks. Some types of arbitration allow a form of appeal. However, the award generally has the force of an adjudicated decision, and can be challenged in court only on narrow grounds, such as misconduct (Cooley, 1986).

The American Arbitration Association has evolved highly formalized, comprehensive sets of rules and procedures for arbitrations under their aegis. There are different rules for different areas – commercial arbitration rules, rules for the arbitration of automotive disputes, construction industry rules, and others. Each of these sets includes an elaborate schedule of fees and penalties for adjournment. Although each industry may have its own procedures, the basic arbitration process forms the core of each procedure.

Many of these statements of rules are quite lengthy. We present here in their entirety a brief set offered by the AAA (1984). Interestingly, these rules are also presented as guides for the mediation process, and they are titled "Alternative Dispute Resolution Procedures". Presumably, one must simply substitute "mediation" whenever "arbitration" is used!

1. Agreement of Parties   These Alternative Dispute Resolution Procedures shall apply whenever the parties have agreed to use them. By mutual agreement, in writing, the parties may modify any provision.

2. Initiation of Alternative Dispute Resolution Procedures   Cases may be initiated by a joint submission in writing, containing a brief description of the dispute with the names and addresses of the parties.

3. Appointment of Neutral   The AAA shall appoint a neutral attorney, knowledgeable in the area of the dispute. The parties shall agree in advance whether the neutral is authorized to issue a binding decision as an arbitrator. When the parties agree that such a decision will be binding, they are deemed to have consented that judgment upon such an award may be entered in any court having jurisdiction. If not authorized to issue a binding decision, the neutral will serve the parties as a mediator.

4. Qualifications of Neutrals   No person shall serve as a neutral in any matter in which that person has any financial or personal interest in the result of the proceeding. Prior to accepting appointment, a person being considered for such appointment shall disclose any circumstances likely to prevent a prompt hearing or to create a presumption of bias. Upon receipt of such information, the AAA

will either replace that person or communicate the information to the parties for comment. Thereafter, the AAA may disqualify that person. Vacancies shall be filled in accordance with Section 3 of these procedures.

5. Time and Place of Mediation Conference or Arbitration Hearing   The neutral shall set the date, time, and place of the first conference or hearing with the parties, seven (7) days advance notice of which shall be given by the AAA to the parties. If the matter is to be mediated, the mediator will arrange an appropriate format with the parties.

6. Representation by Counsel   Any party may be represented at the conference or hearing by counsel or other representative.

7. Adjournment   Conferences or hearings may be adjourned by the neutral for good cause.

8. No Stenographic Record   There shall be no stenographic record of any such proceeding.

9. Arbitration hearing   A hearing may be conducted by the arbitrator in a manner which permits a fair presentation of the case by the parties. Normally, the hearing shall be completed within one day. Only for good cause shown may the arbitrator schedule an additional hearing.

10. Evidence   The arbitrator shall be the sole judge of the relevance and materiality of the evidence offered.

11. Close of Hearing   The arbitrator shall ask whether the parties have any further proofs or testimony to offer. Upon determining that the presentations are concluded, the arbitrator shall declare the hearing closed.

12. Award   The award shall be in writing and shall be signed by the arbitrator. It shall be rendered promptly and, unless otherwise stipulated, not later than thirty (30) days following the close of the hearing. Any settlement reached by the parties may be incorporated in such an award.

13. Delivery of Award to Parties   The parties shall accept as legal delivery of the award the placing of the award or a true copy thereof in the mail by the AAA, addressed to such party at its last known address or to its attorney, or personal service of the award, or the filing of the award in any manner which may be prescribed by law.

14. Expenses   The expenses of witnesses for any party shall be paid by the party producing such witnesses.

15. Interpretation and Application of Procedures   The neutral

shall interpret and apply these procedures insofar as they relate to the neutral's powers and duties. All other procedures shall be interpreted and applied by the AAA.

16. Judicial Proceedings and Immunity   Neither the AAA nor any neutral serving in a proceeding under these procedures is a necessary party in judicial proceedings relating to the arbitration or mediation. Neither the AAA nor any neutral serving under these procedures shall be liable to any party for any act or omission in connection with this service.

VARIATIONS

"High–low arbitration" involves an agreement between disputants to limit the minimum and maximum amount of potential awards; the range of potential loss and gain is thus predetermined before a decision or verdict is returned.

In "final-offer arbitration" the arbitrator is presented the final positions of the two sides. He or she must select one of these two positions. The rationale for final-offer arbitration is this: if the parties know or suspect that the arbitrator will render a compromise decision, perhaps splitting the difference between them, they will each exaggerate their demands. This, of course, is inimical to productive negotiation. But if they know that the arbitrator is forced to choose one or the other position, they will bargain with one another more readily, and they will adjust their final offer in order to cut their potential losses.

A variation of this procedure does not allow the arbitrator to know the two final offers; he or she determines a figure, and whichever of the two positions is closer to that figure becomes the actual award. The exception occurs when the arbitrator chooses a figure exactly between the two sides' final positions, in which case the arbitrator's choice becomes the award.

"Court-annexed arbitration" diverts cases involving a sum of money under some maximum figure from the courtroom to non-binding arbitration. Should either party be dissatisfied with the decision they can request a "trial de novo"; however, a penalty (such as the arbitrator's fee) is often imposed upon the party making such a request. In some cases, if the party is unsuccessful in improving its result, additional penalties may be assessed. This threatened penalty, of course, acts as a coercive measure in keeping appeals from the courts.

"Med-Arb" describes a process in which the third party first attempts to assist the two parties in working out their dispute themselves by mediation. If they cannot agree upon a satisfactory solution to any or all of the divisive issues, then the mediator may make a recommendation (non-binding) or a decision (binding).

According to Ross (1982), the term "med-arb" was coined by Sam Kagel to describe his work in private and public sector contract negotiations. For years many decision making third parties, including judges, arbitrators, and National Labor Relations Board examiners, have been using this procedure informally. Following the trend of many other alternative dispute resolution procedures, med-arb is becoming institutionalized. It is commonly used in public sector collective bargaining where no right to strike exists, in the private sector when the costs of impasse are seen as too high by both labor and management, and even in child custody disputes.

One of the questions about the effectiveness of med-arb is how the potential dual role of the third party might affect the mediation process. Ross (1982, p. 2) points out the skepticism of veteran labor relations practitioners, who wonder how, if the disputants indicate their willingness to compromise in certain areas during the mediation stage, the process might affect the med-arbiter's decision if the case proceeds to arbitration. One party might reduce the chances of resolving the dispute during mediation by sticking adamantly to its initial positions, but get a better settlement by not having weakened its bargaining position. Because of this potential process/role conflict, some med-arb programs separate the roles of mediator and arbitrator. In these programs, another third party will enter the case as arbitrator after the mediation efforts have broken down, and the disputants must present their case anew.

McGillicuddy, Welton, and Pruitt (1987) conducted research at a community mediation center in which they compared the effects of straight mediation, med-arb in which the mediator is also the arbitrator (med-arb same), and med-arb in which there are different mediators and arbitrators (med-arb different). One might expect that disputants in the med-arb same condition would try more to impress the third party with the merits of their position than to problem-solve; however, the results suggest otherwise. In fact, the researchers claim that the disputants in med-arb same produced more problem-solving and were less hostile and competitive than in either straight mediation or med-arb different.

Unfortunately, there were substantial problems with the research.

Case assignment procedures were suspect; no account was made of the different skill levels of the mediators; the sample size was quite small; the dropout rate was incredibly high (68 per cent); the presence of observers may have contaminated the test; and, most incredibly, disputant evaluations revealed that a substantial proportion of those who filled out the questionnaires did not understand the decision making procedures (18 out of 46)! The experiment thus points more to the problems of conducting valid research in field settings than to its presumed results.

Brams (1987) suggests a rather complex process that is an innovative variation of arbitration. The third party does not actually render a decision, but acts as a mutually trusted "referee". Each of two sides in a bargaining situation privately gives its reservation prices or position (the absolute minimum or maximum the parties will accept or give) to the referee. If the offers do not overlap (e.g., one will offer no more than 15 dollars, and the other will accept no less than 20), the referee so informs the parties and the process ends. But should the offers converge or overlap (one offers as much as 20 dollars, the other will accept as little as 15), the referee informs the two parties only of the fact that there is an overlap.

Each party then makes a final offer. If both final offers are within the original overlapping interval (one offers 18 dollars, the other will accept 16), the agreement will be the average of the two offers (18 + 16 = 34; one-half of that is 17). If only one of the offers lies within the original overlap (one offers 14 dollars, the other will accept 18), that offer (18) will be the settlement. If neither remains in the original interval (the final offer is 14, the final acceptance figure is 21), the process ends and the disputants must find another way to settle their differences.

CONCLUSIONS

The main concerns of the arbitration field itself center around the neutrality of the arbitrator. Explicit rules require full disclosure of financial or other association with disputants by the potential arbitrators. In some cases arbitrators actually sign an oath promising to render a fair decision before they hear the case.

Goldberg, Green, and Sander (1985, pp. 189–90) detail a number of advantages that arbitration has over adjudication. These can be distilled as follows: the parties can select as decision maker someone who is an expert within the area of the dispute; an agreement to arbitrate may specify that the decision is final, which allows for a meaningful sense of finality; the arbitration process can be shielded from public scrutiny; procedural rules can be adapted to satisfy the specific requirements of the disputants; both proceeding costs and costs of representation may be lower than going to court; and, the decision may be made in a timely fashion. Edwards (1986) adds that the arbitrator, unlike the judge in many circumstances, is free to exercise common sense.

Another advantage to the disputants in some cases is the flexibility in location. Cases may be heard in the arbitrator's office, in the disputants' home setting, or in other locations convenient to all parties. Conversely, some participants prefer the stately formality of the courtroom and the ceremonial adjuncts to the decision making process. Some arbitrators even duplicate the court and its accessories, such as the American flag, the gavel, the judge's robe, and so forth.

Some of these advantages may be turned against disputants, or may threaten harm to public interests. In cases involving consumer complaints against corporate bodies, an expert is likely to have professional ties to the latter. The finality of the decision, which usually allows no appeal for errors of fact or law, is an advantage only if one assumes that there are never any errors of fact or law, a rather dubious assumption. Private proceedings in certain cases may threaten the First Amendment right of scrutiny over governmental institutions (Gnaizda, 1982). Formal procedural rules can work to balance unequal power; their waiver, then, may act against the interests of the less powerful party. Parties without full representation may not realize their rights.

An unforeseen side effect, inherent in the structure of final-offer arbitration, has been discovered by major league baseball, which uses this procedure in salary disputes. Because management, naturally enough, presents to the arbitrator the problems and weaknesses of the player, many of the players come out of the hearings feeling humiliated and unappreciated. While this decision making procedure thus works at one level (in that it prevents the long hold-outs which used to be common), it can be destructive of relationships.

The recent growth of interest in management, settlement and resolution practices has seen many established procedures being applied in new settings. As this process of extension occurs with arbitration, serious questions about reduction of individual rights and disproportionate benefits to institutionalized interests are raised. The non-voluntary programs such as court-annexed arbitration and Auto Line impose the process upon parties before they can seek redress through standard adjudicatory procedures. Many brokerage firms mandate arbitration agreements, leaving cheated investors no other recourse than a panel of industry people paid by the exchanges (Stern, 1987).

Provided only interests are involved, the diminution of individual rights in exchange for increased efficiency may be a worthwhile bargain. This is unlikely in the majority of cases, and the probability is that values and even human needs, especially of recognition and identity, may be suppressed in what could be a power-dominated process. An arbitrator, without any training to be alert to such circumstances and interested in a quick and authoritative settlement, is unlikely to be aware of deeper issues that could lead to less cooperative behavior by the parties after arbitration.

11 Ombudsmanry

INTRODUCTION

In the broadest terms, an ombudsman (sometimes shortened to "om") is an independent agent whose role is to protect some specified class of people from abuse by a particular authority. Caiden (1983b, p. xvi) describes the ideal function of a governmental ombudsman:

> to protect individuals against possible governmental abuse of public trust and to ensure that all power is responsible and accountable to the public . . . If wrong has been done, the offending agency is expected to make it right . . . But even where no wrong has occurred, it is deemed important to know whether people harbor grievances.

Titles for the same or similar roles include liaison officer, internal mediator, work problems counsellor, dialog, director of personnel communications, and director of employee relations.

Ombudsmanry as known today originated in Sweden, although Stieber (1985) claims that the Control Yuan of China's Han dynasty (200 BC) and the Roman censor of about the same time performed similar functions of scrutinizing administrative officials. According to Caiden (1983b) the institution spread from Sweden to the rest of Scandinavia and to Western Europe. The Russian model, as old as the Swedish one, is also used in Eastern Europe and Israel. British Commonwealth countries and dependencies followed New Zealand in adopting variations of the Swedish model, and were followed by Pacifica and the US. Japan is unique in devising its own ombudsman-like institution.

Sweden's constitution of 1809 called for a "justitieombudsman" to be appointed by the legislature to deal with citizen complaints against the government. The same office, with a different name, had been filled prior to that time by a representative of the king. The change was a significant step in the legislature's move towards greater independence from the king (Rowat, 1985).

In Sweden today the office is still quite prestigious. There are four ombudsmen who, while officers of the legislature, are also politically independent of it. One oversees the tax system, one the courts and criminal justice system, another the social welfare and educational

112

systems, and the fourth the armed forces. They are appointed for four-year terms by agreement of the major political parties. Their power is indirect, in that they cannot make changes themselves in laws or policies, but can only recommend such changes. If their recommendations are not accepted they may bring pressure upon the authorities through publicity in the press.

Their procedures are fast, informal, and inexpensive for the citizens. The bulk of their work involves individual citizen complaints about administrative decisions made by public agencies. These are often minor problems that would not justify formal remedial action, such as would be necessitated by an appeal through the courts.

The Swedish experience has provided a model for the rest of the world, but there are other types of ombudsmen as well. Zagoria (1988) adds two other types of governmental ombudsmen to the legislative-appointment model: the executive model, in which the om is appointed by an elected executive and reflects that executive's power; and the citizen model, in which the om is appointed by a civic commision in conjunction with local government.

Zagoria (1988) details the strengths and weaknesses of each approach. The executive om can be established quickly by executive order. The om may have a good deal of authority, in particular with fellow executive appointees. However, the executive om may be perceived as, and may indeed be, more concerned with the executive's concerns than those of citizens.

The legislative om has a long tradition, dating from 1809, and the experience has proven its worth. Since the office is institutionalized it is relatively free from executive pressure and political concerns. It is, however, subject to budget and personnel dictates of the legislature. The legislative om's powers are limited to making recommendations to agencies for remedial action.

The citizen om can deal with all kinds of complaints and may take a public advocacy role. Because of its broad sponsorship, its recommendations are likely to garner respect. However, funding is uncertain from year to year, which makes it susceptible to pressures from sponsoring organizations.

Whatever their institutional base, ombudsmen have domain over either a specific field or over a specific geographical area. Their responsibility may be to those working within an organization or to clients served by an organization. Ombuds offices have been established to protect the rights of children, of college students and employees, of nursing home residents, of corporate employees, of health-care patients, and of prisoners. Some newspapers have ombudsmen representing the readers' interests. Professional organizations, such as those representing nurses and secretaries, often have ombuds officials. In Norway, there is an ombudsman representing the interests of children (the "barneombudet"). If the organisation is one which provides services to the general public, then the ombudsman represents that public's interest.

According to Rowe (undated, p. 1), ombudsmanry "probably provides the largest number of jobs for neutrals in North America." Professional organizations include the Corporate Ombudsman Association, the University and College Ombudsman Association, the United States Association of Ombudsmen, and the International Ombudsman Institute.

THE PROCESS

Ombudsmen deal with three types of disputes: those involving a specific case, such as when an established procedure was mistakenly not followed; those involving a series of similar complaints, which reveal a pattern of neglect, incompetence, or inadequate staffing in implementing established procedures; and those revealing problems with structure, whose remedy can be only a change of procedures and system.

In some cases, an ombudsman performs a fact-finding or investigatory role at the initiation of a complaint; in others, a final decision making one. When located in one particular field (such as nursing home care), the ombudsman may be required to have a high degree of substantive knowledge of that field. If given more generic responsibility, such as over county or state institutions, conciliation and mediation skills may be more important. Zagoria (1988, p. 18) describes the role as follows:

> part fact-finder, part investigator, part systems analyst, part judge, part conciliator, and, if necessary, part advocate for the citizen. Required is a person with thick skin, good ears, determination, and persistence. It is a demanding job since it often involves dealing with difficult people on both sides.

The ombudsman's involvement in a case is occasionally self-initiated, but it more frequently begins with a complaint, which may be made by telephone, by mail, or by personal contact. In some areas of Australia, the om travels to rural areas to bring the service to the residents. Ombudsmen may hold hearings in the field or in their own office; they may work with as few as two individuals or with the entire membership of an organization.

If a complaint is judged to be within the om's jurisdiction, the om must then determine where and how to intervene. In England, New Zealand, Denmark, and Queensland, Australia, the first step is to address the head of the department or agency with responsibility and power to remedy the complaint (Zagoria, 1988). In other jurisdictions the opposite approach is taken, with the rationale that the official or employee closest to the complainant has the most knowledge of the problem, is most concerned, and deserves a chance to deal with it before superiors are brought in (Zagoria, 1988). However, in some areas, such as Sweden, complaints are immediately made public.

Because there is a wide range of types of complaints handled by any ombudsman, flexibility of response is required. At the lowest level of involvement, the office may simply act as a referral center for individuals unfamiliar with a particular bureaucracy. In these cases, there are already established procedures for dealing with a particular problem, and the om's involvement ends after proper referral has been made. Typical of such cases are complaints about needed street and building repairs or correction of a bill for services.

Ombudsmen might break through bureaucratic red tape, mediate between individuals or groups, make legislative recommendations, and perform any other functions that they see as helpful. An ombudsman may exert both official and unofficial influence, through investigation and private or public criticism, but the ombudsman usually does not have the power to enforce a judgement, although in some cases the om is given authority to initiate legal action.

Despite complaints about the absence, in most positions, of power to order relief, Zagoria (1988) claims that from 90 to 100 per cent of ombudsman recommendations are voluntarily adopted by governments. In several places, if the recommendations are not carried out a response must be made explaining the reasons. Refusal to accept the recommendations may be countered by a public statement of the ombudsman, which in some localities must be accompanied by the institution's reasons for not complying. Some ombudsmen are given regular access to the newspapers.

Indeed, some newspapers and television stations have programs with names such as "action lines" which perform functions similar to those of an ombudsman. The use of persuasion can be more compelling if backed by the threat of large-scale publicity about an institution's failures, whether such publicity is justified or not. Doi (1985) insists as well that the effectiveness of reasoned persuasion depends upon general agreement by administrators and public on a standard, such as law and principles of fairness and equity, used to evaluate administrative performance.

CONCLUSIONS

The future of ombudsmanry is likely to see an intensification of the debate about the effectiveness and, more importantly, use of ombudsmanry. According to Caiden (1983a, p. xvii):

> At one extreme, there are those who hold that the institution is an essential instrument in the modern administrative state to reduce the gap between the administrators and the administered, to open up the operations of government to public gaze, to protect basic human rights against possible infringements by the public bureaucracy, and to improve the quality of public administration. At the other, there are those who maintain that the institution is merely a public pacifier, a device to assuage public critics of government operations at minimal cost without having to change anything fundamental, and should it attempt to do anything more than mediate between public agencies and complainants, should it criticize the administration and embarrass the government, ways are quickly found to neutralize it.

In its ideal form, ombudsmanry protects the rights of individual citizens. As Stieber (1985, p. 61) puts it:

> It is a means of saying "you count" to those who often do not feel they count or are uncertain about their rights . . . The watchdog role counters some of the rigidity, impersonality, and complexity which characterize all large organizations, public and private.

In so doing, however, it also grants institutional legitimacy. Doi (1985, p. 55) as state ombudsman for Hawaii, views his office as an important element in democratic government. He bases this belief on two assumptions about what is required for democratic government:

> (1) Democratic government must be responsive, responsible and accountable to the people. To be so, that government must be

responsive, responsible and accountable to individual members of society; and
(2) To remain viable, democratic government must be committed to self-scrutiny, self-criticism, self-evaluation, and self-improvement.

He believes that the ombudsman performs both of these functions. However, Caiden (1983b, p. xvi) warns that the office may be used by a non-democratic regime "as a carefully managed device to enable the populace to criticize low-level bureaucrats without implying wrongdoing at higher levels of government".

If properly used, individual complaints and disputes can be an early warning of more serious problems. Zagoria (1988) claims that, in some cases, attention paid by ombudsmen to complaints has led to significant systemic change. He suggests that executive and administrative personnel worried about the discovery of problems within their domain should recognize that unremedied faults often grow and lead to worse exposure through lawsuits, media attention, or political opponents. In some settings, the ombudsman is even expected to identify important problem areas and provide senior management with recommendations for policy changes (Hendry, 1987).

Zagoria (1988) also points out that, in many cases, the ombudsman exonerates an official or institution from blame. He claims that the rate of justified complaints in the US in the mid-1980s was around only 20 to 50 per cent. Of course, this finding raises questions about what is considered "justified" and about other standards of evaluation. In settings in which the ombudsman is employed by the agency over which he or she has responsibility, there is a built-in conflict of interest between organizational and individual needs. Obviously, an om whose job was created to reduce the number of lawsuits against an organization or to protect officials from an unreasonable public is going to behave differently than one whose position was created to assist individuals in their dealings with the organization.

Indeed, Kolb (1987) differentiates between a "helping" and "fact-finding" orientation of ombudsmen. The first group tends to create individualized solutions to problems, and the second investigates whether standard procedures were properly followed. The first group is more likely to see their role as independent of the organization or as advocates for people; the second, as embedded in the organization. Evaluation of ombudsmanry, then, depends greatly on the definition of the role. Different expectations create differing criteria for success. Those who view the task focus as one of ensuring due process would use legal or similar criteria for evaluation; those who view it as one of helping people would judge success or failure by client satisfaction, usage rates, cost savings, and organization changes (Rowe, 1986).

Zagoria (1988, p. 37) reports that some om believe that "only an independent, objective ombudsman appointed by a legislative body with full power to investigate complaints against executive departments and agencies is the genuine article". Indeed Rowat (1985, pp. 182–3) has warned that, in public institutions, the title of ombudsman should be given only to politically independent grievance officers. This will protect the integrity of language and, most importantly, avoid having officials who "end up in the vest pockets of chief executives, or as advocates for the administration's point of view".

Yet, paradoxically, the very same independence that ensures objectivity also can create fears of the misuse of political power. In at least one instance, it was reported that an ombudsman's office was cut in half because of concerns that expansion of the office would be too advantageous politically for the officeholder (Mills, 1987).

Caiden (1983b, p. xvi) believes that ombudsmanry is not likely to spread further. He suggests that its ideological roots are likely to grow "only in democratic soil, where the social climate favors humanitarian considerations, equality, civic responsibility, constitutionalism, representative government, and genuine concern for basic human rights". Ironically, it may be most used where least needed – that is, the willingness to use an ombudsman is itself a demonstration of existing sensitivity to the needs of the public.

III
Resolution

12 Introduction: Resolution

We now approach practices that recognize the complexities of conflicts, and seek to match appropriate processes, on the basis of some theoretical explanation. There are, however, a variety of theoretical explanations, leading, therefore, to a variety of practices. They all seek resolution – that is, an outcome that does not rest on the application of consensus norms, or enforcement in any sense; but this is about all that is held in common. There is also confusion within this area of resolution, no less than in management and settlement.

There are those who seem to believe that conflicts between nations and groups arise largely from misunderstandings and misperceptions, perhaps in some cases because of cultural differences. They recommend, therefore, opportunities for citizens and persons close to decision makers to come together in circumstances in which there can be confidence-building, increased trust based on better understandings, and shared experiences. We have examples of shared television programs, student and scholar exchanges, and other such social activities.

There are others who believe that a deeper experience is required, and there is, therefore, T-group Resolution which involves participants in a great deal of introspection. This bears a relationship to processes associated with management problems, for it a process that seeks to alter the perceptions and behaviors of participants. This is a process that can be useful if the participants are those who are directly in conflict. Clearly it is less useful in cases in which participants are representatives of communities or nations.

A further development of these processes has been labeled 'Second Track Diplomacy', that is processes that parallel the official, but carry on informally and in a more exploratory way than would be possible officially. Second Track (or Track Two) Diplomacy, because it is flexible and unofficial, can readily fit in with a variety of theoretical explanations of conflict, and processes will alter accordingly. There are those who stress a psychological or psychiatric dimension. While the language employed, and the cases to which reference is made, suggest that these processes are particularly relevant to international and intercommunal conflicts, they are processes that have a generic application. There is much to be learned from these processes that can be applied to interpersonal and small group conflict. Indeed, the

121

management area would be qualitatively improved by knowledge of these processes and the theories that lie behind them.

Our main focus is, however, on "analytical problem-solving conflict resolution". These are processes that have not developed out of any one discipline, but have taken much from many disciplines. They are processes that rest on generic theories of behavior, and seek to incorporate any insights that can be gained from all other processes. Analytical problem-solving conflict resolution is not a response to crowded courts, and is not an adjunct to judicial, quasi-judicial, advocacy, or power bargaining processes. Its origins lie in theories of behavior and politics. There is here a break-point in the study of processes: the power of human needs becomes the focus in the explanation and resolution of conflict. There is a recognition that in order to deal with street gang warfare, domestic violence, terrorism or any other symptoms of a social problem, it is necessary to delve into and deal with the causal circumstances. Psychological dimensions are not neglected, but it is not assumed that these alone are the source of problems: there are environmental, social, economic, political and institutional sources also. There is a recognition that face-to-face procedures are important; but it is not assumed that better relationships provide an answer to a deep rooted conflict.

Problem-solving conflict resolution can reasonably be regarded as the synthesis and culmination of past and present thinking in the fields of management, dispute settlement and conflict resolution. At the same time its applied relevance is largely confined to deep rooted conflict at high societal levels for the reason that its process is exacting. It provides for the participation of several professionals on a third-party panel, and requires of these professionals an extensive training usually up to and beyond that associated with a doctorate. Its unapplied relevance, however, is particularly significant, for it is the insights from theory and practice at this level that finally permeate all other theories and processes.

It is not meant to imply by this claim that problem-solving conflict resolution has solved its theoretical and applied problems. On the contrary, as will be seen in Chapter 16, there are still different frameworks and approaches. It is a logical claim rather than a content claim: problem-solving conflict resolution strives to provide the synthesis that all seek and from which all can benefit.

So much is this the case that in Chapter 17 we include as a resolution process what we term "Deductive Analysis", the research activities of professionals in the search for universal sources of conflict, and options available in specific situations.

In Part III we outline each of these five resolution processes – Citizen Diplomacy, T-group Resolution, Track Two Diplomacy, Problem-solving Conflict Resolution, and Deductive Analysis – and some of the variations in each.

13 Citizen Diplomacy

"Citizen diplomacy" refers to an entire class of informal and unofficial procedures for application at the international or intercommunal level where there are different cultures and an apparent need for better understanding than can be achieved through more formal contacts and interactions. Different forms of citizen diplomacy are linked under this term because of their shared status of non-professional diplomacy and decision making, using procedures that are outside the normal processes of diplomatic and official activities. The processes are widely varied, including citizen exchange visits, rock concerts, twin city bonds, educational exchanges, joint research, humanitarian aid, and all manner of informal contacts.

A 1986 survey sponsored by the Kettering Foundation (1987) sampled a cross-section of organizations in the US that practice citizen diplomacy in one form or other, ranging from citizen–citizen exchanges to organized discussion of high policy issues. Of the 168 organizations that responded to the questionnaire, 90 per cent believed that they were engaged in some form of unofficial public diplomacy. The majority were primarily concerned with relationships within North and South America, but wide interest was revealed in relations with the Soviet Union, within the Middle East and in Asia and the Pacific. Some were concerned also with domestic relationships. The Mennonite Conciliation Service, for example, has promoted a Victim–Offender Reconciliation Program (VORP) along with some community mediation centers (see Chapter 4).

A SAMPLE

This is not the appropriate setting for a comprehensive survey of organizations that fall within this set. Some examples, however, will make possible the discussion of principles involved, and an assessment of such activities.

A Christian group, Moral Rearmament, started by Frank Buckman in 1938, offered a forum for those who believed that to be effective and non-violent, any change on a grand scale – economic or social, national or international – must be the result of change of persons and their behaviors. There must be individual honesty, love, purity and unselfishness, and accordingly Moral Rearmament is rooted in "a revolutionary change in the heart and character of men" (Entwistle and Roots, 1967, p. 78). The Foreign Service Institute of the US Department of State published an account of the influence of behind-the-scenes activities of Moral Rearmament on the outcome of the Zimbabwe settlement brought about at the Lancaster House conference chaired by Lord Carrington (Bendahmane and McDonald, 1986). In it the claim is made that what has been regarded as a British diplomatic success was in fact due to prior unofficial interactions arranged by a leader of Moral Rearmament.

The Quakers have a long history of citizen diplomacy through conciliation and mediation in international and intercommunal conflicts (see, for example, Oran Young, 1967; Elmore Jackson, 1983; and Sydney Bailey, 1985). On-going activities take place at Friends House positioned close to the United Nations Headquarters at New York, and elsewhere. Bailey set out the role of Quaker intermediaries as follows:

1. Respect must be established with both sides to the conflict
2. There must be sympathy for position of both sides, and there must be impartiality
3. There must be an understanding and sympathy with different cultures and norms and
4. There should be a face-to-face dialog, with the intermediaries seeking to reveal misunderstandings and misperceptions.

The same objectives have been sought in many different ways, including exchanges outside a particular conflict, but where there are high levels of international tension. Chadwick Alger is a professor of international relations at the Mershon Center at Ohio State University. He is far from a sea coast, international relations are seemingly remote. But he can point to activities in the local environment that are part of international relationships. He has sought to close the gap between social science and everyday human experience. One way in which he has sought to do this, one way he has sought to bring global realities to public attention, is to encourage twin city recognition, and in this way provide a framework in which there can be exchanges that include some element of mutual identification (Alger, 1977).

Indeed, in this category must also be included the activities of professional associations with international memberships and participation such as the International Studies Association, the

International Society of Political Psychology, the Consortium on
Peace Research, Education and Development, National Conferences
on Peace and Conflict Resolution, and indeed professional associations of all kinds that promote interactions across national ideological
boundaries. Teaching programs that include foreign students are in
the same category.

THEORETICAL JUSTIFICATIONS

The goal of citizen diplomacy is to break through the barriers of
distrust that characterize relations based on mutual threat. Official
diplomacy operates within a power framework. Attempts to improve
personal relationships are always suspect. No one would deny the
usefulness of promoting improved citizen relationships, and if this
were done on an extensive scale it could influence public policies.

There are two reservations that must be made. First, citizen
diplomacy is subject to the conditions imposed by authorities. In a
"cold war" phase, governments are likely to deny visas, prevent
exchanges, and generally to discourage any favorable perception of
the enemy. Citizen diplomacy is, therefore, an activity that is relevant
when there are openings to be exploited. In Soviet–US relations, for
example, there have been several stages at which citizen diplomacy
has been relevant and has been positive in its effects. These have
been followed by cold war phases, and those who have been brought
into touch have lost touch, and a new beginning has had to be made
at some later stage.

Citizen diplomacy rests on the theory that more direct contacts at
a citizen level can create improved relations that in due course might
spill over to the official level. It shares this view with functionalists
like Mitrany (1966). It is the theory that lies behind the Agency for
International Development (AID) program of the US Department
of State. But experience is that personal relationships that develop
as a result of working together are transitory, and that there is little
accumulated trust as a result. Increased tensions can bring about an
end to such exchanges. The hard realities are that there is more than
relationships involved in most conflict situations. No amount of
interaction between Israelis and Palestinians can alter the structural
problems that are perceived as posing long-term threats to both sides.

Like most endeavors, citizen diplomacy provides one ingredient, for use at appropriate times, that needs to be incorporated into some comprehensive process of conflict resolution.

14 T-group Resolution

INTRODUCTION

The relevance of T-group processes to conflict resolution is a matter of contention. There have been international applications by Doob and his associates, working with East Africans in one instance and Irish in another, which have been heavily criticized (Boehringer *et al.*, 1974; Doob, 1970; and Doob, 1981). There are those whose own personal experience with T-groups or similar training would lead them either to dismiss outright their usefulness for any learning, or, conversely, who are ready to view the small group experience as a panacea for a host of societal woes. Despite the controversy, however, the T-group is widely used by businesses, government agencies, and private organizations to help alleviate intra-organizational conflicts, among other purposes. It is appropriate to review work done in the late 1960s and early 1970s in the light of more recent developments, especially the emergence of the new field of conflict resolution.

THE T-GROUP

The development of training in human relations was both a contributor to and a product of the increasing interest in small group behaviors that began just prior to the Second World War and flourished after the war. The beginnings of the T-group can be traced to a workshop, held in Connecticut during the summer of 1946, that was designed to develop leadership capabilities among participants in government-sponsored programs. The workshop staff, led by the social psychologist Kurt Lewin, met regularly at night to analyze the day's activities. Some of the workshop participants began attending those staff meetings and disagreeing with staff interpretation of their behavior. As the staff began to appreciate the value of the participants' input, they realized that they had discovered a new means of learning. Shaffer and Galinsky (1976, p. 14) relate what occurred:

> As these discussions became more heated, Lewin and his coworkers started to see in them the germs of a related, but more dynamic group – i.e., a "training group" (soon to be shortened to "T-

128

group") . . . The group leader, or "trainer", would not fulfill the group's probable expectations of how a leader should behave, and would instead, in a more indirect and Socratic fashion, ask the kinds of questions and make the kinds of comments that would help the group *learn how to learn* from its experience. Because the group would thus be placed in as pure a culture as possible, the covert group dynamics normally obscured by the pressures, agenda, and structures of ongoing business and bureaucratic groups would be thrown into bolder relief.

Activities vary from one T-group to another. Depending upon the needs of the participants, a group might focus upon topics such as interpersonal relationships or organizational effectiveness. Nonetheless, there are a number of procedures that form the core of any T-group:

1. An ongoing group of 6 to 15 participants
2. 1 or 2 members with specialized skills and training who serve as facilitators or trainers
3. Interaction as a group lasting from 10 to over 40 hours
4. Deliberate minimization by the trainers of conventional structure, organization, and agenda
5. Expectations that group members will take the role of participant/observers in order to learn from their interactions within the group
6. Primary focus upon the present as opposed to the past
7. Minimization of the influence of hierarchical status from the outside world, by avoidance of titles, occupations, or rank
8. On-going analysis by participants about their reactions to the group interaction
9. Trainer commentary upon the group interaction, including presentation of relevant theory and research findings, to give participants a cognitive understanding of their experience.

There are several elements which T-group trainers take pains to assure participants that a T-group does not include:

1. It is not therapy
2. It is not an attempt to get everyone to like one another
3. It is not an attempt by the trainers to get people to behave or think as they do
4. It is no guarantor of change
5. It is not "encounter".

By the mid-1960s, thousands of people each year were participating in National Training Lab (NTL) T-groups offered in Bethel, Maine. Many other organizations and individuals were also offering training, and larger corporations often had in-house trainers. Although not as popular now as at that time, the basic T-group remains an established form of human relations training for government, business, and service organizations. Despite all of this experience, however, important questions about its validity remain unanswered, such as why some individuals respond to the intensive experience better than others, whether individual changes are lasting, or how results can be translated into successful action back home.

Furthermore, we still do not know the extent that learning depends upon the process as opposed to other elements of the T-Group. Rogers (1961) and other researchers of the third-party role have found that success depends less upon process than upon the third party's self-awareness, empathy, and unconditional positive regard for others. Despite the best attempts at controlling conditions as much as possible, there has been no proof that the influence of the T-group process is greater than factors such as the competence of the group leadership or the personality of the participants. Partly because of the unresolved and seemingly unresolvable questions about the small group experience, by the late 1970s the scope of T-group research had decreased considerably.

T-GROUP OBJECTIVES

According to Lakin (1972, p. 5), participants in T-groups have been expected to achieve or begin to achieve these objectives:

1. Developing knowledge about group behavior
2. Developing diagnostic skills regarding group processes
3. Increasing group effectiveness
4. Improving evaluation of behavior in groups
5. Developing self-insight.

Individuals should also be able to gain the following (Lakin, 1972, p. 9):

1. Increasing awareness of interactional styles
2. Increasing sensitivity to others
3. Understanding of group processes and their immediate effects

4. Understanding of how roles are taken up and fulfilled
5. Understanding of how conflicts arise and are resolved.

These goals describe task-specific individual improvement. Bennis (1962) on the other hand, lists a series of meta-goals that are more oriented towards personal growth. These include expanded consciousness and recognition of available choice, a spirit of inquiry, authenticity in interpersonal relations, and a collaborative conception of the authority relationship.

According to Hampden-Turner (1973), the T-group can improve an individual's quality of cognition, including awareness of one's needs and those of others, clarify one's identity, and increase self-esteem.

A more transcendent goal is offered by Benne, Bradford, and Lippitt (1964, p. 15), who claim that "The training laboratory offers opportunities to improve the quality of membership in various associations and of participation in diverse human affairs".

THE T-GROUP AND CONFLICT RESOLUTION

The T-group has been used as a deliberate vehicle for the resolution of two levels of disputes and conflicts. Most commonly, it is seen as one means to alleviate intra-organizational disputes. Businesses, government agencies and private organizations such as churches and charitable foundations have sent officers and personnel in steady streams to NTL locations for one or two weeks at a time to learn how to manage disputes and work together more effectively.

The second type of application has been inter-group conflict. Sensitivity training incorporating T-group elements has been offered to disputants with the intention of increasing awareness of individual needs and concerns and improving communication. In contrast to intra-organizational conflict, however, examples of the latter type of application are rare.

The first conflict resolution effort by Doob and his associates was a long-standing dispute in the 1960s between Ethiopia, Kenya, and Somalia (see Doob, 1970 and 1981; Walton, 1970; Foltz, 1977; Hill, 1982; Fisher, 1972 and 1983). The conflict, manifested through armed clashes along their border, involved many issues, such as ethnic pride, traditional ways of life, dependence upon outside powers, and the assertion of national sovereignty.

The facilitators chose as participants six university professors from Kenya and Ethiopia and six academically trained professionals, including some government officials outside of the foreign ministry, from Somalia. They thus sacrificed more direct access to policy making for the increased flexibility that individuals not directly tied to government responsibility might be able to provide.

The workshop, held in the Hotel Fermeda in the Italian Tyrol, lasted two weeks. It consisted of two phases. During the first phase, mixed-nation groups developed diagnostic skill in group process and communication. Not until the second phase was attention turned towards finding solutions to the substantive issues.

The stated goal of the workshop was for the participants to generate options for resolution separately within the two T-groups, and to reach consensus agreement during a general assembly upon one of those options. Overall assessment of the workshop's success was mixed. Within the T-groups the participants were able to reach agreement with one another; when the total group was together, they failed to do so. Certain individuals exerted disproportionately disruptive influence upon the proceedings. There was also dissension within the various national groups. In addition, a lack of time forced a hasty conclusion to the effort.

With the experience of Fermeda behind them, Doob and his associates were ready to attempt another workshop that would allow them to incorporate what they had learned (see Doob and Foltz, 1973, 1974; Doob, 1981; Foltz, 1977; Hill, 1982; Fisher, 1972, 1983). For a variety of reasons they chose to work in Northern Ireland. Because of the situation there a problem-solving approach, in which the goal was to gain agreement on one solution, did not appear feasible. Foltz (1977, p. 209) stated that "There were no longer any apparent responsible leadership structures occupying equivalent positions on either side of the central social cleavage who might be able to implement ideas generated in a problem-solving workshop. They therefore recruited 56 local leaders for a ten-day program designed to teach each participant to analyze problems of organization and inter-group relations, and thus to improve their effectiveness in their groups at home. According to Foltz (1977, p. 210):

> The purpose, then, was to assist in reversing the trend to local disorganization, in effect to give some local leadership groups greater control over the impact of the surrounding chaos on their communities, and further to establish human communication links

between local Protestant and Catholic leaders that might someday come in handy in building understanding and cooperation at the grass roots.

To accomplish this, the participants were brought to Stirling University in Scotland for the ten days of the workshop, which once again consisted of two stages. The first stage followed a modified Tavistock T-group approach, which provided for much confrontation between young and old, women and men, lower class and middle class, and moderates and extremists. The second stage, less confrontational, followed the NTL approach.

Again, assessment of the workshop results was mixed. Once again, certain individual participants proved to be quite disruptive. Severe criticism given to the effort by two members of the initial management team prevented completion of the project (Boehringer *et al.*, 1974; Alevy *et al.*, 1974).

Lakin's Arab–Jew workshops of 1968 in Israel provide another example of the application of the T-group to inter-group conflicts. With colleagues Lomranz and Lieberman, Lakin (1972, p. 249) intended to "discover ways to diminish 'we–they' feelings and to establish other loyalties which would, at least transiently, overarch in-group loyalties". There were two workshops, one with ten participants in Haifa and one with eleven in Jerusalem; both involved Israeli Arabs and Jews.

The training design included pre- and post-training assessment of participants' perceptions and anticipations, training in communication, and group dialogue in T-group form. Cross-ethnic teams were asked to develop concrete proposals for improved relations to be presented to the total group for discussion. Lakin's assessment of the effort, including such elements as hostility, affection, trust, free interaction, thematic apperception, and participant evaluation, reflected mixed results.

There are a number of other instances in which certain limited aspects or variations of the T-group were employed to assist inter-group conflict resolution. These include the following:

1. A union–management intergroup laboratory run by Blake and his associates in 1964 (Blake, Mouton and Sloma, 1965)
2. Three workshops involving Israeli Arabs and Jews run by Benjamin and Levi (Levi and Benjamin, 1976; Benjamin and Levi, 1979)
3. A laboratory training for police officers (Sata, 1975; Pfister, 1975).

4. A series of workshops offered by Rogers during the 1960s, 1970s, and 1980s (Rogers, 1965 and 1987; Rogers and Sanford, 1987).

ASSESSMENT

Doob's work has been criticized (Kelman and Cohen, 1976) for relying too heavily upon intra- and inter-personal change among the participants as the means of resolving the conflict. Doob (1981, p. 236) asserts that:

> The underlying theory suggests that, although individuals are slow to change or to be creative, under some circumstances rapid changes and creativity can be induced. They are likely to be influenced when they have been transplanted out of their usual milieu, when somehow they have been induced to view a situation quite differently from the way they have in the past or the present, or when a central change within them – as in a conversation – has repercussions for their other values and attitudes.

The T-group was to be the vehicle for seeking that change. Doob (1970, p. 11) foresaw that the T-group could potentially provide:

> an opportunity for individuals to have close and prolonged contact with one another and thus, minimally, at least to perceive diverse viewpoints. It offers a stimulating and intense experience in which the participants learn more about themselves, about their relations to other persons, and hence about their own behavior and roles in real life.

During the Fermeda workshop, the participants completed much of their training and learning prior to dealing with the conflict's substantive issues. Because this approach generated some resistance from the African participants, Doob suggested that future workshops draw the process–issue line less distinctly.

The expectations of Doob and his associates for the African workshop were not based solely upon untested speculation. A number of training workshops incorporating the T-group had been held in West Africa during the early 1960s. These trainings involved a total of about 300 people, mostly employees of government-sponsored agencies, and they were intended primarily to improve the participants' organizational effectiveness. However, trainers and participants alike realized that, as a significant corollary, severe inter-tribal rivalries and hatreds were being interrupted. The potential for larger-scale conflict resolution appealed to one of the trainers for these efforts, who then also participated as one of the trainers for the Fermeda workshop.

Doob and his associates never suggested that individual change alone would suffice to resolve any conflicts. Prior to Fermeda they cautioned that contact might leave participants with unfavorable impressions of one another; that inhibitions, both proactive and retroactive, might prevent or erase learnings; and that too much anxiety might be evoked. In Belfast, they deliberately took pains to caution against any undue expectations of success. Foltz (1977, p. 211) claimed that they were "particularly concerned to puncture the millenial hopes that occasionally were voiced". Rather, they wanted participants to achieve specific limited objectives (Folt Z, 1977, p. 204):

1. a heightened motivation to work for less conflicting relations (or less costly ways of settling conflicts)
2. skills to increase their ability to act on their motivation
3. personal contacts across the line of conflict which can be used when needed, and
4. a bond of trust with other participants which can validate communications across the line, whether those communications originate with and are ultimately destined for participants or the participants are merely contact persons.

Despite the emphasis upon individual motivation, skills, personal contacts, and trust, this was not a simplistic view of the conflicts (Foltz, 1977, p. 203):

We did not, however, assume that all conflicts are based on "misunderstandings" or "prejudices" which rational men can overcome once their hearts and minds have been opened. Rather, we appreciated that substantial material and important symbolic interests were at stake for which men were rationally willing to risk their own lives and those of others, but we felt that painstaking clarification and communication of issues and commitments stood a better chance of improving the lives of the peoples involved than would their continued obfuscation.

A significant question with which all promoters of the T-group grappled was: How can what occurs in the "here-and-now" be transferred into practical application back home? This is a relevant question for all forms of intensive group experience. The question includes a different twist in conflict resolution, since the results sought during the T-group go beyond individual changes in behavior; they include agreements whose implementation must involve others back home. Back (1972, p. 185) criticized the Fermeda workshop for its re-entry failures: "The formal post-meeting evaluations showed the familiar pattern of general medium satisfaction with the experience, and little future effect". Foltz reports of the followup interviews in Belfast that about one-third of the participants reported significant positive change in their personal or public lives resulting from the workshop. While positive individual change certainly can be a valid goal, and may well have been significant for those so affected, it was not the goal of the workshop. But neither he nor Doob can say with any certainty whether or not these changes affected the course of the conflict.

The uncertainty was even greater for the Belfast workshop than for the Fermeda workshop because of differences in how the results were to be transferred into activities back home. Foltz (1977, p. 216) differentiated between the "process-promoting" of Belfast and the "problem-solving" of Fermeda:

> The problem-solving workshop assumes that solutions will be reported back to decision-makers and that any solutions will be implemented through and under the control of those authorities. A process-promoting workshop has a more subversive potential in that the process it promotes may operate quite independently of and indeed counter to the existing authorities and their wishes.

Had participants returned to their homes full of enthusiasm for their experience and ready to suggest major changes in attitudes and policies towards the other side, they might well have received a cold welcome from their own kind. According to Wedge (1970, p. 496), referring to Fermeda:

> Nothing could have been more disastrous for the development of the approach than to have the participants return to their nations fired with enthusiasms for policies unacceptable to the governments and people of their states.

An additional problem intervenors using T-group experiences share with other practitioners is the difficulty of gauging the success or failure of their efforts. This difficulty is compounded in situations where participants are representatives of their respective populations.

In cases such as these, even a workshop experience that exceeds sponsor and participant expectations might have a negligible impact upon their domestic political situation.

The Belfast workshop in particular was severely criticized for the sponsors' failure to attempt a rigid evaluation of participant changes (Boehringer *et al.*, 1974). The book-length report of the Fermeda workshop (Doob, 1970), on the other hand, is unique in terms of case studies of any conflict resolution design and application. It includes lengthy critiques of the effort by organizers, trainers, and – most importantly – the participants. Nonetheless, nobody would claim that this was a fully satisfactory evaluation of that workshop.

Ferguson, one of the Fermeda trainers, provided the clearest assessment of the sources of its successes and failures. He blamed its ultimate failure not upon the T-groups, which he believed mobilized the collaborative and cooperative impulses of the individuals, but upon the formal strictures of the general assembly, which encouraged competition, noncooperation, caginess, resistance, and hostility (in Doob, 1970). He would encourage more careful participant selection, avoiding individuals with serious personality problems and choosing those with more influence within their home setting. He would build national teams before the workshop, including the team of trainers, which suffered from insufficient preparation.

Along with the problems, Ferguson saw many successes. The workshop participants provided a new model of conflict resolution that could be studied, adopted, adapted, or rejected by others. They linked people of those three countries in ways they had never been linked before. They provided two carefully considered plans for the resolution of the countries' border problems. And, finally, they "rallied the energies of many men to seek a solution for the kind of international problems that have caused untold human suffering all through history" (in Doob, 1970, p. 135).

CONCLUSION

A few cases, no matter how well reported, cannot serve as an adequate test of any application. Yet the Fermeda and Belfast workshops, because of the excitement, controversy and, ultimately, disfavor they generated, had a disproportionate effect on the field of conflict resolution. They had served as the definitive studies of the application of T-groups to inter-group conflict resolution and, as a result, a warning to others against their use. But the work of Doob and others can be viewed another way: as the beginnings of exploration of the use of intensive small group activities that allow participants to learn about themselves and their impact on others. Thus, instead of a closed question already presumed to have been answered in the negative – Can the T-group resolve intergroup conflicts? – we can ask a more open-ended question: In what ways can we gain from the wealth of four decades of T-group experience and research? Improving third-party capabilities, preventing destructive intra-party squabbles, and training individuals to resolve their own conflicts, are all areas in which the T-group might contribute in the future.

In certain circumstances, the T-group process may yet prove an aid to inter-group conflict resolution. Given the proper timing for intervention, sufficient time for planning, suitable participants, adequate consideration of transfer and re-entry problems, and knowledgeable third parties, other efforts may well be successful. At the least, the experience of T-group workshops is a resource in the development of other conflict resolution processes.

15 Track Two Diplomacy

"Track Two Diplomacy" is a term used by an official of the US Department of State (Montville, 1987) to describe communication at an unofficial level of matters normally negotiated officially – matters such as arms control or conflicts between and within countries. In Montville's own words:

> Track two diplomacy is unofficial, informal interaction between members of adversary groups or nations which aim to develop strategies, influence public opinion, and organize human and material resources in ways that might help resolve their conflict. It must be understood that track two diplomacy is in no way a substitute for official, formal, "track one" government-to-government or leader-to-leader relationships. Rather, track two activity is designed to assist official leaders by compensating for the constraints imposed on them by the psychologically understandable need for leaders to be, or at least to be seen to be, strong, wary, and indomitable in the face of the enemy . . . Track two diplomacy is a process designed to assist official leaders to resolve or, in the first instance, to manage conflicts by exploring possible solutions out of public view and without the requirement to formally negotiate or bargain for advantage (Montville, 1987, p. 7).

The term, like most terms in this wider field of dispute settlement and conflict resolution, has come to mean other processes as well. It has sometimes been used to designate all citizen diplomacy, and also sophisticated analytical processes that seek to discover hidden sources of conflict. But we have been struggling in this study to give terms as precise a meaning as is possible. For this reason we have not equated Track Two Diplomacy with Citizen Diplomacy. We give it the meaning first intended: unofficial attempts to deal with subject matters normally dealt with at a diplomatic level. It is an interaction of persons who are free from the necessity to hedge, to bargain from strength, and to remain within instructions.

The emphasis is on the unofficial, but the subject matters are those that are discussed officially. It is not surprising, therefore, that Track Two Diplomacy is an activity pursued by former officials, and by scholars and others who have had, and sometimes continue to have, close links with governments.

PUGWASH CONFERENCES

One of the early examples of Track Two Diplomacy was in the immediate post Second World War period when former officials and scholars from the West met regularly, perhaps for a week at a time, with counterparts from the Soviet Union. It has to be remembered that this was a time of great uncertainty in Soviet–US relationships, and even greater uncertainty about the future of weapons of mass destruction. Interestingly, some of the participants had been involved in the development of the atomic bomb used against Japan, and perhaps this was a kind of therapeutic experience: an endeavor to ensure that this invention would not be so used again. The conferences took their name from the first meeting site, Pugwash, in Nova Scotia, Canada.

Initially the belief was that physical scientists, because they were "scientists", could best deal with the complex relationship issues that were involved, but gradually more and more political and social scientists were invited to participate. Meetings became larger and larger, and perhaps lost some of their earlier focus. As participants made this a regular – usually annual – activity, the group tended to become rather like a professional association, and more removed from decision makers than had been the case initially.

DARTMOUTH CONFERENCES

The Dartmouth Conferences have a similar history and function. Sponsored by the Kettering Foundation, and supported by many leading foundations, they commenced in 1960. The initiative seems to have been with President Eisenhower at a time when Soviet–US relations were particularly tense due to the shooting down of the US U-2 spy plane over Soviet territory. The first meeting was at Dartmouth College in Hanover, New Hampshire, US. The rules were that conversations would be behind closed doors, they would be off the record and have no official standing, but conclusions would be communicated to governments. In 1988 this confidential nature of the discussions gave place to more public participation.

The Dartmouth Conferences are referred to by their sponsors as "supplemental diplomacy" rather than Track Two. The alternative track concept is, however, present. It has two implications. First, as pointed out, it is unofficial diplomacy; but second, it recognizes the legitimacy and need for a Track One, a power track, in which communication is by other means, including threat. This is a further reason for distinguishing such activities from other private citizen activities that in some cases are opposed to, or perhaps seek to undermine, the official or Track One process.

THE ADR COMPONENT

It will be seen that this Track Two notion is not unlike ADR in respect of courts. If some way out of a problem can be found by the non-official alternative means, then the suggestion can be referred to the appropriate official institution – a court or a government. As with ADR, Track Two activities depend for their success on the quality of the dialogue, and the basic assumptions and theories held by the participants. In Track Two Diplomacy it is unlikely that a solution to a problem will be discovered only by improved relationships between participants. Their role is to define the nature of the problem, and to be innovative about solutions.

It is here that there is a limitation. Being unofficial does not necessarily alter frames, paradigms, philosophies, interpretations or policies. The limitations of official dialogue are still present. Again, the similarity with ADR is apparent: an alternative to a court, especially acting in conjunction with a court, is most unlikely to pursue norms inconsistent with those of the court. An alternative to official negotiation is unlikely to be able to accomplish more than altering perceptions, clearing away misperceptions, and discovering means of cooperation within existing parameters. This may accomplish a great deal, and in Soviet–US relations a major contribution has been made. It is not a process that is likely to resolve a complex problem of relationships that requires structural and policy changes, as is usually the case in a multi-ethnic conflict, or an international conflict such as in the Middle East, where structures, roles and nationalism are the issues.

UNOFFICIAL OR ANALYTICAL?

Montville includes in Track Two Diplomacy problem-solving dialogues or "workshops" that are far more analytical of particular conflicts than the examples referred to above. The two may go together, but not necessarily. We have, therefore, a separate category, Problem-solving Conflict Resolution, to which we now turn.

16 Problem-Solving Conflict Resolution

Facilitated problem-solving conflict resolution has developed as the behavioral sciences have been applied to situations thought to be too intractable to be settled without overwhelming coercion and force. It includes a variety of approaches whose commonalities are more procedural than substantive. These commonalities include the following:

1. The breaking down of conflict situations into parties and issues
2. Face-to-face interaction between representatives of two parties (at any one time) to a conflict
3. The use of a facilitator or panel of facilitators to assist dialog, and
4. Intense analytical interactions involving one or more seminars or "workshops" of a week or so duration.

The primary activity engaged in by the parties in these seminar workshops is *analysis* – that is, a searching exchange between the parties designed to reveal positions, frustrations, constraints and perceptions. It is because analysis is the basis of the resolution approach that only two parties interact at one time, even though there might be many parties and issues involved. It is out of this analysis that the parties are led to discover options. This analysis becomes of crucial importance when the parties, especially the status quo party, make their costing assessments about the lengths others will go to achieve their goals. Conflict resolution processes do not include separate caucussing, as is sometimes the case in arbitration, for it is important that all participants be fully aware of the total situation as perceived by others.

The role of the third party is a crucial and active one, just as it is in a professional counseling situation. The initial goal of the third party is to help the participants to define accurately the interests that are negotiable, and the basic needs and values that are not, and to assist the parties to discover options that are acceptable in terms of their interests and that satisfy their needs.

In *Conflict: Resolution and Provention* it is argued that there is no problem of scarcity in needs satisfaction: the more identity or security one party has, the more and not the less the other party will

143

experience identity and security. Win–lose elements enter into the process only when the means, the "satisfiers" of needs, are discussed. Scarcity is an issue only when searching for the means. In any problem-solving situation there are many ways by which goals can be achieved. The interaction is, therefore, one concerned with available options. Very often, however, such solutions will require significant changes in social, political and economic systems that shape and, in some cases, generate conflict.

Problem-solving conflict resolution, being concerned initially with the analysis of a situation, does not involve facilitated negotiation or power bargaining. Its analytical thrust makes power irrelevant. The powerful are in a position realistically to predict and cost the consequences of their exercise of coercive power. Vietnams would not occur if there were sufficient knowledge of their nature, including values attached to autonomy and independence. It may be that because of short-term political interests the leaderships of the militarily powerful will finally choose, despite the future costs, to continue the exercise of power. In such a case there will be no resolution, as in situations such as South Africa, the Middle East and in many contemporary ethnic conflicts. At the same time, the process offers "weaker" parties a method of reassessing their longer-term costs of escalated protests. It is, in essence, a process of informed decision making.

As a result, the training required by an intervenor to perform a third party role is extensive. It goes far beyond, though it includes, the training associated with management processes. To repeat, the purpose of the intervention is to assist the parties to a conflict in making a deep analysis of their conflictual relationships, revealing the hidden data of goals and motivations, enabling an accurate costing of their tactics and policies, and finally assisting in the discovery of acceptable options. This requires a wide knowledge of conflictual behaviors and, therefore, of human behavior generally, of structural and institutional sources of conflict, and of options that might be available or that might be created. It is a process that requires theoretical training and professionalism at a post graduate level, together with applied experience.

Analytical conflict resolution in a particular case offers its own findings, thus enriching the basis for future applications. Each resolution of a particular dispute provides a deeper understanding of conflictual relationships generally, and points to means of resolving other disputes. In addition to resolving a particular problem, conflict resolution seeks to find explanations useful to the solution of all such cases. This makes it a policy resource and, as we shall see in Part IV, a means of conflict avoidance as well as conflict resolution in a particular case.

A THEORETICAL BASIS GIVING RISE TO A PARADIGM CHANGE

Holistic theories of behavior that are relevant to the applied processes of conflict resolution have emerged only in recent decades, and only as a consequence of the breaking down of the boundaries of separate disciplines. Human needs theory, which was the framework of *Conflict: Resolution and Provention*, and the subject matter of *Conflict: Human Needs Theory*, provides a holistic theory. It makes possible an analysis and a deduced problem-solving approach that can be applied at all societal levels.

No doubt this theory, still in its infancy, will be modified and developed. What can be said now is that it seems to be on the right track logically. It is a theory of human behavior that takes into account ontological human needs – the logical starting point of any analysis of human relationships – in sharp contrast with traditional theories that were absorbed with ways in which individual and national behaviors could be contained and manipulated so as to conform with societal requirements.

Conflict resolution of the problem-solving type takes on, therefore, an image of a political philosophy. Those whose material interests are already threatened by unresolved conflict, and those whose interests lie in longer-term political and social stability, such as major corporations anticipating a continued existence, are likely to be attracted to the cost calculations involved in making assessments and predictions of the consequences of unresolved conflicts. Others may perhaps opt for legal processes and alternatives through which they can achieve or preserve some immediate gain, regardless of future costs.

THE INTERNATIONAL SCENE

In this review we make no distinction between levels of conflict. We are treating conflict as a generic phenomenon, and trying to get to its roots before deducing means of dealing with it.

In practice it is impossible to separate that which is national from that which is international. There are over a hundred violent conflicts in the world society which are of international concern, even though they may not be defined as international and, therefore, do not fall within the jurisdiction of the United Nations. These are the ethnic, boundary, liberation and other conflicts within nations that spill over into the international system and attract the interest and participation of external powers. Any separation of that which is national from that which is international becomes artificial. All have common sources in structural conditions which appear to frustrate goals and values of some of those affected. The United Nations as originally conceived was, and remains, largely irrelevant to the total world society in which it seeks to maintain peace. The majority of conflicts are outside its jurisdiction. In any event, they cannot be resolved by Security Council decisions, mediation and peace keeping.

EXCLUDED AREAS

At this international level, however, as at the domestic level, there are areas of study we exclude by reason of our definition of conflict resolution.

There are movements associated with arms control, protests designed to eliminate some forms of weapons, non-violent means of protest, and related activities. There are institutes which focus almost exclusively on criticisms of weapon systems and defense tactics. These are serious studies, but they do not relate to conflict resolution as we use the term. There appears to be an unstated assumption that the problem to be faced is the existence of the arms, rather than the reasons why the arms exist. Rarely in these studies is there any reference to the existence of deep rooted problems in international relationships which must be resolved before there are likely to be any significant arms reductions.

Nor are we concerned with the area which can be described as strategic studies. These are studies of means of defense, sometimes by those who are seeking means of arms reduction, sometimes by those seeking more effective means of deterrence. There is, once again, little interest shown in the sources of conflict, and how conflict itself might be tackled rather than merely managed or deterred.

LAW, DIPLOMACY AND CONFLICT RESOLUTION AS POTENTIALLY COMPLEMENTARY

Conflict resolution has, however, potentially close links with legal studies, as suggested in the Introduction to this book. It is through legal and related practices that conflict resolution must evolve and be institutionalized. The practical link between the legal processes and conflict resolution is the general attorney, and special associates with appropriate training. Attorneys have a duty to represent a client. It has generally been the goal of attorneys to settle disputes outside court processes. The formal legal process may in many cases be the appropriate one, especially where a dispute involves interests which can be assessed on the basis of acceptable legal and social norms. But to represent clients adequately in cases in which human needs are involved, the attorney cannot be in an adversarial negotiating situation. To link law with conflict resolution the traditional role of representing one client has to change, for in conflict resolution the third party serves all parties to the dispute. Attorneys may be required to work together far more in the interests of clients, bringing clients together and taking into account behavioral elements that are not adequately considered by courts and out-of-court settlements.

Two steps are required. First, attorneys representing contending parties must adopt procedures whereby they are not adversaries in representing their clients, but act more like a panel of facilitators in a conflict situation. Second, attorneys must, as a further step, evolve processes whereby they can have as clients all parties to a conflict. To achieve this both theoretical and process training would be required. The effect would be to shift from legal norms to norms based on human needs, legal norms becoming no more than a fall-back position in the event of failure.

It is the same at the international level. Diplomats and persons with special training in non-bargaining, problem-solving techniques need to work together in much the same way as attorneys and conflict resolution specialists need to work together. There are situations in which bargaining and compromise are required – as, for example, in the majority of trade negotiations. But there are also situations in which there is a need for a deep analysis of situations. In most international relations the issues are not simple matters of right and wrong, calling for sanctions or reprisals: there are problems to be solved. When the Indian population in Fiji outnumbered Fijians, the Fijians responded by rejecting the "democratic" (majority rule) philosophy. Situations like this do not call for sanctions by other nations. They call for imaginative solutions, derived from some form of facilitated interaction, which would, in the example we used, allow Fijians to preserve their identity and traditional roles, while also allowing Indians their rights to recognition. In arms control negotiations, there is a role for negotiators, but there is also a role for those who can look at the problem more deeply, and ask relevant questions about the felt need for arms, and alternative ways in which these apparent needs can be satisfied.

The institutionalization of conflict resolution processes must ultimately be through attorneys, diplomats and others in traditional occupations who can adapt to new insights into human behaviors. Institutionalization cannot be through institutions such as the United Nations, for power political institutions based on the separate nation-state are unlikely to make such a paradigm shift.

DECISION MAKING, AND INTEREST DISPUTES AND NEEDS CONFLICTS

From this institutionalized perspective conflict resolution would be a supplement and complement to existing domestic and international decision making processes. Before any such steps are taken, however, it is necessary to determine which cases should be subject to formal or traditional proceedings, and which should be handled by conflict resolution processes.

These distinctions, however, are difficult to make in specific cases. The Falklands/Malvinas situation was a dispute between the United Kingdom and the Argentine, debated in terms of historic and legal claims to sovereignty. But it was also a conflict involving the autonomy of the inhabitants, and some deep rooted resentments against Britain for its past treatment of Argentinians as a people. Such situations require both negotiation and analytical processes. Usually it is not until disputes and conflicts are being treated that their nature is revealed.

There is evidence that the overall problem of conflict and its resolution is at last being tackled. There have been fundamental changes in thinking, in questioning traditionally held assumptions, and in gathering together knowledge which has been scattered throughout different disciplines. Basically this shift in thought is from control, suppression or settlement of disputes by bargaining, negotiation, mediation, coercion and power in one of its many forms, to an acceptance that a conflict, especially a situation of violence, presents a problem to be solved. This shift in thinking is at an early stage. As is always the case when a paradigm shift is involved, we must first experience anomalies, unanswered questions and failures. This provokes thought, then clear conceptualization and exposition of some alternative. Only then will societies be prepared to move from one position to another.

SOME DIFFERENT APPROACHES

Now we turn to describe a sample of different approaches that fall within this category of problem-solving conflict resolution.

Blake, Mouton and Sloma (1965) pioneered the laboratory approach within the field of industrial relations. Their work preceded the work of social scientists such as Walton (1969, 1970) and others who were concerned more with international relations, such as Doob (1970, 1981); Doob and Foltz (1973, 1974); Lakin (1972); and Benjamin and Levi (1979). These early approaches tended to be directed toward sensitivity development.

Subsequently there were more therapeutic approaches such as those of Carl Rogers (1965, 1987) who in the last years of his life applied his individual and group therapy experience to inter-group conflicts within many countries. He viewed the ultimate source of conflict as a psychological matter. In his view, conflicts involving seemingly irreconcilable differences were not over material resources, but over the mutual convictions that the self is right and good, while the other is wrong and evil. Resolution, accordingly, begins when the parties change these perceptions and learn to understand and to respect each other.

A somewhat different psychological assumption was later made by Vamik Volkan (1987) working with Demetrios Julius (1988) and a US State Department official, Joseph Montville (1987). They sought to apply their psychiatric and psychoanalytical knowledge to international situations of conflict, while seeking also to take note of political and social conditions. Assumptions such as some inherent need for an enemy were important in their explanation of conflicts.

Rogers and Volkan and his colleagues all adopted procedures which are part of a problem-solving exercise, that is face-to-face interactions facilitated by a neutral yet contributing third party.

TOWARDS A SYNTHESIS

This movement from sensitivity development, based on an assumption that conflict is due to false perceptions, toward a more intense analysis of unconscious behavioral predispositions, based on an assumption that conflict has its sources in individual problems of adjustment to situations, was followed by a holistic approach, by which we mean taking the totality of the person and the environment into account.

It should be noted, however, that there is a paradigm shift implied here which is not always perceived when comparing approaches. The emphasis is still on the person, and behavior. But while in sensitivity, psychological and psychoanalytic explanations and processes there is the implication that the problem is with personality abnormalities and the need for education and adjustment, when a holistic approach is adopted and environmental conditions are included, the emphasis shifts away from the person as the source of conflict towards institutions. What emerges is a structural theory of conflict. The processes, and the remedies that arise out of these processes, are more directed toward institutional and system change, and far less toward changes in behaviors.

This structural approach was initially pursued by John Burton (1969) and Herbert Kelman (1979) and others working with them. At the heart of the theory and practice of Burton is the hypothesis that all peoples, no matter how they differ in culture and education, share certain human needs that are ontological, and therefore universal. Governments through their norms and laws, and societies through their cultures, seek to socialize the individual into certain behaviors. The gap between what is expected of the person by authorities and by traditional consensus norms, on the one hand, and the inherent needs of persons, on the other, is the measure of the lack of legitimization of authorities. If no means of satisfying human needs exist within the boundaries of social norms and institutions, the individual and identity groups will act outside these boundaries. As institutional responses become even more defensive and opportunities of protest increase, so conflicts within national and international societies increase.

It follows that resolution depends on a thorough analysis of both the needs to be satisfied, and the failings of societies to satisfy them. While Burton has been primarily concerned with the development of theory, and the processes that are deduced from theory, Kelman has a specific interest in applying this approach to the Middle East situation (1979). The two have worked together on several occasions.

Both of these theorist-practitioners have published widely, and their publications are readily available. In an Appendix to this book we have included substantial extracts from a publication by Burton, *Resolving Deep-Rooted Conflict: A Handbook* (1987), as such a detailed description of a process, based on practice, is unusual.

17 Deductive Analysis: the Discovery of Options

It has been emphasized in the discussion on resolution, and it is emphasized even more in the "rules" of procedure contained in the Appendix to this book, that the parties to a conflict must explore options that meet their needs after they have made an adequate analysis of the total situation. It is also emphasized that they will need help in discovering options, for they will be thinking only of those within their knowledge and experience. The third party has a special role in deducing options from the analysis in an exploratory and imaginative way.

This points to the need for preparation by intervenors in advance of acting as a third party. Indeed, given an adequate theoretical framework, a third-party panel should be in a position to predict in most cases the kinds of options that are appropriate once they have some additional knowledge of the local situation. Multi-ethnic situations, for example, have similarities that seem to dominate the differences that emerge in different situations.

Implied here is that there are two sets of factors. First, there are "universal" components that if present have predictable consequences and invite predictable options – components such as ethnicity, class, discriminations, non-legitimized institutions and boundaries drawn as a result of invasions rather than by natural geographical or human features. Second, there are local conditions – for example, national histories, leadership personalities, economic conditions and others – which modify the options which would otherwise seem to apply.

The existence of conditions which have a universal application, and their pervasive influence, suggests an important stage in conflict resolution that does not involve an interaction between the parties. This initial analysis is an essential part of the preparation by a panel for an intervention. Indeed, it could in most cases be the most significant part of the total process.

Take, for example, the protracted conflict in South Africa. A mediator could attempt to move into the situation and engage the parties at one level or another, as many have attempted to do, with no basic knowledge other than some knowledge of process. The assumption would be that given a controlled interaction the parties could arrive at some agreed option. This would be most unlikely. Or someone with a conflict resolution background could seek to engage the parties and to conduct with them an analysis of the total situation, and find that at the stage of deducing agreed options there were only two: one-man-one-vote on the one hand, and some modification of the status quo on the other, neither of which would be acceptable.

The situation would be quite different if a preliminary mini-analysis had taken place. This would involve the panel, together with other professionals, making a preliminary analysis and applying to the situation as they know it whatever theoretical knowledge they have of such a situation, and any empirical knowledge they have of other situations in the same category (for example, multi-ethnic). They would then bring into the discussion a specialist in the geographical area who could supply the data that was specific to the situation, its history, the factions, the geographical location of factions and other such details. There would then emerge one or more options that could be deduced from both universal theory and specific conditions.

In *Conflict: Resolution and Provention* the case of South Africa was dealt with in this way. It was argued that one-man-one-vote was no more likely to be acceptable there than in any other similar situation, such as Cyprus or Sri Lanka. As an option the model of the international system was put forward – that is many separate entities, with close functional relationships. The constitutional pattern would be many separate units, including some separate black factions, brought together not in a federation which would again raise the numbers and voting problem, but in a functional system in which each unit had a veto. If the system were valued, as is the international one (many functional agreements governing transport, communications, health and others are observed even in times of international tension), then the veto would not be exercised. Whenever the veto was exercised that particular functional area would have to be reexamined.

This was given as the kind of imaginative option, amongst others, deduced from knowledge of that type of situation, that a panel likely to be involved should explore in advance. No doubt local circumstances could make impossible such a deduced option, despite the fact that it could meet the requirements of the universal ethnic condition. The exercise in discovering and testing possible options is preparation involving a synthesis of the knowledge available to a panel prior to its meeting with the parties concerned.

There is revealed here a sharp division between those, on the one hand, who regard intervention as being within a "democratic" framework in which the mediator has no more than a process role, and who warn against any positive role by a third party and those, on the other, who regard the role of the third party as being an active participatory one over and above any process role. This is probably the difference between management and conflict resolution processes. Where there are deep rooted conflicts both their analysis and the discovery of options are likely to be beyond the capacities of the parties who are caught up in their conflict. This is one reason why training programs in conflict resolution should be formal and extensive.

This exploratory and advisory process is not unusual in other professions. In the medical, legal, engineering and other professions, consultants give advice to practitioners who are dealing with particular cases. Where conflict resolution processes differ is in the reality that the parties themselves remain the final arbiters, and even when there is general acceptance of an option, they must be responsible for its details, its negotiation and implementation.

THEORY DEVELOPMENT AS A PROBLEM-SOLVING PROCESS

Here we approach the important topic of the relationship between theorist and practitioner. This, in turn, touches on the problem of institutionalization of conflict resolution practices. There are university institutes and privately funded organizations that seek to intervene in disputes and conflicts. In many cases the problems giving rise to the disputes and conflicts relate to institutions and policies that are quite outside the scope of the conflict resolution process. Take, for example, conflicts between street gangs in some major industrial cities in various countries. Settling or resolving one such confrontation does little to prevent the next. The drug problem in the US, and its associated violence, cannot be dealt with by resolving specific conflicts that end in murders. These are situations that must involve government agencies.

The theorist, however, has a practical role to play in such situations. Government policies can succeed only if the problem is defined accurately. Gottfredson and Hirschi in their book, *A General Theory of Crime* (1990), stated that the basic assumptions on which US "drug war" policies were based were false. In particular they pointed out that crime of all kinds is carried out predominantly by young people between the ages of 10 and 25, and they argued that incarcerations beyond the age of which there is the probability of committing a crime must be dysfunctional. Needs theorists might be able to explain why there tends to be more alienation and anti-social behavior at this stage of development. These would be contributions to policy, and therefore, part of a process of problem-solving. The same considerations apply to specific situations of conflict. There is a role for the theorist in helping to define the problem on the basis of theories that have a universal application.

Theory and practice are often separated in the division of labor, but the two are intimately interdependent. Conflict resolution processes are effective instruments only to the extent that those applying them are in a position accurately to define the situation into which they are intervening, and can advance explanations of the conflictual behaviors being treated. It may be a great mistake for a third party to enter that role without extensive consultations and preparations, especially a consideration of the components of a particular conflict that are universal within the set of conflicts in which it belongs.

For this to be possible an adequate theory of human behavior is required: indeed this is the starting point of any analysis of any situations of conflict. It is for this reason that further development and understanding of needs theory must be regarded as the core of the study of conflict, its analysis and resolution.

IV
Provention and
Education

18 Introduction: Provention and Education

We have been concerned with processes and practices in management, problem-solving, dispute settlement and conflict resolution. But we live in societies and at a time at which such processes cannot keep pace with the rising levels of problems, disputes and conflicts. There are limits to which prison populations and arms expenditures can increase, and limits also on the diversion of professional skills to problems of management, disputes and conflicts. The process that is called for is decision making that is designed to avoid or treat at source these problems.

We are not always aware of the magnitude of the social problems we seek to tackle. In developed countries we treat Gross National Product as though it were a measure of well-being, and assume that its growth should reduce the number of disputes and conflicts at all societal levels. This is a mistake from two points of view. Even if GNP were such a measure of growth, it masks income and opportunity inequalities. As the rich get richer and the poor poorer (nationally and internationally), so the incidence of conflict rises. But GNP is not a measure of well-being. Even in the most prosperous of countries as measured by GNP, quality of life is declining at an exponential rate. It takes a greater and greater effort to maintain standards; one wage earner is no longer sufficient in the family; there are environmental costs, transport problems, street and home security problems, ethnic conflicts, and a host of others which increasingly detract from quality of life.

As quality of life decreases human needs satisfactions decreases, and disputes, conflicts and violence increase. The gap between the two is escalating at an exponential rate. This gap will not be reduced by dispute settlements and conflict resolutions. It can be reduced only by removing those conditions that create it, allowing an improvement in the quality of life for all.

It is in this wider perspective that assessments of processes must be made. It is not sufficient to make assessments on the basis of particular cases. Processes are valuable, first for the insights they provide into the fundamental causal problems, and second for the contributions they make to bringing about conditions that address

159

these fundamental problems.

It has to be noted that in many cases, perhaps most cases, mediation processes do more harm than good from this perspective. They provide an answer to the particular case and, if very successful, help to preserve that system or set of circumstances that give rise to the cases being treated. This may be good for professional business – there will always be further cases to treat – but it raises some ethical questions.

In this Part IV, and also in Part V, we wish to address some of these issues. In Part IV we look at *pro*vention as a decision making process, and as an extension of conflict resolution. We have not included a discussion on decision making since this was covered in *Conflict: Resolution and Provention*. We do, however, dwell on the importance of education in the nature and handling of conflicts, especially of the young, as a major part of provention.

19 Provention

The term *pre*vention has the connotation of containment. The term *pro*vention has been introduced to signify taking steps to remove sources of conflict, and more positively to promote conditions in which collaborative and valued relationships control behaviors (our note on p. ii of this book).

Dispute settlement and conflict resolution processes seek to settle or to resolve a particular dispute or conflict. Even if they get to the roots of the problem, they do not prevent another case of the same type occurring.

Provention is a more fundamental study and exercise. It is a decision making process in which the future is analysed and anticipated, and as a result policy decisions are taken to remove the sources of likely disputes and conflicts. Were consideration for the future given priority, civilizations would be threatened only by an inadequate understanding of human relations and systems operations. But civilizations have yet to discover the representative political system that gives priority to the future. Provention, a study of conflict avoidance, would be the core of such a political philosophy.

This is a subject that was discussed in the final chapters of *Conflict: Resolution and Provention* and there is no need to repeat the observations made there. In the context of processes, however, provention requires some consideration. It is a new subject. Decision making, and even academic decision making models, have not included provention except to the limited degree to which any preventive strategy discovers that there are situations to be provented, such as in health care or in environmental pollution. Indeed, it is this distinction between deterrent strategies that seek *pre*vention, and the problem-solving strategies that seek *pro*vention by the removal of causes, which prompted the introduction of the word *provention*.

There are signs of change. In *Conflict: Readings in Management and Resolution* there is one contribution which seeks to link conflict resolution and the newly emerging political philosophy of the "Greens". Provention, looking to the future, is the basis of Green philosophy: the initial interest of the Greens was to look ahead and focus on the way in which the environment was being destroyed for some immediate gain, at the expense of the future. Once a thought system is extended beyond the environment to the economy, and to

161

political life generally, there emerges a wholly new political approach to decision making. The Green interest in the environment is politically safe. Extending the same thinking to other problems, such as the prevention of crime by providing education and opportunities, is politically less acceptable, but the Greens seem to be heading in such directions by anticipating the future. By giving attention to the future the Greens have appealed to thinking people regardless of ideological persuasions: they may have within their grasp a political philosophy that could break through contemporary party-political expediency and enable representative government to avoid its short-sighted approaches to public policies.

In at least one State in the US, Virginia, there is a Council on Coordinating Prevention, which in 1989 presented to the Governor a Comprehensive Prevention Plan which set out

> goals and strategies to help localities reduce a wide array of social problems, from teen substance abuse to teen pregnancies, from illiteracy to crime . . . It stresses the need to pull together state and local service agencies, private businesses and individuals, parents, churches and schools and to coordinate the efforts towards the purpose of prevention (Stansbury, 1989).

The plan suggested that funds must be reallocated from treatment to prevention in certain areas of public policy. This is an early step. Probably provention requires substantial changes in the organization of societies. Capitalism, with its profit incentive, appears to contain within it the sources of corruption and exploitation, leading to poverty, discriminations and violence. Communism, designed to prevent this and to provide a sharing society, has been found to lack the necessary incentives for the production of that which is to be shared. Early face-to-face societies were cooperative and sharing to a high degree; large industrial civilizations are still seeking institutions and processes that are at the same time cooperative and to some degree sharing, and also sufficiently representative and productive to maintain an acceptable quality of life. Political philosophies based on knowledgeable provention could be a solution.

It is clear that provention must rest heavily on the theory and practice of conflict resolution as the means by which insights are obtained into the nature of problems. Provention is an extension of analytical conflict resolution. It is the decision making process by which theoretical and empirical findings regarding particular cases of conflict are generalized and translated into policies.

Pragmatism is, accordingly, excluded in provention, at least to the extent that there is an adequate knowledge base. Provention must rest on reliable theories of human behaviors, and accurate predictions of environmental circumstances. This will rightly be regarded as impossible. But what is possible is a deliberate attempt to focus on the future, and to predict within the limits of knowledge – something that is not a normal part of decision making at any societal level.

We have, for example, theories and empirical evidence that the source of a great deal of anti-social behavior stems from adverse living conditions. Yet there is little attempt to avoid the costs and consequences of deviant behaviors and incarcerations by diverting adequate resources to housing, education and health. Whether the conflict be drug violence or ethnicity conflict, there are means of provention that are probably less costly to society than attempts at control.

It follows that decision making theory is the starting point of provention. In *Conflict: Resolution and Provention* there is a series of diagrams to show how thinking on decision making has changed. While some decades ago the human dimension was at last introduced into decision making models, the future as a prime concern has still to be introduced.

KEY SUBJECT AREAS

Conflict resolution theory and practice, with its focus on the satisfaction of human needs, provides a direction for conflict provention policies. These are being pursued gradually in relevant disciplines. One of the most obvious areas of investigation is child education and support. Studies such as *The Friendly Classroom for a Small Planet: A Handbook on Creative Approaches to Living and Problem Solving for Children* (Prutzman *et al.*, 1978) are evidence that there is a growing appreciation of the sources of social problems. As we shall see in Chapter 20, there are many other initiatives of this kind in education, and also in health.

The practical social problem, however, is one that such initiatives can do little about. There is an accumulation of people who have been neglected, and catching up is impossible in the absence of major shifts in priorities, especially in developed industrial countries. The general problem is being made even more difficult by immigrations and the emergence of deep rooted ethnicity discrimination that legislation alone cannot control. Social problems that arise out of the existence and accentuation of both class and ethnicity are likely to overwhelm many societies. Resolution processes will require the backing of planned provention on a scale commensurate with the kind of defense expenditures that so distorted economies in the 1980s.

This is a book about dispute settlement and conflict resolution. We find that we must finally turn to provention if we are to tackle these problems effectively. This means a focus on political philosophy generally, and decision making in particular. It is this focus on the future, the avoidance of problems, that must be at the core of training and in the minds of any intervenor, whether the intervention be in management, disputes or conflicts.

20 Education

INTRODUCTION

The growth of interest in new means of dealing with management problems, disputes and conflicts, has resulted in the creation of four major fields of educational practice.

One of these fields – training in negotiation and mediation skills for businesses, government and non-governmental organizations, and community volunteers – has become a major business. Many third-party practitioners and organizations devote the bulk of their time to developing, marketing, and giving these trainings.

In another of these fields, teaching at the university level, a number of graduate programs incorporate the study and practice of management, dispute settlement, and conflict analysis and resolution.

The two fields with the most far-reaching implications exist at the primary and secondary school level. These fields, if carefully developed, have the potential to move one step beyond decision making provention. The first, "cooperative learning" or "cooperative education", involves the restructuring of standard classroom educational practices. The second field, "student conflict manager" programs, involves teaching a core of selected students to act as mediators for their peers. We will now consider these latter two fields.

COOPERATIVE EDUCATION

Elie Wiesel (1989) tells of an old Talmudic legend in which certain angels gave God contradictory advice about the creation of Humankind. The Angel of Love favored creation, certain that humans would have to love one another to survive; the Angel of Truth was opposed, certain that existence would necessitate lies. The story pits those who view humans as essentially good and cooperative against those who see us as naturally destructive and competitive. The same argument has continued for centuries, and continues today, around the answers to various forms of the same question: are humans (or certain divisions of humans: men, certain races, various nationalities) inherently and necessarily aggressive, warlike, competitive, and dominance seeking? And, if so, should this behavior be accepted as inevitable and even beneficial?

In secondary education, many social psychologists and educators answer both questions with a definitive, No! There exists today a virtual cottage industry for promoting, teaching and testing the results of cooperative learning in the classroom. Dozens of books and training manuals are published each year. The International Association for the Study of Cooperation in Education (IASCE) publishes a newsletter and sponsors conferences, and the social psychology and education journals contains numerous studies of various forms of cooperative education.

This industry is relatively new in its current institutionalized form. According to Schmuck (1985), however, its roots extend at least to the work of John Dewey and Kurt Lewin. From Dewey came the moral imperative to teach and model cooperative democracy in the schools; from Lewin, the heritage of group dynamics.

Kohn (1986) distinguishes between structural competition and intentional competition. Structural competition is situational, as in the competition for acceptance into college, for grades and for the favors of the teacher. Intentional competition is attitudinal. Structural competition involves a situation designed to allow (or even mandate) mutually exclusive goal attainment, what Deutsch (1973) terms "contrient interdependence." Both structural and intentional competition involve what is known popularly as a "win/lose" orientation.

This characterization may also be extended to cooperation. Structural cooperation involves situations designed so that what benefits any individual also benefits the group, what Benedict (1959) termed "synergy," or Deutsch "promotive interdependence": a "win/win" orientation.

The developers of cooperative learning programs are attempting to create a classroom environment that eliminates all of the structural competitive aspects of the educational process, and many of the intentional aspects, by instituting instead structural and intentional cooperation.

Axelrod (1984) suggests three categories of means by which the strategic setting of a relationship may be altered to promote cooperation: make the future more important relative to the present; change the payoffs to participants; and teach values, facts, and skills that promote cooperation. It is the latter two means, the combination of inducements with learned values and skills, that are the core of cooperative learning processes.

In order to get a sense of the field we will examine the methods of two of the most prominent groups of researcher-practitioners, Elliot

Aronson and his confederates (1978) and the Johnson brothers, David and Roger (1985; 1987a,b).

Responding to problems with desegregation in the schools of Austin, Texas, Aronson's group created a technique of classroom instruction that used small groups and peer teaching to induce cooperative behavior among classmates. Theorizing that racial tension was exacerbated by the prevailing competitive norms of the classroom, their intention was to build into the institution, in this case the classroom, the structures that prevent those tensions.

The "jigsaw" technique they devised is quite simple. Before students are introduced to various learning tasks (which are similar to standard curricula), they are taught team-building techniques. In small groups of four or five, students learn listening and evaluative skills, brainstorming methods, and leadership skills. They are also taught how to express feelings constructively. The group learns about dealing with problems through instruction and role playing. Extremely disruptive students get extra training before they go into the group.

It is only after students (and teachers) have completed training that they are ready to tackle their substantive assignments. Each member of the group is responsible for learning one aspect of a group assignment and for teaching it to the others. Hence the title, "jigsaw": each student may be seen as one piece of the puzzle, whose pieces must come together to create the whole.

The results of "jigsaw" include an increase in liking the members of one's own group, while maintaining the same level of liking for the others in the class; an increase in liking school; improved self-esteem; and decreased competitiveness. Students learn to view their classmates as resources and gain more ability to empathize. Minority (Black and Hispanic) scores on standardized tests improve, while white scores remain the same (Aronson *et al.*, 1978).

However, not all researchers agree about the effectiveness of the method. While several researchers report positive results, others find none; for instance. Moskovitz *et al.* (1985) report a great variety in the implementation of jigsaw, and no positive effect on the variables of student attitudes, achievement, attendance or behavior.

The Johnson brothers (David W. and Roger T.) at the University of Minnesota have become well-known both inside and outside the field of social psychology because of publicity they have received through their numerous books and articles, public appearances, and coverage in popular journals such as *Psychology Today*. Since the early 1970s they have been researching not just cooperative learning, but the relative impact of cooperative, competitive, and individualistic learning experiences. Their primary research method has been the field experiment, performed in schools.

Their typical study is as follows (Johnson and Johnson, 1985). They recruit three teachers for a three-week study. Each teacher receives 90 hours of training on how to implement three learning situations: cooperative, competitive, or individualistic. Differences in individual teachers are controlled by rotating the teachers across conditions each week. Students are randomly assigned to each group, with equal divisions of gender, race, and ability. The curriculum for each group is identical. Teachers are assigned a script for each day and are observed daily as well. The researchers also observe and analyze how the students interact with one another.

Twenty-one out of 26 of the Johnsons' studies found that cooperative learning promoted higher achievement, with 2 studies having mixed results and 3 showing no differences. Among the findings was that higher ability students also benefited from working with medium and low ability students. They also found that cooperative learning experiences result in greater interpersonal attraction and more positive relationships than do competitive and individualistic learning experiences.

In addition to their field experiments, the Johnsons have studied entire school districts, through surveys, and performed several laboratory experiments. They also conducted a meta-analysis of all the research on the relative effects of cooperative, competitive, and individualistic efforts on achievement and productivity (D. Johnson, Maruyama, R. Johnson, Nelson and Skon, 1981). They analyzed 122 studies with 286 findings completed between 1924 and 1981. Their conclusion was that cooperative learning produced higher achievement than competitive and individualistic learning experiences, with the average person in the cooperative mode at about the 80th percentile of students working within the competitive or individualistic modes.

They also conducted a meta-analysis of research on the relative impact of cooperative, cooperative with intergroup competition, interpersonal competitive, and individualistic learning experiences on interpersonal attraction (D. Johnson, R. Johnson, and Maruyama, 1983). In their analysis of 251 findings in 98 studies, from 1944 to 1982, they found greater interpersonal attraction in the cooperative mode among homogeneous students, students from different ethnic groups, handicapped students, and non-handicapped students.

The Johnsons also have developed a process, "Constructive Controversy", for conducting classroom research so that it is not destructive in its competitiveness (Johnson and Johnson, 1987b). The class is divided into groups of four. Each pair within the group studies the arguments from opposing sides of a controversial issue. Each pair then presents the case for their side, while the opposing side listens and asks clarifying questions only. Each side then challenges the other's arguments. The pairs then switch sides and present the case for the opposition. After that, the team members as a whole analyze the issue for eventual presentation of a report, a summary of which all sign.

STUDENT "CONFLICT MANAGERS"

Student "conflict manager" programs are the most recent and mainstream development of the movement begun in the 1960s and 1970s by religious and peace activists. Their desire has been to inculcate in children both the desire and ability to create a more peaceful world. From these beginnings of occasional isolated efforts have come several organizations, and the growth of what may now be legitimately called a social movement.

There are several national organizations in this field. Children's Creative Response to Conflict Program (CCRC), begun in 1972, is affiliated with the Quaker Fellowship of Reconciliation. The acronym "CCRC" also stands for the organization's four basic themes: cooperation, communication, affirmation, and conflict resolution. CCRC sponsors an annual "gathering", publishes a regular newsletter, and produces training materials, including a teacher's handbook, *Friendly Classroom for a Small Planet* (Prutzman *et al.*, 1978).

Educators for Social Responsibility was formed in 1982. A membership organization for educators, it sponsors a variety of activities and resources, as it moves beyond its original emphasis on peace education in a nuclear age.

The National Association for Mediation in Education (NAME), begun in 1984, represents over 500 members from around the country. NAME publishes an annotated bibliography on school based mediation, and sponsors conferences, a newsletter (*The Fourth R*), and other resource materials. It also serves as a general clearinghouse for information about who is doing what and where, both through its newsletter and through its directory of school-based programs.

Perhaps the organization most active in instituting programs and extending the boundaries of the field is Community Boards of San Francisco. Community Boards is involved with youth at several levels, by establishing school "conflict management" programs through their School Initiatives Program, by training 14–18 year-olds as community volunteers for diversion of youth offender cases, and by training youths in communication and other skills in California rehabilitation and treatment facilities. Community Boards also provides training for those interested in institutionalizing student conflict manager programs. They also serve as a resource center, producing items such as a school curriculum, training manuals, and training videos.

Davis and Porter (1985) have catalogued a number of goals and benefits of a school-based mediation program. These can be grouped in three categories: benefits to the school administration, benefits to the disputants, and benefits to the student "conflict managers".

They suggest that conflict is a natural human state, better approached with skills than avoidance. Expulsion, suspension, court intervention, and detention are neither appropriate nor effective in dealing with problems in schools. Mediation can improve communication between and among students, staff, and parents. It can reduce violence, vandalism, and chronic absence. By shifting responsibility for their disputes to the students, teachers and administrators can concentrate more on teaching and less on discipline.

They claim that mediation training also allows youths and teachers to understand more about themselves and others. Mediation is uniquely suited to the personal nature of young people's problems for they would not ordinarily take to authority figures. Recognition of student competence in resolving their own disputes encourages their growth and gives them life skills such as listening, critical thinking, and problem-solving, each of which is basic to all learning.

Davis and Porter's final claim is that mediation training increases citizenship interest and participation. With its emphasis upon respect for others' views and the peaceful resolution of differences, it prepares students to live in a multicultural world.

Typically, student conflict management programs combine some general education for all students in the school with specialized training for the actual "conflict managers". These mediators may be selected by the administration or by their fellow students. They often wear brightly colored T-shirts during recess or lunch time as they deal informally with arguments. In some programs mediators work in more structured sessions during or after class.

The mediation processes used by the students are similar to those taught to volunteers at community mediation centers. Indeed, many programs have begun as initiatives of local mediation centers. Typically, the process begins as co-mediators, or a panel of mediators, introduce themselves and the process to the disputants. Groundrules, such as "no name-calling" and "no interrupting", are explained, and participants often must agree to abide by the rules before they proceed.

The mediators are taught to bring out both the facts of the dispute and the feelings of the disputants. The parties are encouraged to work out solutions to their problems themselves. The mediators push for solutions that can reasonably be expected to be carried out, that are specific, and that actually solve the problems. If an agreement is reached, all participants sign it. These agreements are checked later to see how well they have worked.

These programs are sold to school boards and administrators on the basis of promised tangible results such as reduced violence, lower drop-out rates, and improvement in learning climate. The proponents of these programs, however, are more likely to have the more global concerns mentioned earlier in mind. As Davis (1986, p. 294) points out, these differences point to two dilemmas with these programs. The first concerns are that the means proposed to facilitate the administration of the system may contain the seeds of system change:

> The shared values . . . include emphasis on the benefits of collaboration in contrast to the costs of combativeness, and an appreciation that the morality of care is just as important as the predictability of proceduralism and rules. These values threaten many. At the school level they call for an examination of the competitive way learning is structured and the authoritarian means used to achieve discipline.

The second dilemma faced by advocates for this movement is that by stressing the connections between interpersonal conflict and these larger goals, especially international peace making, they will generate opposition from those who would view these programs as soft, misguided, or even unpatriotic.

While many individuals working in this field are aware of potential problems, such awareness has not been actualized beyond discussions at seminars and workshops. What exactly are students being taught – conflict resolution, or obedience? Unlike the cooperative learning field, there is almost no research into the effects of these programs, and evaluation is heavily affected by wishful thinking. More research, and more critical analysis, must precede any satisfactory evaluation.

V
Conclusions

21 Assessment

BASES OF ASSESSMENT

We have examined samples of processes in management, dispute settlement and conflict resolution as they have evolved in recent years. We have sought to put these processes in the context of decision making and provention – means of avoiding the situations with which the processes are designed to deal.

In assessing processes there must be some criteria:

1. Do we assess processes within the limited context of their declared goals – that is, allaying specific arguments, disputes and conflicts as they emerge in the organizations and societies in which they take place? On this basis most practitioners could claim some successes.
2. Do we assess them as contributors to harmonious relationships in the wider social environment in which they take place? A settlement of a wage dispute within a monopolistic industry that had the effect of raising prices to consumers might not be assessed as a success on this basis.
3. Do we assess processes on the basis of their outcomes in the future? Some environmental settlement that satisfied parties in the present might not be assessed positively on the basis of its future consequences.
4. Do we assess processes for the extent to which they deal with disputes and conflicts that are rampant in underprivileged segments of societies? Most processes, from courts to all manner of ADR processes would probably fail on this test – we have been examining processes that are essentially middle class means of dealing with relationship problems.

It is understandable that those involved in management processes would make their assessments on results within the organization or social unit concerned: some agreement would be regarded as a success regardless of wider social consequences, or subsequent breakdowns in the agreement. Those concerned with dispute settlement would similarly make "within-system" assessments. Conflict resolution processes, because they involve wider perspectives, are more difficult to assess, for there may be institutional changes required that have longer-term implications.

When, however, we introduce a provention perspective, then the basis of assessment of any process must be the extent to which it contributes to the elimination of the conditions which promoted the problem in the first place, and the manner in which it contributes to societal quality of life now and in the future.

ASSESSMENT AND NORMS

Ultimately we seek processes that achieve their immediate or within-system goals, that is, deal effectively with the situation at hand and at the same time reflect the longer-term interests of society. This has been the purpose of legal processes, and of established arbitration and related processes. They have sought to settle disputes on the basis of consensus norms of justice, thus meeting the requirements both of the parties and of the wider society. The observance of certain norms has been there as a guide, and a basis for assessment.

The issue we raise here is not, however, whether judicial processes and their alternatives, together with conflict resolution and provention processes, are based on social and legal norms. That has been the traditional basis for assessment, but it fails to address a far more important reference point. The issue we confront is whether the norms which guide judicial and alternative processes are those that lead to outcomes that contribute to the solution of the source problems, and to quality of life in the society.

The issue we raise is not whether decisions are based on norms, but the source and quality of those norms. Norms based on tradition and precedent do not take into account discovery and increased knowledge, especially knowledge of human behavior. Take, for example, the problem of segregation of minorities in education. On the basic norm of non-discrimination, integration by bussing could be a policy legally required. This leads to all manner of logistic problems in addition to complaints by those who wished to be educated within their local communities. If, however, the basic norm were individual development, then attention would be given to improving the standards of education in the minority areas so as to make them attractive to all in the community. Norms, whether they be legal norms or social norms, must reflect changing circumstances, altered knowledge especially about the human condition, and emerging values, if they are to serve their purpose as the basis of conflict resolving and proventive decision making.

A THEORETICAL FRAMEWORK

We have tried in this study to place processes in an evolutionary context, meaning that as behavioral theories have advanced so have the processes that are derived from them. What has become apparent is that judicial processes, based on legal norms and not behavioral norms, cannot resolve problems of deep rooted conflict. Nor can arbitration and most forms of coercive mediation. With more understanding of human behaviors and the ways in which societies have evolved, we develop more understanding of structural sources of conflict and the need to seek institutional policy options that cater to human requirements. These insights have yet to be translated into norms and into institutionalized processes of dispute settlement and conflict resolution.

The human needs theoretical framework is part of this evolution. No doubt there will be further developments, especially in defining more precisely what these needs are, and in exploring institutional satisfiers. At the present time it leads us to categorize *disputes over interests*, on the one hand, and *conflicts over values and needs* on the other, leading to processes of *settlement* and *resolution*. If specific cases can be placed reasonably in one of these categories, then the appropriate deduced processes can be applied. Case assessment is then possible.

We should note in passing that we are giving "settlement" a special meaning – that is, the acceptance, perhaps under power bargaining or judicial circumstances, of an agreement that does not satisfy expectations, demands or even the requirements of justice. But such settlements may be wholly acceptable in the circumstances, and in this sense some disputes could be regarded as "resolved". We find it useful, however, to keep the distinction between settlement relating to disputes, and resolution relating to conflicts, to maintain a distinction between situations involving interests that are negotiable, and others that involve non-negotiable human needs.

A TRANSITION PERIOD

The present may be a transition period in means of dispute settlement and conflict resolution – a transition from traditional judicial processes applied to certain kinds of cases, to alternative dispute settlement and conflict resolution processes. Underlying this transition is a far deeper and more significant one. This is a transition from the ideal of a centralized democratic political system seeking to cater to the legitimate needs of the total society, with an authority assumed to have a legitimized monopoly of power by which to enforce its decisions, to the political reality of a society in which political power is possessed by interests and factions. In the most "democratic" of societies we see the way in which institutions are controlled, not by electorates, but by special interest groups. In such a society the educationally and economically underprivileged are, for all practical purposes, outside the political process, and struggle to establish their own means of survival, by violence against each other if necessary.

This is a transition from a system of traditional institutional power and elite-dominated norms, whether they be applied through courts or alternatives, to a system driven by the power of human needs that *will* be pursued regardless of legal norms and constraints. In conditions in which authorities have little legitimized status because they represent only elite interests, in which significant proportions of the total population have no valued relationships with society that would control their behaviors, and in which the means of violence are readily available, law and order based on traditional legal and societal norms is no longer possible.

Supplements and alternatives to courts may seem to have a special role in such conditions, but their processes are just as likely to escalate further existing levels of dispute and conflict. They cannot provide a substitute for legitimized authorities and their institutions of control.

The transition which societies, regardless of ideology, are presently undergoing is not, therefore, a superficial one concerning processes. It is a fundamental and historical transition brought about by the challenge to social norms which cater to power-elite interests and which in so doing deny human needs. While the individual pursuit of human needs can promote the social good in conditions in which the individual values social relationships and consequently observes societal norms, that same human drive can in other circumstances be destructive of society and of self.

This transition situation is, indeed, a confused and difficult one. It raises questions of ethics, relevance, justice, constitutional rights, human rights, human needs and a host of others. It is a transition away from authoritative decision making toward something, the nature of which is far from clear. A clear picture of the desired future, and agreed steps toward it would seem necessary. The management and dispute settlement processes which we have examined do not provide these. Problem-solving conflict resolution, leading to provention, may be on the right track, but is still at an immature stage.

DEFINING THE PROBLEM

The final means of assessment is the extent to which processes contribute to the solution of the societal problems that call them into existence. What are these problems and what are their solutions? Applying the processes of conflict resolution we must first define the problem before we can deduce possible solutions.

The problem is not overcrowding of courts, and the solution is not, therefore, some supporting alternatives. There is the prior question of why courts are overcrowded and why enforcement agencies cannot contain conflict and violence. Underlying this is the question: What is the source of an escalating level of disputes, conflicts and violence?

We have in *Conflict: Resolution and Provention* sought to reveal the sources of conflict, and were led to human needs theory as the framework in which to make the analysis. We deduced that conflict could be resolved and provented only by structures, institutions and policies that gave first priority to the satisfaction of human needs, especially needs of recognition and identity, rather than requiring the individual in society to adjust to the institutions of society. To the extent that the individual is required so to adjust it can be only as a result of values attached to relationships within and with the society.

That being the definition of the problem, we are led to reexamine the norms of society, and in particular the norms that are applied in judicial processes: to what extent do they rest on interests and the preservation of institutions, and to what extend do they cater to the human needs of individuals?

SOME EMPIRICAL EVIDENCE

There has been to date little such assessment of the many different and sometimes competing processes that are employed in the management, dispute and conflict fields. Pragmatism still dominates, and pragmatism, being a subjective orientation, justifies itself. We are dealing, let us recognize, with recent innovations. Those assessments that are made must be inconclusive in the absence of some recognized theoretical framework from which can be deduced the source of the problem and its appropriate treatment.

To make an analogy, the treatment of a health problem must first be assessed by reference to its explanation. Loss of weight and fatigue can have many causes, and the remedy depends on diagnosis. Assessments of treatment unrelated to diagnosis are as reliable as those made by a witch doctor. So, too, with interventions in disputes and conflicts: it is the validity of the definition and explanation of situations that must first be assessed. Quite separately the process of diagnosis and the effects of the deduced remedy require assessment, but it is the justification of the process based on a preliminary analysis of the situation that is of importance.

So far the various fields of dispute and conflict resolution have by-passed this issue. It is difficult in most cases to determine why some process has been introduced or what is its justification. The fact that courts are crowded might justify alternatives, but does not of itself justify some particular alternative. There have developed many face-to-face techniques for improving personal relationships. It could be that attempts to improve personal relationships by direct interaction are not adequate, and in some cases even dysfunctional in the longer term.

Ordinary social and organizational problems of *management* which we have differentiated from the fields of dispute settlement and conflict resolution, and which comprise the bulk of tensions in societal relationships, are also likely to involve interests and human needs in some degree. So, too, disputes and conflicts involve problems of management. As we have emphasized, these *management, dispute* and *conflict* categories are ideal types. The corporate body may have common goals, but there are usually personal interests and needs below the surface. The probability is that many situations in the management category fall into the dispute and resolution categories also, but are not treated as such by third parties whose training is in management processes only. As professional organizations tighten professional qualification requirements, and as there is more under-standing of the nature of human relationships, it will be found that the processes relating to this management category will be confined largely to straightforward organizational and management relationships where all that may be required is some process by which consensus choices can be made.

There is another danger with the indiscriminate use of such processes generally, and this is the way in which management problems and disputes can escalate over time, simply through the dynamics of process poorly understood and applied. An argument can become a dispute, and even a conflict, if not professionally managed. The conclusion of the mediator is likely to be that the problem was with the parties, whereas an objective and analytical assessment might find that it was with the mediator.

AN EMERGING DISQUIET

There are the beginnings of disquiet and concern as the alternative fields enlarge and claims of success proliferate (Abel, 1982; Hofrichter, 1987; Harrington, 1985). Amy (1987), to whom we referred earlier, has made a valuable assessment by examining ADR procedures employed in relation to environmental mediation. He is able to generalize his observations to apply to other areas also. He observes that most writing on the topic has been by mediators and those who champion this new alternative to courts and to government decision making. A closer look casts doubt on the procedures. In the case of environmental disputes, for example, he observes that they can turn out to be chiefly a public relations exercise, and a means of letting accountable authorities off the hook with interest group and public opinion. Amy regards the procedures as potentially manipulative, and subject to political bias, without necessarily being faster, less confrontational or less costly. He sees scope for abuse, as power pressures finally win out. His conclusion seems to be that, "Environmental mediation does deserve a place in environmental politics, but its role should be a relatively small one". And again, "On balance, environmental mediation is a process that should be approached with such caution and skepticism" (Amy, 1987, pp. 224–5). In an Epilogue he extends these warnings to such mediation in other areas also. There is a growing critical literature on the role of ADR, and lawyers are showing concern. There is criticism of "ad hoc negotiation processes", the way in which "ADR becomes a tool for diminishing the judicial development of legal rights for the disadvantaged", and the way in which "ADR will lead to a second-class justice" (Edwards, 1986).

It would seem more practical in changing circumstances to adapt processes already institutionalized, rather than keep inventing new ones. Those involved in alternatives to courts seem to assume that there will be no changes in judicial procedures, and the norms on which decisions are based. Does the invention of alternatives to courts mean that courts will in due course become less and less relevant? Or does it mean that legal processes will alter to accommodate to new insights into behaviors, perhaps as rapidly as can alternatives, and reoccupy their dominant role in dispute settlement, and extend this even to conflict resolution? Judging by the way many lawyers are responding, the latter might well be the case (Bush, 1984).

There are some important preventive issues raised here, in particular how to avoid the persistence and escalation of confusion and injustice. If courts are crowded, and if they are not attuned to some types of disputes and conflicts, there are remedies other than rejecting a highly institutionalized and professionalized institution. In evolutionary terms the future in the handling of disputes and conflicts is likely to be a combination of legal processes, in which legal rights rather than human needs are assessed, and analytical problem-solving conflict resolution processes, in which human factors are of prime interest. Beyond that future there is likely to be a merging of these two approaches such that consensus norms of social control, and the human needs norms that require problem-solving processes, become the guides for social behavior and social control. Rather than commence an array of processes, few with any theoretical basis, might it not be better to seek to alter the general education and specific training of attorneys, and ultimately the norms on which judicial assessments are based?

THE POLITICAL NEED FOR A PARADIGM SHIFT

These observations should be placed in their political context. The increase in disputes, conflicts, crime, violence and ethnic wars is confronting authorities globally with situations beyond their control, regardless of the coercion employed. The greatest of powers is defeated by a smaller power, and nationally and internationally drug barons can defeat judicial processes, police and armies. Governments are led into practices which, performed by others, would be described as terrorism and murder.

In short, there is something self-defeating in traditional norms if they require for their defense just those behaviors they seek to control. Anomalies such as this clearly call for some fundamental rethinking. The paradigm shift from power-elite norms toward human needs norms would seem to be the one required, a shift that could take place over time once the power of human needs were understood, the costs of their frustration appreciated, and the appropriate alternative processes tested and practiced.

We are led to pose the question whether the way forward is the invention of alternatives, and in due course alternatives to alternatives, or is it also or mainly the adaptation of existing institutions and practices to changing circumstances, including increased knowledge of the human condition?

This is an issue that reaches beyond the judicial–ADR debates. Courts, after all, are institutions designed to interpret the law, and the establishment of legal norms is at least in part a function of decision making at a high level. There cannot be, at least in any short term, any major alterations in legal norms that are not initiated by authorities and relevant decision makers. The future of dispute settlement and conflict resolution, like the development of provention, depends on political decision making.

Many centers dealing with public policy disputes have been created, especially in the US. These are free standing – that is, not connected to courts. Some are privately funded, some are agencies of local, state and federal governments. They deal with environmental problems, and the many decision making problems authorities face. Some also deal with organizational problems in corporations. They are, in effect, adjuncts to decision making processes rather than alternatives to courts. A criticism is that there are no norms being applied other than the power norms of society that control such decision making. Change in legal norms under pressure of cases is more likely to take place, even in the absence of political decisions, than change in power bargaining norms.

We must conclude that advances in dispute settlement and conflict resolution at all societal levels will not come about only by creating new institutions, public or private, but by injecting into decision making in every sphere, from the family to the world society, greater understanding of human behaviors and the need for social, economic and political change on a continuous basis so as to cater to human needs in changing circumstances. In due course this could affect legal norms. If this were to be the case alternatives to courts and to legal processes would not be required or even desirable. But for lawyers not to be confrontational and adversarial, and to seek to solve problems, would require a different training, and different codes of professional ethics.

Some attorneys are already employing persons with relevant training to assist them with the high proportion of cases which they attempt to settle or resolve outside formal judicial processes. It is in this institutionalized way that there can best be the meeting point of disputes and conflicts, settlement and resolution, judicial processes and analytical problem-solving.

There is one other traditional and institutionalized process that, like law, must be preserved and similarly developed, and this is the general area of "management". Advice, assistance, support and constructive interventions have always been a normal part of social life at all societal levels. Important developments in mutual help and in "provention" – though it is not called this – are taking place in many societies at the community level. There is probably no better means of tackling problems of alienation and conflict than by collaborative local inputs into education, individual development, social responsibility and environmental preservation, thus improving quality of life and reducing the incidence of disputes and conflicts. Courts are a fall-back institution. These community activities, however, must reflect the greater knowledge that is available now about the human condition, as must the norms and procedures of courts.

These considerations apply at the international level also. It is most unlikely that there will be any institutionalized process of conflict resolution within the framework of the United Nations' political institutions. The United Nations Security Council is not a problem-solving body. The Secretariat is so recruited and organized that there is little prospect of analytical problem-solving thinking being absorbed and applied to the many situations, domestic and international, that currently disturb international relations. There is, consequently, no body to which parties can turn to help resolve their conflicts which can, at the same time, protect them from being seen to be weakening in their conflictual resolve. Typically they cannot agree to meet face-to-face, and any alternative is not a satisfactory way of arriving at an agreement based on a deep analysis of their problems.

The International Court is as yet a wholly unacceptable body, for no party to a conflict can submit matters of vital concern to the uncertainties of adjudication. No party can enter a forum that accepts the assumption that there is "right" and "wrong" in a situation. As yet it is unlikely that the Court will tackle problems on a problem-solving basis. But the same winds of change operate at the international level as at the domestic: little by little it is being realized that conflicts cannot be suppressed, that agreements cannot be forced by mediation and compromise, and that there is a felt need for neutral and professional interventions that delve into the source of conflicts, and discover options that satisfy the parties, and also the wider community. The International Court remains the only international institutionalized body that could enact the role of a third-party facilitator to determine parties and issues, and be creative in putting forward proposals that meet the needs of the parties concerned. It should at least be challenged, as ADR is challenging national courts, to catch up with theory and reality, and to begin to alter norms, procedures and staffing accordingly.

There is one existing national institution, diplomacy, that in the international field parallels community-based interventions. If foreign offices were to have teams of professionally trained diplomats who could use the facilities and contacts of their local embassies as suitable neutral locations, many disputes and conflicts could be dealt with at an early stage and in confidence. Unfortunately the tendency for governments is still to take sides in a conflict, rather than view conflicts as a problem to be solved, thus inhibiting the work of professional diplomats.

The contemporary focus on "alternatives" reflects a false definition of the problem societies face. Whether it be at the domestic or the international level, it is not necessarily alternatives that we seek, but institutions, whether existing or supplementary, that are designed to reflect all available knowledge, and to cater for the needs of those they purport to serve. Inventing alternative institutions cannot be a substitute for deeper analysis and changed thinking.

22 Ethical Considerations

PROFESSIONAL ETHICS

We have described the present as one of transition in social control, one that is inevitably full of uncertainties and contending approaches. It is one, therefore, in which professionalism is being challenged constantly: are new modes based on expediency, or do they have a firm base in theory? do alternatives to courts play into the hands of the powerful at the expense of the underprivileged? are palliatives useful when what is required are substantial changes in institutions and policies? One can go on and on to no avail, and with little prospect that any practitioner will be diverted from his or her special orientation and trade.

What is objectively clear is that professional ethics in interventions cannot be based in any society on just any existing societal and legal norms and conventions. These are based on tradition, and historically are likely to reflect elite interests rather than human needs and societal interests. They are part of the problem, not part of the solution. Applying them is merely reinforcing the structural causes of disputes and conflicts.

Neither can ethics be based on the personal and subjective value systems of the intervenor. An intervenor is inevitably the product of a culture and will tend to be supportive of the status quo even in cases in which circumstances, over which parties to a dispute or conflict have no control, are responsible for the confrontation.

Nor can it be claimed that it is ethical either to be neutral or biased in favor of one party. Bias is merely a personal projection likely to prejudice the success of any process. Neutrality, meaning impartiality, is nothing more than a necessary condition without which no facilitating process can work.

Nor can it be claimed that to be "democratic" is ethical, or to act in the ways in which the parties to a dispute or conflict wish. An intervenor is acting on behalf of society as well as the parties, for in the longer term an agreement between the parties that prejudices the wider social interest will not be in their interests.

From a humanitarian point of view it could be argued that it is proper to help parties to disputes and conflicts to find an accommodation, even though this kind of activity could direct attention away

186

from the source of problems and even defer temporarily the felt need for social and political change. This could be regarded as socially praiseworthy behavior, but not necessarily ethical.

Professional ethics must be assessed on the basis of available knowledge, predictions as to the future, and the longer-term quality of life outcome for any persons or groups directly or indirectly affected by an intervention. This means that the source of professional ethics is in the type of training that has been received in relation to particular roles.

Process training alone may be sufficient in cases in which there is intervention under supervision, just as clinical staff operate under the directions of a qualified doctor. An important part of process training, however, is to provide an awareness of unusual circumstances that signal that the process may not be suitable, and that other advices are required.

Professional organizations have begun to tackle these problems of ethics and professionalism. In the US, the Society of Professionals in Dispute Resolution (SPIDR) discusses at annual conferences and in their publications whether and how mediators can be evaluated. So far there are no clear answers – perhaps because there is no theoretical framework on the basis of which assessments can be made. There is as yet no professional organization that deals specifically with conflict resolution, and we have all manner of shuttle diplomacies carried out by persons with little or no professional training. The tendency remains to try to apply settlement and mediation techniques even to situations in which there can be no compromises and no coercion. Nor is there any professional organization that is concerned with the professional ethics of decision makers.

In assessing ethics we are forced back to the position in which we found ourselves when trying to determine how to assess success and failure in the application of different dispute settlement and conflict resolution processes: the assessment must be made on the basis of the validity of the theoretical framework being followed. If the theory is valid, if prediction is reliable, if outcomes prove beneficial to all parties concerned, if problems are provented, then the processes employed are positively assessed, and the intervenors and decision makers are acting ethically.

This is a book about processes, not theories. But whether it be process, professional ethics, justice or any other concept relating to social policy, finally we are led back to a theory of human behavior that can put forward specific goals in relation to which assessments can be made. Goals such as individual development, recognition and identity are widely recognized; but we still lack precision in identifying these needs in practice. It is here that we need research and discussion before we can make progress on practices and their assessment. But that knowledge which now is available, and it is considerable, must be reflected in processes if practitioners are to be judged to be ethical.

Appendix: Facilitated Conflict Resolution Procedures[1]

INTRODUCTION

As stressed throughout this book, processes and procedures for handling a conflict are deduced from the theoretical or explanatory framework in which decision makers operate. If there is a power framework, conflict management will take one form, if a problem-solving framework then interactive and analytical procedures will logically be appropriate.

In every case certain regularities or "rules" are necessary. In a game, as in any social relationship, there have to be rules or regular patterns of behavior so the players (or members of society) can reliably predict the behavior of others. Everyone then knows what is expected of them and how to respond. It would be impossible to play a game if the rules were subject to alteration or modification during it. In facilitated conflict resolution, where tight control of discussion is required to ensure a comprehensive analysis, it is most important that the rules are clearly understood, consistently observed by the facilitator(s) and respected by all concerned.

If rules were interpreted merely as guidelines, they might be ignored or applied pragmatically according to the pressures of circumstances. However, the delicate nature of facilitated interactions between parties to a conflict requires the application of tested procedures and does not allow for innovations except as a result of careful prior consideration.

For example, when the person sponsoring a facilitated interaction between parties is asking the leading representative of a party to a conflict to nominate participants and is explaining the procedures to be followed, he or she may be tempted into a discussion of some aspect of the conflict. This prior discussion could prejudice the perception of the neutral role of the third party. To take another example, during discussions the panel may be tempted *not* to control dialogue when participants stray from the current agenda item and attempt to advance proposals before the analysis is complete. Experience has shown that this can derail the whole process.

No set of rules will prove perfect, and this element of rigidity could seem to be claiming too much for a particular set of rules. The rigidity is, however, more in relation to the principles on which the rules are based than to their specific application in all situations.

For example, in industrial dispute settlement a mediator frequently favors "caucusing" or separate meetings of each of the parties with the third party. The attempt is to find how far one party is prepared to compromise and to adjust to the other. While caucusing could be useful in a management or an interest bargaining situation, it would destroy the credibility of a third party

189

in a tense situation of deep rooted conflict. More importantly, it would destroy the central purpose of the facilitated process – that is, to reveal directly to each party the attitudes and motivations of the other, and the costs of various policy options.

In the following statement of rules there tends to be a focus on more conspicuous conflicts such as international and communal conflicts. The generality of the principles on which these rules are based should not, however, be missed in adapting them to domestic and other situations.

THE RULES OF SPONSORSHIP

Facilitated conflict resolution is an intervention into social relationships. It is important in conflict resolution at the interstate, intercommunal and small group and personal levels that no interventions occur unless they are based on theories of behavior that have been adequately tested in practice, and unless they are carried out by persons who have had the appropriate training and experience. Our first rule restricts the sponsor – that is, the person or institution which initiates and arranges for the facilitated conflict resolution process.

Rule One
A sponsor should not approach parties to a dispute with a view to facilitating a resolution unless the sponsor can provide facilitators who possess the required training and skills.

Conflict situations are often costly in lives and in resources; people involved are desperate and have high expectations for an intervention of this kind. Unless there can be adequate follow-through, sufficient monetary and personnel resources, and the ability to sustain the project over an extended period of time (perhaps in exceptional cases up to a year or more), interventions should not be attempted.

Rule Two
A sponsor should not approach parties to a dispute without being sure it is possible to stay with the situation until the services offered are no longer required.

The sponsor's first step after being approached by a party to a conflict, or in taking an initiative in a particular situation, is to identify the parties involved so that appropriate approaches can be made to their leaders or decision makers.

This is usually not a simple task. Indeed, sponsors are likely to have to adjust their perceptions as they proceed. A simple and atypical case is one in which there are only two parties, and in which the issues can be defined clearly. In these cases, identifying the parties presents few problems. In the more typical case it will be discovered that there are many parties and different issues relating to each. When a conflict has been protracted, there will be many sub-parties because the protracted nature of a conflict leads to divisions within each party and to the emergence of rival leadership groups.

In these circumstances a comprehensive list needs to be made of parties and issues and, insofar as is possible, set out in an order that reflects the degree of each party's involvement in the conflict. For example, in a conflict in which the parties each have external backing, the resolution process should commence with those whose transactions are most affected, not with the external parties even though they appear to be more influential.

Conflict resolution will not be complete until all parties and issues on this list have been brought into the resolution process. The list may be amended by the sponsor as further insights into the nature of the conflict require.

Rule Three
The first task of a sponsor is to identify, as far as is possible, the parties and issues relevant to the conflict, and their degrees of involvement. This task is to be accomplished prior to initiating any approaches to the parties involved.

The facilitated conflict resolution process, being intensely analytical by nature, must be limited in regard to both parties and issues. The parties to a complex conflict are not all brought in together. The problem-solving process requires the separate treatment – that is, separate facilitated discussions – of those issues that relate to particular parties. However, such separate treatment must be carried out in the context of the whole situation. The discovery of options at one level enables movement of the process to more peripheral levels.

In all conflicts there are those who are immediately concerned and others who have interests in the conflict and its outcome. In industrial relations there are those immediately concerned within the company affected, and unions and other interest groups that might be affected by outcomes. In an ethnicity conflict that has wider strategic implications, the resolution of the conflict between the parties immediately concerned tends to be treated by external parties as less important than its control, which may occur through coercive means, within some great power strategic plan. In the longer term this approach is self-defeating as it leads to protracted, though perhaps submerged, conflicts, evidenced by terrorism and other means of protest.

The tendency in traditional conflict settlement procedures is for the more powerful parties to be brought into discussion, and for them to deal first with the issues that are relevant to them. This approach frequently pushes aside the central sources of the conflict. Facilitated conflict resolution seeks to begin with the core issues, and the parties directly concerned with them.

Rule Four
The starting point in the analysis and resolution of any conflict is where the closest relationships have broken down – that is, within parties involved in a conflict, or between communities within a state. The analysis then moves outward until all parties and issues are dealt with.

We have been looking at the problem of parties and issues from the perspective of an ideal situation in which a large number of facilitators is available, and in which adequate resources are available. Typically sponsors have limited resources at their disposal and are forced to concentrate at any one time on a few parties and the issues that involve them. For this reason it is important that the sponsors keep the remaining parties informed of their planning.

Rule Five
If the sponsor is not in a position to organize more than one seminar series at a time, a list of parties and issues (with some indication of the order in which they will be tackled) should be communicated to all parties. The communication should clearly point out that no discovered option that affects others will be implemented until there is discussion of it with all concerned.

SPONSORS AND DECISION MAKERS

The notion of "problem-solving" means leaving decision making in the hands of the parties until an agreement is reached which satisfies the needs of all concerned. It also involves the separate conceptualization of needs and interests. It is based on the theory that common or universal needs of both sides can be met, and that a "win–win" outcome is possible. These ideas are all outside the traditional conceptual framework of decision makers who view relationships as being based on relative power. The "entry" problem for a sponsor of facilitated conflict resolution is, therefore, a difficult one.

Even though the parties to a conflict may be aware of this problem-solving approach, they may still hesitate to seek assistance. In the case of a communal or international conflict interaction with the opposing party would be interpreted as treason. Besides, a willingness to communicate with the other side is usually perceived as an admission of weakness. This applies to all levels of interaction. For this reason, at least until there is some change in conventional wisdom, the sponsor must make the initial approaches to parties in conflict, and should not expect to be approached formally. Moreover, the sponsor must make the approaches to both parties simultaneously so that both can respond without an appearance of weakness.

The most effective method is to approach heads of governments or leadership of communities and institutions directly since it is their interest and knowledge of the process that is finally important. It is usually necessary to set out the approach in writing, to invite participation in the same form and simultaneously to all parties, and to follow up with personal visits. Experience has shown that such leaders often respond positively and quickly to the idea of informal exploratory discussions, (perhaps in the first place at an academic level), for which they do not have to take any public responsibility.

Rule Six
All communications to parties should be directly to those involved, and in the cases of large groups, at a leadership or near leadership level, or at least with the knowledge of leadership.

It is most important that sponsors are, and are seen to be, neutral and to remain neutral during the whole process. Neutrality does not imply absence of sympathy. The fact that the sponsor wants to deal with a conflict situation, and the sponsor's ability to identify with the parties concerned can, however, be misinterpreted by parties, leading to their rejection of the invitation.

Rule Seven
Communications should be simultaneous and identical with no issues raised in invitations. Follow-up visits in support of invitations should be confined to a description of the processes and detailed arrangements.

In the case of large groups, such as nations, the parties are invited to nominate representatives who are once-removed from decision makers – for example, members of parliament, personal friends in whom there is confidence, and others. The possibility of failure will then be of less political concern, and there cannot be complaints about talking with the enemy. (In many cases parties to disputes do not "recognize" each other or are at war and, therefore, cannot be seen to be involved in any direct way.) Often scholars selected by leaders can represent a party well in initial meetings because of the analytical nature of the process. An additional advantage of meetings of scholars is that the unofficial nature of the process is emphasized, and it is more acceptable to political leaders.

Rule Eight
Parties should be invited to send participants who are not official representatives, but who have easy access to decision makers.

The participation of oppositions within a ruling political party, or others whose support for agreed proposals would be required, is important because oppositions have to be supportive of results. Their involvement at an early stage helps both in the analysis of the situation and in the re-entry. However, including rival political party representatives on a team causes some difficulties since they are, especially in party parliamentary systems of government, often reluctant to help the governing party resolve a problem.

Rule Nine
The participation of all factions within a party should be sought.

ENTRY RULES

There is an obligation on the sponsors to communicate back to leaders at each significant stage, for example, after a seminar series. This will be done by participants from their own perspectives, but a report direct to decision makers maintains the link with the sponsor and the process. This link has a specific value. First, it is often necessary to interpret a final agreed statement in the light of the total proceedings, to assess the value of subsequent meetings from a perspective that is not confined to one party, and to arrange subsequent meetings perhaps with some different participants. Furthermore, a stage is reached at which there should be a transition from informal and exploratory discussions to official negotiations. It is for the sponsor to suggest when this stage is reached, and to facilitate the transfer.

There is an important confidentiality issue involved in reports to decision makers. The participants have been invited to a private discussion. It should be communicated to participants that reports to those who nominated them may be made and the reasons for making them. It may be the case that in the views of the participants the stage is not yet ripe for such reports, and the panel should take these views into consideration.

Rule Ten
Sponsors should make reports to the leadership of the parties involved after each workshop series, or at agreed stages in the total process.

Once viable options have been discovered it may be desirable to negotiate details, and for this purpose to transfer the discussions to a more official level. If some participants represent minority views within a party to the dispute, it may be appropriate at this stage to limit participation to those who represent the point of view of the formal decision makers. Participants – for example, from opposition leaderships or political parties – may play a constructive role in defining the problem and exploring a solution, but may have divided loyalties that cause them to undermine the drafting of an agreement which could give credit to the current group leadership or political party in power.

In particular, it will be necessary to work out the transition that may be necessary from exploration of options with opposition members present, to a later stage when only the representatives of decision makers may formally be involved. This is a stage for considering tactics, rather than substance. In some cases the transition may be by holding informal discussions between officials nominated by leadership within the same facilitated unofficial and quasi-academic framework. In others it may be necessary to arrange for non-official participants to be briefed on official views, and to arrange a means of direct communication during seminar discussions.

Rule Eleven
Sponsors should give special consideration to the transition stage between the unofficial discussions (which sometimes include participants representing opposition leadership or parties) and the official negotiations, and to take whatever steps are required to prepare for this even before viable options have emerged in the seminars.

This need for transition raises issues of publicity. The unofficial problem-solving process is understood to be confidential. Sometimes not even the existence of discussions is made public. The format can be perceived as an exploratory exercise, having nothing to do with decision making. In some cases an academic image is particularly valuable. However, there are bound to be leaks, especially when oppositions are included. They may wish credit, they may wish to embarrass, or they may wish to push the group leaders or government further and quicker than the latter believe they can go.

Rule Twelve
The panel should seek from participants specific agreement on what, if any, publicity is desired and generally seek to avoid any dysfunctional consequences of publicity.

PREPARATORY RULES

Inevitably there are financial problems inherent in the process. For example, governments cannot be seen to be taking an active interest in discussions with "the enemy" or the factions "in rebellion". Financial support would indicate such an active interest. Factions in rebellion usually do not have financial resources. Small groups within a union are not in a position to meet the costs involved in facilitated processes, especially when these are located in a foreign country. Minorities generally are not in a position to take time off, to travel, to pay for accommodation and incidental expenses. Furthermore, the first meeting, as has been stated, has to be at the invitation of the sponsors. The result is that the sponsors may have to be prepared to meet all the expenses, fares, maintenance, etc. of at least the first meeting. There are preparation costs, fares for visits, the costs of documentation and research. During the seminars there are all manner of ancillary costs – participants phoning home, receptions, etc.

Rule Thirteen
Before approaches are made to parties to a conflict there should be adequate funds for a first meeting so there are no unnecessary anxieties and economies.

Once the process has been initiated and when the parties have had time to establish their own funding, they should be encouraged to meet all their own expenses. This adds to their commitment. However, in many cases the parties will not be in a position to raise the substantial funds required for travel and accommodation.

Rule Fourteen
Participants should be encouraged to organize within their own communities and to contribute to their transport and accommodation costs after the first meeting.

Furthermore, experience shows that opportunities for "entry" occur suddenly and sometimes without more than a few days warning. Sometimes it is necessary to make quick visits or frequent telephone calls to "enter".

Rule Fifteen
Reserve funding is necessary so that opportunities are not missed.

Location is an important consideration for several different reasons. It is necessary to have a neutral meeting point. At the same time it must be one that enables communication among participants and those who nominated them. It should be as convenient as possible to participants and facilitators. The cost factor also enters in here.

Rule Sixteen
The sponsor must reach agreement with those who are nominating participants on the location of the meeting place, a neutral environment being the main concern.

Accommodation raises some important issues. In some cases when parties are in violent conflict there are tensions when they meet and it is less embarrassing for all concerned if they are accommodated separately. Even when this is not the case it is desirable that parties be accommodated separately to prevent interactions outside the facilitated structure of the workshop.

Rule Seventeen
Parties should be met separately and housed separately if possible.

Seating can present some problems. Each situation has to be handled differently according to circumstances. For example, when participants are in a violent conflict and feel deeply about, for example, "atrocities", they have difficulty in being polite even over coffee. In the beginning they do not like to sit facing each other during discussions. Panel members must be in easy verbal contact with each other and so must members of each party. Usually it is convenient for the panel to be at its own table facing the participants. As there are only two parties involved each party can have a table facing each other and the panel at an angle of 45 degrees – forming a triangle. This helps to ensure that communication is through the panel and not direct. It also enables the parties to be in a face-to-face dialogue when they are ready for that.

Rule Eighteen
Thought needs to be given in advance to seating arrangements, and changes should be made if, for any reason, the group dynamics require this.

It will be noted that no seating is provided above for observers or recorders. The presence of any persons other than panel members is a constraint, and recording – except the notes taken by participants and the panel – inhibits the kind of interaction sought.

There is only one exception to this rule, and that is the presence, when it is really necessary, of an interpreter. Often translation can be effective by seating participants whose knowledge of the language being used is inadequate next to participants in the same party who have no problems with it. Formal interpreting can be disruptive of interaction and should be avoided if it is clear that there is no real problem.

When an interpreter is employed, it should be not merely a professional interpreter, but one who also knows the language of conflict resolution. The concepts used in discussing conflict resolution are not readily translated and a thorough knowledge of the language to be interpreted is necessary, rather than just a conversational knowledge.

Rule Nineteen
There should not be any observers nor should there be any provision for recording, even though the parties express no objections. However, appropriate interpreters should be available as required.

At times there is a need for discussion within parties or within the panel during seminar sessions. Sometimes separate meeting places are required at short notice, for example, when there is disagreement amongst members of a group.

Rule Twenty
There should be provision for small conference rooms near the main meeting room in which parties and the panel can each meet separately.

The aim of the facilitated discussion is to encourage direct interaction resulting in the greatest accuracy in interpretations of motivations and intentions. The environment needs to assist this in every way.

Rule Twenty-One
The sponsor should ensure that the general environment of the meetings and the comfort of the participants contributes to the facilitated discussions.

Sometimes parties will be from different cultures and have difficulty over names. There will be introductions at the outset, but adequate reminders are necessary. Name tags on the person are not required and would not be worn after the first day. Place names are useful.

Rule Twenty-Two
There should be lists circulated of participants and panel members, and clear name displays in front of each.

It is important that the participants understand the process. They should know what is expected of them before they meet in seminar sessions, what kind of expositions will be required of them at the initial meeting and generally what the rules are. Some information will have been conveyed in the invitation and the follow-up visit. But some clear indication in advance of what will take place at the first meeting is important.

Rule Twenty-Three
Parties should be prepared for the first meeting, know what is expected of them, be aware of the role that will be enacted by the panel, and generally be made to feel comfortable about the process.

THE THIRD PARTY

The fact that the facilitated process is an analytical one requires that the parties concerned can come together to examine each other's underlying motivations and goals in a direct interactive way. It must also allow them to define issues and make reliable assessments of the costs of their positions regardless of whether the parties are nations, communities, small groups or individuals, community and central authority, or community and community.

This process is in contradistinction to traditional practices in which the third party tends to consult separately with those involved in a dispute. It is clearly at variance with traditional and diplomatic practices, in which relations are severed at times of high tension and conflict and in which governments operate through "protecting powers". The absence of direct interaction has been a handicap for mediators who move to and fro between parties. Hence the next rule is indispensible for facilitated conflict resolution.

Rule Twenty-Four
Parties to conflicts must be placed in a direct analytical and non-bargaining dialogue.

The above rule implies the likely failure of processes involving direct bargaining from predetermined positions, or mediation or other processes that rely upon a third party to put forward proposals or to apply normative considerations. Yet direct interaction clearly requires the presence of a third party to offset any tendency for contending parties to see only that which they expect to see, and to prevent them from lapsing into bargaining or adversarial interaction. In advising parties, sponsors should emphasize the need for a third party in any situation of tension, and should discourage direct interaction except during the facilitation process.

Rule Twenty-Five
A third party should be present in any dialogue among conflicting parties who are seeking to understand their conflict and to find an agreed resolution.

The role of a third party is not to mediate in the sense of suggesting seemingly reasonable compromises. The third-party role is to facilitate in the ways suggested above. This distinction between *settlement* and *resolution* is important. There can be a settlement of a dispute by the use of superior power, or by an enforced ruling from a court. Equally, an obligation to accept the findings of a mediator can lead to a settlement. The current consensus view is that compromise is the best possible outcome of a conflict. However, in facilitated resolution of serious conflicts, compromise must be avoided because the issues being discussed are ones on which there cannot be compromise: identity, security, recognition, and others to which reference has already been made. There may have to be compromise on interests, which can be made the subject of some bargaining, but human needs, and sometimes cultural values, are not subject to compromise. Attempts to arrive at compromises are a reason for stalemates in negotiation.

For the same reason a distinction must be made between goals and tactics. The goals cannot be compromised, but the means to reach the goals can. For example, possession of territory can be a tactic for attaining the goal of security. But security itself can best be secured by tactics that do not threaten or lessen the security of others.

Rule Twenty-Six
The role of the panel in conflict resolution is not to seek compromises. It is initially to facilitate analysis so that goals and tactics, interests, values and needs, can be clarified, and later to help deduce possible outcomes on the basis of the analysis made.

The third party has a key function to ensure that neither it nor the participants are working on false basic hypotheses about the nature of the particular conflict under discussion. There will be preconceived notions drawn from the media and official statements. It must be discovered whether the conflict is due to aggressiveness and leadership problems, fundamental drives of identity, recognition and distributive justice, or confusion over needs and interests. The panel must ensure that the opposing parties have every opportunity to assess each other's motivations, and accurately to determine for themselves the nature of their conflict.

To make this possible, panel members must know what questions to ask, how to distinguish tactics from goals, and how to encourage the parties to reveal their deep motivations, values and intents. These tasks require panel members not merely to have a broad knowledge of their own speciality and of conflict theories, but also to be familiar with theories of functionalism, institutions, legitimacy and such relevant topics. They must have a knowledge of the way in which the normative and power/coercive philosophy has evolved, and must recognize its strengths and weaknesses. Further, they must understand the logical relationships between traditional assumptions based on the dominance of authorities and institutions, and the defensive strategies that these theories produce, since this is the conceptual framework in which parties to disputes will be arguing. Similarly, panel members must be informed fully of the alternative human needs approach, the problem-solving strategies that are its logical outcome, how it has evolved from traditional thought, and relevant interdisciplinary studies.

Rule Twenty-Seven
Panel members should be drawn from several key disciplines, they should be widely informed of different approaches in their own fields, have an adequate knowledge of conflict theories, and be experienced in the facilitation process, so as to help the parties to arrive at an accurate definition of the situation under examination.

One perspective which is clearly important is the gender perspective. It is important to have panels that comprise both sexes. Sometimes an ethnic or class perspective may be important.

Rule Twenty-Eight
It is necessary to have balanced viewpoints and perspectives represented on the panel, including gender, and where relevant, ethnic and class perspectives.

In the final analysis the parties to a conflict are the real experts. The conflict is theirs and they must determine its nature by their own analysis of it. The data, facts and interpretations must come from the perceptions and experiences of the opposing parties, not from the panel. For this reason panel members must not be prejudiced by preconceived views based on so-called expert knowledge of local conditions, as may easily be the case if a panel member is exclusively a specialist in respect to that conflict. All persons who serve on the panel should have the capability of placing the particular situation in the wider perspective of social relationships.

Rule Twenty-Nine
The panel should not include persons who have made an exclusive speciality of the particular conflict being analysed, or of the region in which it takes place.

From time to time in all areas of thought there are significant paradigm shifts. In the analysis and explanation of conflict a consensus could emerge in support of one particular philosophical approach. Such a consensus would make it seem unnecessary for different philosophies and disciplines to be taken into account by the panel. However, even within an approach wholly oriented towards one particular philosophy, the testing function remains an important one. In some conflict situations leadership roles may seem to play a dominant part. For example, it may appear that there is a clear struggle between two factions for political power for its own sake. The power struggle could be a sufficient explanation of the conflict, suggesting the need for some third-party intervention to control the violence. Within a problem-solving framework the primary purpose of the interaction would be to demonstrate the costs and consequences of leadership interests and to include them within the problem-solving process.

Rule Thirty

Endeavors should be made to bridge the traditional explanations of power rivalries and problem-solving approaches by considering all and incorporating the relevant ones into the problem-solving process.

Panel members are likely to have different approaches, particularly if they come from different disciplines. They may have some difficulty in communicating with one another. Yet in their role as a panel they must work together to ensure that the right questions are asked at the right time, that the parties are not confused by different approaches, that the testing and constructive analyses are followed through logically on the basis of an agreed process.

Rule Thirty-One

Panel members must prepare and confer before and during the seminar, even adjourning discussions for this purpose, so that they are always acting together and with mutual understanding.

In order to have a spread of disciplines and approaches, and yet keep the numbers small enough for group dynamics to operate, the ideal panel is composed of four or five members, with about ten participants who are involved in the dispute. This can present a problem, for panel members ideally should know each other well, interact well, be selfless in not wanting to intervene or to make presentations merely to enact a role, be prepared to spend the time necessary in preparation and follow up, and be present all of the time at future discussions.

Rule Thirty-Two

Panelists must be selected, not only for their professionalism in facilitation, but also for their talents and abilities to work within a team, and even then, only if they can be available as and when required.

THE ANALYTICAL STAGE

The workshops or seminars are meetings, four or five days in duration, that comprise one stage or phase of discussion. There may be several seminar series conducted before the discovery of agreed options. In addition, there are likely to be other seminars concerned with the details of potential official agreements. Before discussion at each of the stages, a few general observations on the process and on the rules should be elaborated either by the sponsor or a panel member.

During the seminar sessions no communication of substance should take place except across the table in front of the panel. Private communications on matters of substance – as occur in a bargaining or negotiating framework – are dysfunctional. All concerned should share any communication, observation or interpretation. In a second or subsequent series of meetings, when participants know each other, this is sometimes difficult to control. Some participants try to pursue their own personal interests and proposals privately. Nonetheless, if the panel itself is aware of the need for open communication it can influence behavior in this respect.

It is particularly important for panel members not to communicate privately with participants. Participants naturally scrutinize relationships between panel members and participants from the other side. While they themselves try to communicate particular observations privately with panel members – frequently about how deceptive the other side is – they lose confidence in panel members if they observe them communicating with others.

It will be found convenient to have lunches and sometimes evening dinners together. They tend to be working sessions. It is desirable, therefore, if a round table can be found to accommodate everyone, for it assists in making conversation a group activity, rather than many separate conversations.

Rule Thirty-Three
Participants should be asked not to discuss matters of substance outside the conference room. Coffee breaks, lunches and other social occasions should be organized to discourage participants from communicating privately either with other participants or with panel members on matters of substance. Panel members should not communicate with participants separately except on a social basis.

There are reasons for limiting personal interactions between members of the opposing parties, contrary to what may be thought intuitively to be desirable. One task of the panel is to ensure that participants do not alter significantly their own value systems and perceptions of the nature of the conflict as a result of the group dynamics and friendships which develop during the process. When they "re-enter" their own society they will have a problem conveying any new ideas to decision makers in a convincing way if this happens. They have to return with an option that meets the needs of their constituency who have not undergone the facilitated experience, and they have to be in a position to sell it, not on the basis of some altered personal relationship or changed perception of the opposing party, but on the basis of the merits of the option discovered.

Rule Thirty-Four
In its procedures and in its observations and advisements, the panel must keep in mind the re-entry problem of the participants.

The panel operates as a team, throwing the ball to the player whose specialization or participation seems to be most relevant at the time. In a panel in which members know each other, have prepared adequately and have had experience, there should be no need for a chairperson as such.

There is, however, a need for a person who acts in the role of host or hostess. This person could be the sponsor. This person may or may not otherwise play an active role. This person calls the meeting to order, outlines the program, decides when breaks are needed, and deals with organizational matters. The host chairperson also observes participants and ensures that all participants are given the opportunity to express themselves during the intense discussions. Panel members focussing on some particular aspect are apt not to observe participants who are not taking an active part at the particular moment. However, panel members also need to observe participant responses for consideration later during panel consultation.

Rule Thirty-Five
The panel acts as a unit in conducting the seminar, with one member acting as the host/hostess and informal chairperson.

There is no formal agenda, but there is a clear understanding among the panel on successive steps. The panel moves the discussion from a consideration of the situation as perceived by the parties when they arrive, through analysis of the situation and the values and goals sought, to the discovery of options.

Rule Thirty-Six
The step-by-step progression from initial perceptions, through analysis of the situation, to evaluation of these perceptions and to finding an agreed definition, to exploration of options that meet the needs of all, should be maintained. However, there should be no fixed agenda of either specific items or timing.

The panel must exercise tight control of the discussions among participants to ensure that the rules of procedure are observed. Sometimes panel members, accustomed to academic free-flowing seminar discussions and the exercise of a great deal of mutual tolerance, are reluctant to intervene and control in this way. However, in a facilitated conflict resolution situation such control is an essential part of the process. If exercised early and consistently there is less difficulty at later stages, when deep feelings are being vented.

Rule Thirty-Seven
The panel asks the participants to observe certain rules of procedure and makes it clear that it is the role of the panel to ensure that these are observed, that this is part of the process, and that this control is necessary for the success of the discussions.

If analysis is to be successful it is important to prevent presentation and discussion of any particular proposal until analysis is complete. There may be participants who are sure they have the answers, and even though they are discouraged by the panel from putting forward proposals, they will present all their questions and comments in relation to them. The panel should seek to control this situation. It is this process which makes the analytical-facilitated discussion distinctively different from the bargaining and negotiating framework where there are usually rival proposals being discussed from the outset.

Rule Thirty-Eight
There should be no proposals put forward by any side until the analysis of the situation is complete and a definition of the situation is agreed.

After the participants have given their first presentations it is necessary to allow for questions of clarification. Such questions, however, can quickly get out of control and become point-making or debating questions. This possibility draws attention to the need for control of discussion by the panel, and to achieve this members must be mutually supportive. If debate occurs at this stage the analytical process is threatened. If control seems impossible, as it sometimes is when levels of tension and suspicion are high, then it is better not to have questions of clarification until all presentations have been completed, and then only after a summary presentation which the panel makes when it feeds back to the participants the main points they have made.

Rule Thirty-Nine
The initial exposition should be heard without interruptions. Following this only questions of clarification should be asked by participants.

The panel should tell participants that the opening statements should deal primarily with the *values* and *goals* at stake in the conflict. Participants will usually deliver the standard type of initial exposition, for at this stage they will confuse values and goals with tactics and their immediate conflict objectives. However, the request from the panel puts participants on notice that the panel is focussing on values and goals. It should also be recognized that participants may not have thought deeply about these matters.

Rule Forty
When the panel asks the participants to make their opening statements, they should ask them to focus on the values and goals at stake in the conflict situation.

After all the participants have made their opening statements, and after controlled questions of clarification, the panel will pose questions of clarification, especially in relation to values and goals. These subjects will have been touched on indirectly or by implication, rather than stated. The rest of the first day is usually spent on such clarifications.

Rule Forty-One
The panel poses questions of clarification, especially in relation to values and goals.

At this stage the panel should have sufficient information to make some analysis of values and goals, shared and in conflict. At a private evening meeting the panel should then prepare a discussion paper for the next day.

Rule Forty-Two
The panel should prepare (overnight probably) a statement of what appear to be shared and unshared values for submission to the participants.

When the participants receive the discussion paper, they will maintain that they have been misunderstood and attempt to restate their views, and they will disagree over values that the panel has stated are not shared. At this stage, some real analysis begins and stated positions tend to be pushed aside. The participants will tend to address each other rather than the panel.

Rule Forty-Three
The panel should allow discussions which help to clarify values to proceed freely, while intervening constantly to ensure that the dialogue remains analytical and does not regress to point-scoring debating exchanges.

From this point on the subjects for discussion have to be decided more pragmatically. The values discussion may be the most revealing, but it will be found that the participants need a lot of help in understanding the expositions of the opposing side. There will be disbelief, hints of deception, and a high level of distrust when values are expressed in a way that does not accord with preconceived notions.
It is at this stage that the panel has an important professional role to play, for a great deal of psychology and political psychology becomes relevant. At this stage the panel should be prepared to play an academic role and place the particular conflict in the context of other conflicts which have similar features. Panel members should also explain the significance of needs and values and how they differ from interests.

Rule Forty-Four
The panel should take the opportunity to communicate any relevant knowledge which will help the participants to interpret what is being said. The panel may refer to other cases of conflict, to research findings on perception, and to theories of behavior.

When the input from the panel is received, the participants will learn a great deal, adopt a different language, and employ new concepts, at least when the input from the panel is relevant. If it is not relevant, the participants will show boredom and restlessness. Incidentally, this is a learning opportunity for panel members also, providing valuable information on conflict. At this stage political philosophies, approaches and theories of cooperation and conflict are put to the test. It is in this sense that the total process should be regarded and treated as a research project with each seminar series leading to refinements of theory and practice.

Rule Forty-Five
The panel must be sensitive to audience response for there will be viewpoints and theories that are quickly absorbed because of their relevance, and others that will provoke no response because they are deemed not to be relevant to experience.

During the clarifications of values and goals, several key issues will emerge that go to the heart of the conflict. These may include leadership problems, identity issues, fears for the preservation of cultural values, and others.

Rule Forty-Six
The panel should move the discussion to the key issues once there has been clarity of goals and values. They should ensure that all discussions be kept within the analytical framework that has been established.

At this stage the panel will be considering the main propositions to include in an agreed conclusion. These propositions will be short statements based on issues and concerns and agreements that emerged during all of the discussions. Sometimes an interjection or a passing comment will contain a hint of some concern which will indicate that a proposition should be explored. In preparation for the drafting of agreed propositions, and to structure discussion of the many issues on the table, it is useful for the panel to prepare general propositions for consideration. As these will be more explanatory than the short statements which will appear in a final statement, they will help the participants to articulate and explain the propositions that will be agreed finally. This practice is designed to reinforce the learning and understanding process, and to help the participants in their own exposition, thus preparing them for their "re-entry".

Preparation of a list of proposals, really a summary in proposition form of all that has taken place, is a major task for the panel. It usually has to be accomplished overnight. The panel will have taken notes of discussions from their different perspectives, and their task now is to ensure that all viewpoints are covered. It is important to include propositions which seem to be in doubt, which may have been implied but not articulated, and others which may have been mentioned but passed over without discussion.

Rule Forty-Seven
The panel should prepare a statement of the general behavioral propositions that have emerged. This list will be discussed in great detail.

The end goal of the first seminar series can usually be no more than a short statement of propositions on values and goals – that is, a definition of the conflict. The discussion of special issues will have clarified the values even more. It will be found that even if there were more time (and four days is about the limit that is possible for participants to be available) it could not be employed usefully. There will be fatigue, some euphoria, and a sense that this is about as far as the discussion can go prior to reporting back.

Rule Forty-Eight
The panel should prepare a draft statement of agreed propositions. It should be submitted to the participants when the panel feels they are ready to give it their detailed consideration.

THE SEARCH FOR OPTIONS

Whether it be at the first seminar series (which is unlikely) or at a second some months later after discussions with leaders who have nominated participants, the next step is for facilitated discussion in which the parties are helped to deduce from the agreed propositions what changes in structures, institutions and policies are required to implement them. At this stage interests surface, especially the interests of those who fear the consequences of change. There is less analysis and far more assertion and defense of positions.

There will be a tendency for the status quo party to be law-and-order oriented and it is necessary to break away from the traditional notions of power, majority control, power balances, human rights conferred on minorities, and other traditional power notions that have led to failure of mediation and negotiation. The role of the panel is twofold, first to make sure the real costs of change and refusal to change are assessed (for example, the likelihood of continued conflict, a deteriorating economy, adverse foreign relations and so on), and second, to be creative regarding possible options.

Options must be deduced from agreed statements of values. Whatever conclusions emerge as a result of logical deductions from values, they should be translated into policies, institutions and structures, even ones that seem novel.

Rule Forty-Nine

The panel should help the participants to deduce from the agreed propositions those changes in structures, institutions and policies that are required to carry agreed propositions into effect and should seek discussion on them.

In many cases it will be found that participants are not ready to look ahead to future options. They will discuss the longer-term goals in principle, but they are living in a complex conflict situation that has a momentum of its own, due to vested interests in the conflict itself. It will be necessary to give consideration to transition steps. However, care must be taken to relate transition to ultimate goals so that the former will not destroy the latter.

There is a warning note to be sounded in this regard. In a complex conflict situation there is always a tendency to seek tension-reduction measures as a means to improve confidence and move toward an agreement. Tension-reduction measures, however, can have the opposite effect. They can make the conflict bearable, create role and other interests in the continued conflict and institutionalize it. While every proposal must be considered on its own merits, this danger needs to be kept in mind.

Rule Fifty

Attempts should be made to arrive at some transition steps that pave the way for longer term solutions.

At this point the panel has to show imagination. While there are universal patterns of conflict behavior, each conflict situation has its own unique environmental, cultural, political and external dimensions. If the conflict involves communities, resolution may be achieved only by a break from traditional institutional forms of government and a consideration of forms of decentralization or zonal systems that border on separation. Similarly in industrial conflicts some radical changes in structure might seem appropriate – for example, some interactive decision making between management and work force.

Options must evolve from the specific needs and interests of the parties and not from some catalogue of available structures. The participants, however, are usually too caught up in their own problems to consider alternative solutions. Usually they do not have the knowledge background to design innovative approaches. The success of the facilitation process will, in large part, depend on the abilities of panel members to come up with possible models for participants to consider. It may be appropriate to illustrate models by symbolic drawings or to make some further elaboration on needs theory and its applications. (A drawing board should be available.)

Rule Fifty-One
The panel must assume a responsibility for putting forward a range of possible options for discussion without putting forward any firm proposals.

POLICIES

A stage emerges at which it is relevant to discuss policies, especially the policies to be followed during transition from conflict to peace. Typically industry will have been disrupted in a prolonged industrial conflict. In a communal conflict economies will have been destroyed, armed forces will be in control at ground level, and communication will have been disrupted, both physically and behaviorally. The panel will not be informed on local details and it cannot be of much help except to maintain the controlled dialogue.

It may be necessary for the sponsor to make arrangements for many ad hoc seminars on particular issues between those concerned. The sponsors must be guided by the parties, but should not regard the work as complete until discussions on transition policies which look to the future can take place readily between the parties.

Rule Fifty-Two
Toward the end of the discussions on values, goals and structures, the panel should make sure to include a preliminary discussion on transitional policies. It should also find out what special seminars may be required in the future.

RE-ENTRY AND FOLLOW-UP

If circumstances allow, the first seminar series should result in agreement to meet again, and in establishing a means for the parties and the panel to stay in communication. Participants should be asked to agree to relay all communications to all participants, not just to certain selected individuals. Such communications will relate mostly to organizational matters and not to issues of substance.

The re-entering parties should be encouraged to establish a base so that they can widen their contacts, and thus both promote the process and prepare the relevant audience to consider the outcomes.

Rule Fifty-Three
The panel should ensure adequate time on the last day of a seminar series for discussion of next steps and means of continued communication pending a further meeting.

Both during and between seminar series there is frequently a need for discussion within parties. If participants represent different factions within a party, differences among them will emerge that need to be sorted out before there can be further progress. Sponsors and panel members, aware of time constraints, tend to keep the participants at work in seminars even in the evenings. This practice can prove to be dysfunctional. It may also be dysfunctional to convene a seminar series too early. As differences within parties may not come to the notice of the sponsors, a good general rule is to allow free time during a seminar series and to allow the participants to set dates for future meetings.

Rule Fifty-Four
The panel must be alert to differences arising within parties and provide time for discussion within and between seminar series. If there are conflicting factions within the parties, it may be necessary to provide for the facilitation of their conflicts before proceeding with another seminar series.

There is a danger that participants will become an in-group and be alienated from others at home who may know less about the process, but who wish to be part of it. As the agenda shifts from one seminar series to another, participants should be changed, with some overlap to ensure continuity and make unnecessary the preliminary steps of initiation into the process.

Rule Fifty-Five
Each meeting should build on the last so there is a natural progression from analysis of the conflict, to a deduction of the required political structures, to negotiation of the interests involved in making the required changes, and to the discussion on policies. Participants should be selected accordingly.

A related danger is that the meetings may become institutionalized and have no end point. While situations vary, generally two or three seminar series should be sufficient to arrive at options for authorities to consider. Any further meetings should be confined to specific aspects of the general problem. Sometimes such ad hoc meetings are best located at the scene of the conflict.

Rule Fifty-Six
The panel should always have in mind the earliest possible termination of the seminar series, moving as quickly as possible from definition and options to consideration of consequences and implementation.

ELECTRONIC COMMUNICATION

Perhaps the main problem to be encountered in facilitated conflict resolution is direct yet private communication between parties in conflict. In practice all manner of subterfuges are adopted. There has been no experience so far with facilitated conflict resolution employing fax and modem methods of communication which simulate a controlled interaction around the table. Looking to the future this could well be the norm at least at an early stage of interaction. Certainly, the training of facilitators should include the use of such communication techniques.

NOTE

1. This Appendix comprises adapted extracts from John W. Burton (1987) *Resolving Deep-Rooted Conflict: A Handbook*, Lanham, Md: University Press of America.

References

ABEL, RICHARD L. (ed.) (1982a) *The Politics of Informal Justice, Volume 1: The American Experience*, New York: Academic Press.

ABEL, RICHARD L. (ed.) (1982b) *The Politics of Informal Justice, Volume 2: Comparative Studies*, New York: Academic Press.

ADMINISTRATIVE CONFERENCE OF THE UNITED STATES (1986) "Agencies' Use of Alternative Means of Dispute Resolution," §305.86–3.

ALEVY, DANIEL I., BUNKER, BARBARA B., DOOB, LEONARD W., FOLTZ, WILLIAM J., FRENCH, NANCY, KLEIN, EDWARD B. and MILLER, JAMES C. (1974) "Rationale, Research, and Role Relations in the Stirling Workshop," *Journal of Conflict Resolution*, 18 (2):276–84.

ALGER, CHADWICK F. (1977) "'Foreign' Policies of U.S. Publics," *International Studies Quarterly*, 21(2).

ALGER, CHADWICK F. (1978–9) "Role of People in the Future Global Order", *Alternatives IV*, 233–62.

AMERICAN ARBITRATION ASSOCIATION (AAA) (1984) "Alternative Dispute Resolution Procedures."

AMERICAN ARBITRATION ASSOCIATION (AAA) (1986) "Mini-Trial Procedures."

AMERICAN BAR ASSOCIATION (ABA), Family Law Section (1984) "Standards of Practice for Lawyer Mediators in Family Disputes," *Family Law Quarterly*, 18: 363–8.

AMERICAN BAR ASSOCIATION, Standing Committee on Dispute Resolution (1987) *ADR: An ADR Primer*.

AMERICAN BAR ASSOCIATION, Standing Committee on Dispute Resolution (1988) *Dispute Resolution*, Issue 23.

AMERICAN BAR ASSOCIATION, Standing Committee on Dispute Resolution (1989) *Dispute Resolution*, Issue 25.

AMY, DOUGLAS J. (1987) *The Politics of Environmental Mediation*, New York: Columbia University Press.

ARGYRIS, CHRIS (1983) *Reasoning, Learning, and Action: Individual and Organization*, San Francisco: Jossey–Bass.

ARONSON, ELLIOT et al. (1978) *The Jigsaw Classroom*, Beverly Hills, Calif.: Sage.

ASSOCIATION OF FAMILY AND CONCILIATION COURTS (1984) "Standards of Practice for Family Mediators," *Family Law Quarterly*, 17: 455–60.

AUERBACH, JEROLD (1983) *Justice Without Law?*, New York: Oxford University Press.

AXELROD, ROBERT (1984) *The Evolution of Cooperation*, New York: Basic Books.

BACK, KURT W. (1972) *Beyond Words: The Story of Sensitivity Training and the Encounter Movement*, New York: Russell Sage Foundation.

BAILEY, SYDNEY D. (1985) "Non-Official Mediation in Disputes: Reflections on Quaker Experience," *International Affairs*, 61 (2): 205–22.

BARNETT, RANDY E. (1981) "Restitution: A New Paradigm of Criminal Justice," in Galaway, B. and Hudson, J. (eds), *Perspectives on Crime Victims*, St Louis: The C. V. Mosby Co.

BENDAHMANE, DIANE B. and McDONALD, Jr, JOHN W. (eds) (1986) *Perspectives on Negotiations: Four Case Studies and Interpretations*, Foreign Service Institute, US Department of State.

BENEDICT, RUTH (1959) *Patterns of Culture*, New York: New American Library.

BENJAMIN, A. J. and LEVI, A. M. (1979) "Process Minefields in Intergroup Conflict Resolution: The Sdot Yam Workshop," *Journal of Applied Behavioral Science*, 13 (4): 507–19.

BENNE, KENNETH D., BRADFORD, LELAND P. and LIPPITT, RONALD (1964) "The Laboratory Method," in Bradford, L. P., Gibb, J. R., and Benne, K. D. (eds), *T-Group Theory and Laboratory Method*, New York: John Wiley.

BENNIS, WARREN G. (1962) "Goals and Meta-Goals of Laboratory Training," *Human Relations Training News*, 6 (5): 1–4.

BINGHAM, GAIL (1986) *Resolving Environmental Disputes: a Decade of Experience*, Washington, D.C.: The Conservation Foundation.

BLAKE, ROBERT R., MOUTON, JANE SRYGLEY, and SLOMA, RICHARD L. (1965) "The Union–Management Intergroup Laboratory: Strategy for Resolving Intergroup Conflict," *Journal of Applied Behavioral Science*, 1(2): 25–57.

BLAKE, ROBERT R. and MOUTON, JANE SRYGLEY (1985) *Solving Costly Organizational Conflicts*, San Francisco: Jossey–Bass.

BOEHRINGER, G. H., BAYLEY, J., ZERUOLIS, V. and BOEHRINGER, K. (1974) "Stirling: the Destructive Application of Group Techniques to a Conflict," *Journal of Conflict Resolution*, 18(2): 257–75.

BOLDUC, DANIELLE S. (1989) "Implications for Restorative Justice: Mediator Styles and Mediator Behavior," paper presented at the North American Conference on Peacemaking and Conflict Resolution (NCPCR).

BRADLEY, RICHARD H. (1988) "Managing Major Metropolitan Areas: Applying Collaborative Planning and Negotiation Techniques," *Mediation Quarterly*, 20: 45–56.

BRAMS, STEVEN J. (1987) "New Rules for Resolving Disputes," unpublished paper.

BROOME, BENJAMIN J. and KEEVER, DAVID B. (1986) "Facilitating Group Communication: The Interactive Management Approach," Fairfax, Va: Center for Interactive Management.

BRUBAKER, DAVE and KRAYBILL, RON (1987) "Finding a Field," *Conciliation Quarterly* (Winter).

BURTON, JOHN W. (1969) *Conflict and Communication: The Use of Controlled Communication in International Relations*, London: Macmillan.

BURTON, JOHN W. (1987) *Resolving Deep-Rooted Conflict: A Handbook*, Lanham, Md: University Press of America.

BURTON, JOHN W. (1990) *Conflict: Resolution and Provention*, New York: St Martin's Press.

BURTON, JOHN W. (ed.) (1990) *Conflict: Human Needs Theory*, New York; St Martin's Press.

BURTON, JOHN W. and DUKES, FRANK (eds) (1990) *Conflict: Practices in Management, Settlement and Resolution*, New York: St Martin's Press.

BUSH, ROBERT BARUCH (1984) "Dispute Resolution Alternatives and the Goals of Civil Justice: Jurisdictional Principles for Process Choice," *Wisconsin Law Review*, 893: 932–62.

BUSH, ROBERT BARUCH (1988) "Defining Quality in Dispute Resolution: Taxonomies and Anti-Taxonomies of Quality Arguments," Disputes Processing Research Program, Working Papers 8–9, Institute for Legal Studies, University of Wisconsin–Madison Law School (June).

CAIDEN, GERALD E. (ed.) (1983a) *International Handbook of the Ombudsman, Vol. I: Evolution and Present Function*, Westport, Conn.: Greenwood Press.

CAIDEN, GERALD E. (1983b) *International Handbook of the Ombudsman, Vol. II: Country Surveys*, Westport, Conn.: Greenwood Press.

CAMPBELL, LINDA E. G. and JOHNSTON, JANET R. (1986) "Multifamily Mediation: The Use of Groups to Resolve Child Custody Disputes," *Mediation Quarterly*, 14/15: 137–62.

CARPENTER, SUSAN L. and KENNEDY, W. J. D. (1988) *Managing Public Disputes*, San Francisco: Jossey–Bass.

CENTER FOR DISPUTE RESOLUTION (1986) "Merits of Mediation."

CHRISTAKIS, ALEXANDER N. and KEEVER, DAVID B., (1984) "An Overview of Interactive Management," Fairfax, Va: Center for Interactive Management.

COATES, ROBERT V. (1985) "Victim Meets Offender: An Evaluation of Victim–Offender Reconciliation Programs," Valparaiso, Indiana: PACT.

COMMUNITY BOARD CENTER FOR POLICY AND TRAINING (undated) "The Conciliation Process: Objectives and Work."

COMMUNITY MEDIATION CENTER OF CHARLOTTESVILLE–ALBEMARLE (1985) "By-Laws."

COMMUNITY RELATIONS SERVICE (undated) "Groundrules and Procedures Governing Mediation of Court-Referred Disputes."

COOLEY, JOHN W. (1986) "Arbitration vs. Mediation – Explaining the Differences," *Judicature*, 69(5): 263–69.

COULSON, ROBERT (1982) "The Functions of Arbitration," *Peace and Change*, 8(2/3): 65–72.

COULSON, ROBERT (1983) *Fighting Fair: Family Mediation Will Work for You*, New York: Free Press.

COUNCIL ON THE ROLE OF COURTS, Jethro Lieberman (ed.) (1984) *The Role of Courts in American Society*, St. Paul: West.

DANZIG, RICHARD (1973) "Towards the Creation of a Complementary, Decentralized System of Criminal Justice," *Stanford Law Review*, 26(1): 1–54.

DAVIS, ALBIE M. (1986) "Teaching Ideas: Dispute Resolution at an Early Age," *Negotiation Journal*, 2(3). 287–97.

DAVIS, ALBIE M. and PORTER, KIT (1985) "Tales of Schoolyard Mediation," *Update on Law Related Education*.

DAVIS, ALBIE M. and SALEM, RICHARD A. (1984) "Dealing with Power Imbalances in the Mediation of Interpersonal Disputes," *Mediation Quarterly*, 6: 17–26.

DELGADO, RICHARD (1988) "ADR and the Dispossessed: Recent Books About the Deformalization Movement," *Law and Social Inquiry*, 13 (1): 145–54.

DEUTSCH, MORTON (1973) *The Resolution of Conflict: Constructive and Destructive Processes*, New Haven, Conn.: Yale University Press.

DOI, HERMAN S. (1985) "A Statutory Classical View of the Ombudsperson," in Society of Professionals in Dispute Resolution, *The Elements of Good Practice in Dispute Resolution*, 1984 Proceedings, Twelfth Annual Conference.

DOOB, LEONARD W. (1981) *The Pursuit of Peace*, Westport, Conn.: Greenwood Press.

DOOB, LEONARD W. (ed.) (1970) *Resolving Conflict in Africa*, New Haven, Conn.: Yale University Press.

DOOB, LEONARD and FOLTZ, WILLIAM J. (1974) "The Impact of a Workshop Upon Grass-Roots Leaders in Belfast," *Journal of Conflict Resolution*, 18(2): 237–56.

DOOB, LEONARD W. and FOLTZ, WILLIAM J. (1973) "The Belfast Workshop," *Journal of Conflict Resolution*, 17(3): 489–512.

DRUCKMAN, DANIEL (1986) "Four Cases of Conflict Management: Lessons Learned," in Bendahmane, D. B. and McDonald, Jr, J. W. (eds), *Perspectives on Negotiation*, Foreign Service Institute, US Department of State.

EDWARDS, HARRY T. (1986) "Alternative Dispute Resolution: Panacea or Anathema?," *Harvard Law Review*, 99: 668–84.

EMERY, ROBERT E. and WYER, MELISSA M. (1987) "Divorce Mediation," *American Psychologist*, 42(2): 472–80.

EMERY, R. E., SHAW, D. S. and JACKSON, J. A. (1987) "A Clinical Description of a Model of Child Custody Mediation," in Vincent, J. P. (ed.), *Advances in Family Intervention, Assessment, and Theory*, vol. 4, Greenwich, Conn.: JAI Press.

ENTWISTLE, BASIL and ROOTS, JOHN McCOOK (1967) *Moral Re-Armament*, Los Angeles: Pace Publications.

ESSER, JOHN P. (1988) "Evaluations of Dispute Processing: We Don't Know What We Think and We Don't Think What We Know," Disputes Processing Research Program, Working Papers 8–10, Institute for Legal Studies, University of Wisconsin–Madison Law School (August).

FEDERAL MEDIATION AND CONCILIATION SERVICE (FMCS) (1981) "Mediation and Labour Management Relations in the Federal Service."

FELSTINER, WILLIAM L. F., ABEL, RICHARD L. and SARAT, AUSTIN (1981) "The Emergence and Transformation of Disputes: Naming, Blaming, Claiming . . .," *Law & Society Review*, 15(3–4): 631–54.

FISHER, ROGER and URY, WILLIAM (1981) *Getting to Yes: Negotiating Agreement Without Giving In*, Boston, Mass.: Houghton Mifflin.

FISHER, RONALD J. (1972) "Third Party Consultation: a Method for the Study and Resolution of Conflict," *Journal of Conflict Resolution*, 16(1): 67–94.

FISHER, RONALD J. (1983) "Third Party Consultation as a Method of Intergroup Conflict Resolution," *Journal of Conflict Resolution*, 27(2): 301–34.

FISS, OWEN (1984) "Against Settlement," *Yale Law Journal*, 93.

FOLBERG, JAY and TAYLOR, ALISON (1984) *Mediation: A Comprehensive Guide to Resolving Conflicts Without Litigation*, San Francisco: Jossey–Bass.

FOLTZ, WILLIAM J. (1977) "Two Forms of Unofficial Conflict Intervention: The Problem-Solving and the Process-Promoting Workshops," in Berman, M. R. and Johnson, J. E. (eds), *Unofficial Diplomats*, New York: Columbia University Press.

FRIEDMANN, JOHN (1988) "Reviewing Two Centuries," *Society*, 6: 7–15.

GALLAGHER, WILLIAM T. (1988) "The Transformation of Justice: Hofrichter's *Neighborhood Justice* and Harrington's *Shadow Justice*," *Law and Social Inquiry*, 13(1): 133–43.

GALTUNG, JOHAN (1976) "Feudal Systems, Structural Violence and the Structural Theory of Revolutions," in Galtung, J., *Essays in Peace Research*, vol. III, Copenhagen: Christian Ejlers.

GETMAN, JULIUS (1985) "Labor Arbitration and Dispute Resolution," in Goldberg, S. B., Green, E. D. and Sander, F. E. A. (eds), *Dispute Resolution*, Boston: Little, Brown & Co.

GNAIZDA, ROBERT (1982) "Secret Justice for the Privileged Few," *Judicature*, 66(1): 6–13.

GOELTNER, C. (1987) "The Computer as a Third Party: A Decision Support System for Two-Party Single-Issue and Two-Party Multi-Issues Negotiations," Working Paper 1958–87, Alfred P. Sloan School of Management, Massachussetts Institute of Technology.

GOLDBERG, STEPHEN B., GREEN, ERIC D. and SANDER, F. E. A. (eds) (1985) *Dispute Resolution*, Boston: Little, Brown & Co.

GOTTFREDSON, MICHAEL and HIRSCHI, TRAVIS (1990) *A General Theory of Crime*, Stanford, Calif.: Stanford University Press.

GREENBAUM, MARCIA L. (1984) "Ethical Considerations in Dispute Resolution," in Society of Professionals in Dispute Resolution, *Ethical Issues in Dispute Resolution*, 1983 Proceedings, Eleventh Annual Conference.

GULLIVER, P. H. (1979) *Disputes and Negotiations*, Orlando, Florida: Academic Press.

HAMMOND, KENNETH R. and ADELMAN, LEONARD (1976) "Science, Values, and Human Judgment," *Science*, 194: 389–96.

HAMPDEN-TURNER, C. M. (1973) "An Existential 'Learning Theory' and the Integration of T-Group Research," in Golembiewski, R. and Blumberg, A. (eds), *Sensitivity Training and the Laboratory Approach*, Itasca, Illinois: F. E. Peacock Publishers, Inc., (2nd edn).

HARRINGTON, CHRISTINE B. (1985) *Shadow Justice: The Ideology and Institutionalization of Alternatives to Court*, Westport, Conn.: Greenwood Press.

HARRINGTON, CHRISTINE B. and MERRY, SALLY ENGLE (1988) "Ideological Production: The Making of Community Mediation," *Law and Society Review*, 22(4): 709–35.

HARTER, PHILIP J. (1986) "Regulatory Negotiation: An Overview," in NIDR, *Dispute Resolution Forum*: 3–14.

HAUGHTON, RONALD (1984) "Dispute Resolution: Analyzing the Explosion," in Society of Professionals in Dispute Resolution, *Ethical Issues in Dispute Resolution*, 1983 Proceedings, Eleventh Annual Conference.

HAYGOOD, LEAH V. (1988) "Negotiated Rule Making: Challenges for Mediators and Participants," *Mediation Quarterly*, 20: 77–91.

HENDRY, JAMES B. (1987) "Ombudsmanry and the Exercise of Choice," in Society of Professionals in Dispute Resolution, *Dispute Resolution: An Open Forum*, 1986 Proceedings, Fourteenth International Conference.

HILL, BARBARA (1982) "An Analysis of Conflict Resolution Techniques," *Journal of Conflict Resolution*, 26(1): 109–38.

HOFRICHTER, RICHARD (1987) *Neighborhood Justice in Capitalist Society: The Expansion of the Informal State.* Westport, Conn.: Greenwood Press.

HUNT, JOAN E., KOOPMAN, ELIZABETH J., COLTRI, LAURIE and FAVRETTO, FRANCINE (1989) "Incorporating Idiosyncratic Family System Characteristics in the Development of Agreements: Toward an Expanded Understanding of 'Success' in the Mediation of Custody Disputes," in Rahim, M. A. (ed.), *Managing Conflict: An Inter-Disciplinary Approach*, Westport, Conn.: Praeger.

JACKSON, ELMORE (1983) *Middle East Mission*, New York: Norton.

JOHNSON, DAVID W. (1987b) *Creative Conflict*, Edina, Minn.: Interaction.

JOHNSON, DAVID W. and JOHNSON, ROGER T. (1985) "Internal Dynamics of Cooperative Learning Groups," in Slavin, R. *et al.* (eds), *Learning to Cooperate, Cooperating to Learn*, New York: Plenum Press.

JOHNSON, DAVID W. and JOHNSON, ROGER T. (1987a) *Learning Together and Alone: Cooperative, Competitive, and Individualistic Learning*, Englewood Cliffs, N.J.: Prentice-Hall (original, 1975).

JOHNSON, D. W., MARUYAMA, G., JOHNSON, R., NELSON, D. and SKON, L. (1981) "Effects of Cooperative, Competitive, and Individualistic Goal Structures on Achievement: A Meta-Analysis," *Psychological Bulletin*, 89: 47–62.

JOHNSON, D. W., JOHNSON, R. and MARUYAMA, G. (1983) "Interdependence and Interpersonal Attraction Among Heterogeneous and Homogeneous Individuals: A Theoretical Formulation and a Meta-Analysis of the Research," *Review of Educational Research*, 53: 5–54.

JULIUS, DEMETRIOS A. (1988) "The Practice of Track II Diplomacy in the Arab–Israeli Conferences," paper presented at Conference on Interdisciplinary Approach to Unofficial Diplomacy, Charlottesville, Va. (April).

KAHN, MARK L. (1984) "The Supply of Arbitrators: Who's 'Making It?'," in Society of Professionals in Dispute Resolution, *Ethical Issues in Dispute Resolution*, 1983 Proceedings, Eleventh Annual Conference.

KELLY, JOAN B. (ed.) (1989) "Empirical Research in Divorce and Family

Mediation," *Mediation Quarterly*, 24.

KELMAN, HERBERT C. (1979) "An Interactional Approach to Conflict Resolution and its Application to Israeli–Palestinian Relations," *International Interactions*, 6(2): 99–122.

KELMAN, HERBERT C. and COHEN, STEPHEN P. (1976) "The Problem–Solving Workshop: A Social-Psychological Contribution to the Resolution of International Conflicts," *Journal of Peace Research*, 13(2): 79–90.

KELTNER, JOHN W. (1987) "Mediation: Toward a Civilized System of Dispute Resolution," ERIC Clearinghouse on Reading and Communication Skills, and Speech Communication Association.

KETTERING FOUNDATION (1982) "Negotiated Investment Strategy."

KETTERING FOUNDATION (1987) "A Map of the Field: a Summary and Analysis of a Questionnaire on Public Diplomacy."

KNUDTEN, MARY S. and KNUDTEN, RICHARD D. (1981) "What Happens to Crime Victims and Witnesses in the Justice System?," in Galaway, B. and Hudson, J. (eds), *Perspectives on Crime Victims*, St. Louis: The C. V. Mosby Co.

KOHN, ALFIE (1986) *No Contest: The Case Against Competition*, Boston: Houghton Mifflin Co.

KOLB, DEBORAH M. (1983a) *The Mediators*, Cambridge, Mass.: The MIT Press.

KOLB, DEBORAH M. (1983b) "Strategy and the Tactics of Mediation," *Human Relations*, 36(3): 247–68.

KOLB, DEBORAH M. (1987) "Corporate Ombudsman and Organization Conflict Resolution," *Journal of Conflict Resolution*, 31(4): 673–91.

KOOPMAN, ELIZABETH J. and HUNT, JOAN E. (1988) "Child Custody Mediation: An Interdisciplinary Synthesis," *American Journal of Orthopsychiatry*, 58(3): 379–86.

KRAYBILL, RON (1984) Training Materials, Mennonite Conciliation Service.

KRESSEL, KENNETH and PRUITT, DEAN G. (1985) "Themes in the Mediation of Social Conflict," *Journal of Social Issues*, 41(2): 179–98.

LAKIN, MARTIN (1972) *Interpersonal Encounter: Theory and Practice in Sensitivity Training*, New York: McGraw-Hill.

LAMBROS, THOMAS D. (1986) "The Summary Jury Trial – An Alternative Method of Resolving Disputes," *Judicature*, 69 (5): 286–90.

LARMER, BROOK (1986) "After Crime, Reconciliation," *The Christian Science Monitor* (June 24).

LAUE, JAMES H. (ed.) (1988) "Using Mediation to Shape Public Policy," *Mediation Quarterly*, 20.

LAUE, JAMES H., BURDE, SHARON, POTAPCHUK, WILLIAM and SALKOFF, MIRANDA (1988) "Getting to the Table: Three Paths," *Mediation Quarterly*, 20: 7–21.

LEITCH, M. LAURIE (1986) "The Politics of Compromise: A Feminist Perspective on Mediation," *Mediation Quarterly*, 14/15: 163–75.

LEMMON, JOHN ALLEN (ed.) (1988) "Establishing Standards for Performance and Evaluation," *Mediation Quarterly*, 19.

LENTZ, SYDNEY SOLBERG (1986) "The Labor Model for Mediation

and its Application to the Resolution of Environmental Disputes," *The Journal of Applied Behavioral Science*, 22(2): 127–39.

LEVI, A. M. and BENJAMIN, A. (1976) "Jews and Arabs Rehearse Geneva: A Model of Conflict Resolution," *Human Relations*, 29 (11): 1035–44.

MADIGAN, DENISE, McMAHON, GERARD, SUSSKIND, LAWRENCE and ROLLEY, STEPHANIE (1986) *New Approaches to Resolving Local Public Disputes*, National Institute for Dispute Resolution, NIDR Teaching Materials Series.

McGILLICUDDY, NEIL B., WELTON, GARY L. and PRUITT, DEAN G. (1987) "Third-Party Intervention; A Field Experiment Comparing Three Different Models," *Journal of Personality and Social Psychology*, 53 (1).

McGILLIS, DANIEL (1986) *Community Dispute Resolution Programs and Public Policy*, National Institute of Justice.

McKNIGHT, DOROTHY (EDMONDS) (1981) "The Victim Offender Reconciliation Project," in Galaway, B. and Hudson J. (eds), *Perspectives on Crime Victims*, St Louis: The C. V. Mosby Co.

MENDELSOHN, BENJAMIN (1963) "The Origin of the Doctrine of Victimology," *Excerpta Criminologica*, 3 (3).

MERCER, NORMAN A. (1987) "Arbitration," *Encyclopedia Americana*, Danbury, Conn.: Grolier, Inc.

MILLS, MICHAEL P. (1987) "The Craft of Ombudsmanry," in Society for Professionals in Dispute Resolution, *Dispute Resolution: An Open Forum*, 1986 Proceedings, Fourteenth International Conference.

MITRANY, DAVID. (1966) *A Working Peace System*, Chicago: Quadrangle Books.

MONTVILLE, JOSEPH (1987) "The Arrow and the Olive Branch: A Case for Track Two Diplomacy," in McDonald, J. and Bendahmane, D. (eds), *Conflict Resolution: Track Two Diplomacy*, Foreign Service Institute, US Department of State.

MOORE, CHRISTOPHER W. (1987) *The Mediation Process: Practical Strategies for Resolving Conflict*, San Francisco: Jossey–Bass.

MOSKOWITZ, JOEL M. *et al.* (1985) "Evaluation of Jigsaw, a Cooperative Learning Technique," *Contemporary Educational Psychology*, 10(2): 104–12.

MUMMA, EDWARD W. (1984) "Mediating Disputes," *Public Welfare* (Winter).

NADER, LAURA (ed.) (1969) *Law in Culture and Society*, Chicago: Aldine.

NADER, LAURA (1980) *No Access to Law*, New York: Academic Press

NATIONAL ASSOCIATION FOR COMMUNITY JUSTICE (NACJ) (1989) *NACJ News*.

NATIONAL CENTER ON WOMEN AND FAMILY LAW (1983) Statement of 14th National Conference on Women and the Law, Washington, D.C. (April).

NATIONAL INSTITUTE FOR DISPUTE RESOLUTION (NIDR) (1987) "Statewide Offices of Mediation: Experiments in Public Policy," *Dispute Resolution Forum* (December).

NATIONAL INSTITUTE FOR DISPUTE RESOLUTION (NIDR) (1988a) "Programming the Process: An Examination of the Use of Computers in Dispute Resolution," *Dispute Resolution Forum* (April).

NATIONAL INSTITUTE FOR DISPUTE RESOLUTION (NIDR) (1988b) "The Status of Community Justice," *Dispute Resolution Forum* (December).

NATIONAL INSTITUTE FOR DISPUTE RESOLUTION (NIDR) (1989) "The Report of the SPIDR Commission on Qualifications," *Dispute Resolution Forum* (May).

PACT INSTITUTE OF JUSTICE (1984) *The VORP Book*, Valparaiso, Indiana.

PAQUIN, GARY W. (1988) "The Child's Input in the Mediation Process," *Mediation Quarterly*, 22: 69–81.

PFISTER, GORDON (1975) "Outcomes of Laboratory Training for Police Officers," *Journal of Social Issues*, 31(1): 115–21.

POMPA, GILBERT G. (1987) "The Community Relations Service," in Sandole, D. J. D. and Sandole-Staroste, I. (eds), *Conflict Management and Problem Solving*, New York: New York University Press.

PRUITT, DEAN G. (1981) *Negotiation Behavior*, New York: Academic Press.

PRUITT, DEAN G. and KRESSEL, KENNETH (1985) "The Mediation of Social Conflict: An Introduction," *Journal of Social Issues*, 41(2): 1–10.

PRUTZMAN, PRISCILLA, BURGER, M. LEONARD, BODEN-HAMER, GRETCHEN and STERN, LEE (1978) *The Friendly Classroom for a Small Planet: A Handbook on Creative Approaches to Living and Problem Solving for Children*, Wayne, N. J., Avery Publishing Group.

RAIFFA, HOWARD (1982) *The Art and Science of Negotiation*, Cambridge, Mass.: Harvard University Press.

ROEHL, JANICE A. and COOK, R. F. (1985) *Journal of Social Issues*, 41(2): 161–78.

ROGERS, CARL (1961) *On Becoming a Person*, Boston: Houghton Mifflin.

ROGERS, CARL (1965) "Dealing With Psychological Tensions," *Journal of Applied Behavioral Science*, 1 (1): 6–24.

ROGERS, CARL (1987) "Steps Toward Peace, 1948–1986: Tension Reduction in Theory and Practice," "The Underlying Theory: Drawn from Experience with Individuals and Groups," "Inside the World of the Soviet Professional," and with Ruth Sanford, "Reflections on our South African Experience (January–February 1986)," *Counseling and Values*, 32(1): 12–75.

ROSS, JEROME H. (1982) "The Med-Arb Process in Labor Agreement Negotiations," SPIDR Committee on Research and Education, Occasional Paper, 82–1 (February).

ROWAT, DONALD (1985) *The Ombudsman Plan: The Worldwide Spread of an Idea*, Lanham, Md: University Press of America.

ROWE, MARY P. (undated) "Becoming an Ombudsman in North America."

ROWE, MARY P. (1986) "The Corporate Ombudsman," presented at the Industrial Relations Research Seminar, Sloan School, MIT, Cambridge, Mass.

SARAT, AUSTIN (1988) "The 'New Formalism' in Disputing and Dispute Processing," *Law and Society Review*, 21(5): 695–715.

SATA, LINDBERGH S. (1975) "Laboratory Training for Police Officers," *Journal of Social Issues*, 31(1): 107–14.

SCHMUCK, RICHARD (1985) "Learning to Cooperate, Cooperating to Learn: Basic Concepts," in Slavin, R. *et al.* (eds), *Learning to Cooperate, Cooperating to Learn*, New York: Plenum Press.

SCHULMAN, J. and WOODS, L. (1983) "Legal Advocacy v. Mediation in Family Law," *The Women's Advocate*, 4: 3–4.

SEBENIUS, JAMES K. (1981) "The Computer as Mediator," *Journal of Policy Analysis and Management*, 1 (1).

SHAFFER, JOHN B. and GALINSKY, DAVID M. (1976) *Models of Group Therapy and Sensitivity Training*, Englewood Cliffs, N. J.: Prentice-Hall.

SHONHOLTZ, RAYMOND (1984) "Neighborhood Justice Systems: Work, Structure, and Guiding Principles," *Mediation Quarterly*, 5: 3–30.

SHONHOLTZ, RAYMOND (1987) "The Citizens' Role in Justice: Building a Primary Justice and Prevention System at the Neighborhood Level," *Annals*, AAPSS, 494: 42–53.

SILBEY, SUSAN S. and MERRY, SALLY E. (1986) "Mediator Settlement Strategies," *Law and Policy*, 8(1): 7–32.

SIMON, HERBERT A. (1960) *The New Science of Management Decisions*, New York: Harper & Row.

SOCIETY OF PROFESSIONALS IN DISPUTE RESOLUTION (SPIDR) (1984) *Ethical Issues in Dispute Resolution*, 1983 Proceedings, Eleventh Annual Conference.

SOCIETY OF PROFESSIONALS IN DISPUTE RESOLUTION (SPIDR) (1985) *The Elements of Good Practice in Dispute Resolution*, 1984 Proceedings, Twelfth Annual Conference.

STANSBURY, BETH (1989) "Problem Prevention to Take Teamwork," *The Daily Progress* (July 25).

STERN, RICHARD L. (1987) "We Wuz Robbed," *Forbes* (December 28).

STIEBER, CAROLYN (1985) "The Ombudsman in Academe and Elsewhere," in Society of Professionals in Dispute Resolution, *The Elements of Good Practice in Dispute Resolution*, 1984 Proceedings, Twelfth Annual Conference.

STRAUS, DONALD (1974) "Computer Assisted Negotiation," American Arbitration Association.

SUSSKIND, LAWRENCE (1986) "Regulatory Negotiation at the State and Local Levels," *Dispute Resolution Forum*, NIDR (January).

SUSSKIND, LAWRENCE and OZAWA, CONNIE (1985) "Mediating Public Disputes: Obstacles and Possibilities," *Journal of Social Issues*, 41(2): 145–49.

SUSSKIND, LAWRENCE and CRUIKSHANK, JEFFREY (1987) *Break-*

ing the Impasse: Consensual Approaches to Resolving Public Disputes, New York: Basic Books.

TOMASIC, ROMAN and FEELEY, MALCOLM M. (eds) (1982) *Neighborhood Justice: Assessment of an Emerging Idea*, New York; Longman.

TYLER, TOM R. (1988) "The Quality of Dispute Resolution Processes and Outcomes: Measurement Problems and Possibilities," Disputes Processing Research Program, Working Papers 8–9, Institute for Legal Studies, University of Wisconsin–Madison Law School (June).

UMBREIT, MARK (1986a) "Victim Offender Mediation: A National Survey," *Federal Probation*, 50: 53–6.

UMBREIT, MARK (1986b) "Victim Offender Mediation and Judicial Leadership," *Judicature*, 69(4): 202–4.

VOLKAN, VAMIK (1987) "Psychological Concepts Useful in the Building of Political Foundations Between Nations," *Journal of the American Psychoanalytic Association*, 35(4): 903–35.

WAHRHAFTIG, PAUL (1982) "An Overview of Community-Oriented Citizen Dispute Resolution Programs in the United States," in Abel, R. L. (ed.), *The Politics of Informal Justice. Vol. I: The American Experience*, New York: Academic Press.

WAHRHAFTIG, PAUL (1987) "Institutionalizing Community Dispute Resolution Programs," *Conflict Resolution Notes*, 5(2).

WALL Jr., JAMES A. (1981) "Mediation: An Analysis–Review, and Proposed Research," *Journal of Conflict Resolution*, 25(1): 147–80.

WALL Jr., JAMES A. and RUDE, DALE E. (1985) "Judicial Mediation: Techniques, Strategies, and Situational Effects," *Journal of Social Issues*, 51(2): 47–63.

WALTON, RICHARD E. (1969) *Interpersonal Peacemaking: Confrontations and Third Party Consultation*, Reading: Mass.: Addison–Wesley.

WALTON, RICHARD E. (1970) "A Problem-Solving Workshop on Border Conflicts in Eastern Africa," *Journal of Applied Behavioral Science*, 6(4): 453–89.

WARFIELD, JOHN N. (1976) *Societal Systems: Planning, Policy and Complexity*, New York: John Wiley.

WARFIELD, JOHN N. (1982) "The Consensus Methodologies," *General Systems*, 27.

WEDGE, BRYANT (1970) "A New Kind of Dialogue," *Journal of Applied Behavioral Science*, 6(4): 494–6.

WIESEL, ELIE (1989) "Are We Afraid of Peace?," *Parade* (March 19).

YARROW, MIKE (1978) *Quaker Experience in International Conciliation*, New Haven, Conn.: Yale University Press.

YOUNG, ORAN R. (1967) *The Intermediaries: Third Parties in International Crises*, Princeton, N.J.: Princeton University Press.

ZAGORIA, SAM (1988) *The Ombudsman: How Good Governments Handle Citizens' Grievances*, Washington, D.C.: Seven Locks Press.

ZARTMAN, I. WILLIAM and TOUVAL, SAADIA (1985) "International Mediation: Conflict Resolution and Power Politics," *Journal of Social Issues*, 41(2): 27–45.

ZEHR, HOWARD, and UMBREIT, MARK (1982) "Victim Offender Reconciliation: An Incarceration Substitute?," *Federal Probation*, 46(4).

Index